Praise for *Bivocational and Beyond*

For congregations with a history of professional clergy, the emphasis on the priesthood of all believers will address the invitation scripture provides that all are called to make disciples and carry out the mission of the church.

- The Rev. Dr. SanDawna Gaulman Ashley, Transitional Synod Leader, Synod of the Northeast, Presbyterian Church (U.S.A.)

Bivocational and Beyond *is a comprehensive discussion of bi/multivocational ministry that offers cultural insights on multivocational ministry beyond the mainline church purview, while noting the challenges such ministries present to congregations and educational institutions. . . . a solid reference for any minister or congregation considering the possibilities that may be beneficial from a broader view of collaborative ministry.*

— The Rev. Dr. Renée C. Jackson, Minister for Ministerial Formation, United Church of Christ National Offices

Bivocational and Beyond *is a crucial book for this pivotal moment in church history. It brings into focus the unmet educational needs that surface, both for clergy and laity, in settings where a pastor brings a bivocational or multivocational approach.* Bivocational and Beyond *does a masterful service by exposing the vast gap between what's needed and what's actually provided in higher theological education today.*

— The Rev. G. Jeffrey MacDonald, Author, *Part-Time is Plenty: Thriving without Full-Time Clergy*

Darryl W. Stephens opens a world of exposure through this edited volume that has the potential of radically reshaping theological education as we know it. This work is quite timely, considering the changing landscape of theological education—prompted by shifts in academy-denominational relationships, declining memberships in many Catholic and Protestant denominations, the browning of student populations in ATS institutions, feedback from ATS graduating student questionnaires about their expectations around ministry options, and recent pedagogical and curricular designs prompted by the impact of COVID-19.

The Rev. Dr. Mary H. Young, Director, Leadership Education, Association of Theological Schools in the United States and Canada

"This book addresses a significant topic in ministry and theological education . . . There are some books on bi/covocational ministry, but they tend to focus on congregational life. I do not know of any books that spend as much time as this one does thinking about how theological education needs to adapt to serve these ministers and their communities."

— The Rev. Dr. Ted A. Smith, Almar H. Shatford Professor of Divinity, Candler School of Theology

Bivocational and Beyond

Educating for Thriving Multivocational Ministry

EDITED BY DARRYL W. STEPHENS

ATLA OPEN PRESS
Chicago - 2022

Published by Atla Open Press, an imprint of the American Theological Library Association (Atla), 200 South Wacker Drive, Suite 3100, Chicago, IL 60606-6701 USA

Published in the United States of America in 2022

ISBN-13 978-1-949800-28-9 (PDF)
ISBN-13 978-1-949800-29-6 (EPUB)
ISBN-13 978-1-949800-30-2 (Paperback)

Cover artwork by Cecily A. Stephens
Cover design by Simply Aesthetic

Table of Contents

Abbreviations .... *i*

Foreword .... *iii*

Preface and Acknowledgments .... *vii*

Introduction *1*

Part I: Landscape

1. *Bivocational Ministry as the Congregation's Curriculum* *17*
2. *British Perspectives on Bivocational Ministry* *37*
3. *Changes in Ministry and Bivocational Ministry since the 1960s* *53*
4. *Black and Bivocational* *65*
5. *Black Student Perspectives* *81*

Part II: Leadership

6. *Calling in Multivocational Ministry* *95*
7. *Pitching Our Tent with Bivocational Ministry* *111*
8. *Exploring Distributive Ministry* *133*
9. *Incarnating Christ through Bivocational Ministry* *149*
10. *Bivocational Ministry as a Path of Unexpected Spiritual Growth* *161*
11. *The Bivocational Congregation* *179*
12. *Bivocational Ministry and the Mentoring Relationship* *193*

Part III: Learning

13. *Empowering the Full Body of Christ* 211

14. *Preparing to Educate for a Thriving Bivocational Ministry* 225

15. *The Multivocational Plans of Students in Graduate Theological Education* 253

16. *Preparing to Teach a Bivocational Ministry Seminary Course* 277

17. *A Mentored Practice Approach to Bivocational Ministry Education* 297

18. *Seeking Information Mastery in Multivocational Ministry* 313

19. *Reimagining Theological Education with a Multivocational Mindset* 327

Contributors 351

Abbreviations

ATS	Association of Theological Schools in the United States and Canada
BIPOC	Black, Indigenous, and People of Color
CoE	Church of England
COVID-19	coronavirus disease 2019
LGBTQ+	lesbian, gay, bisexual, transgender, and queer or questioning
LTS	Lancaster Theological Seminary
NIV	New International Version of the Bible
NKJV	New King James Version of the Bible
NLT	New Living Translation of the Bible
NRSV	New Revised Standard Version of the Bible
UK	United Kingdom (adjectival form)
UCC	United Church of Christ
US	United States (adjectival form)

Foreword

A pastor for every church, and a church for every pastor? Through the years, many congregations and church leaders assumed that the goal for every church was to have a full-time pastor with a seminary degree. However, this model has never been the actual staffing pattern for many congregations. History, tradition, and financial realities have led many churches to meet their pastoral leadership needs in a variety of ways, including the deployment of part-time, bivocational, and shared pastors, along with lay leaders and volunteers.

In recent times, it appears that the staffing patterns of congregations are changing more significantly. One major factor is the considerable increase in the number of very small churches, with the consequent economic limitations these churches face in providing pastoral leadership. Fewer congregations now can financially support a full-time pastor.

Between 2000 and 2019, it was common for the overall number of churches within many denominations to decline, while at the same time the number and percentage of very small churches (with an average worship attendance of 25 or fewer) increased. In the Church of the Nazarene, for example, the number of those very small churches increased by 81% and, as of 2019, represented 29% of all churches in the denomination (Kubichek 2021).

The immediate result of this change is that far more churches are served by part-time pastoral leadership now than in 2000. Similarly, in 2000, 27% of United Methodist congregations had part-time pastoral leadership. By 2019, 42% had a part-time pastor. A major reason for this change is that there were 2,059 more United Methodist churches with attendance of 25 or fewer in 2019 than in 2000, according to the General Council on Finance and Administration of the United Methodist Church. Many of these small churches share a pastor with another church or churches. In other cases, the pastor does not serve another church while providing part-time ministry to the congregation. It is this latter group of pastors to which this book is devoted and for whom it can be so valuable.

As the authors illustrate, bivocational ministry is far broader than the term might denote to many. The specifics of how bivocational pastors and their congregations shape their lives cover a broad range of patterns. There is no one dominant approach. Some have full-time jobs beyond their church work while others have jobs that are part-time. For some, the "other" vocation is retirement, family care, or volunteer work. The Church of the Brethren, as one illustration, is a denomination in which most of the churches are served by part-time and bivocational pastors. A Church of the Brethren survey found that 22% of those serving congregations have full-time jobs outside of pastoral ministry. Another 23% have part-time jobs, and 11% have multiple part-time jobs in addition to their ministry work. The diverse life situations of these part-time pastors are illustrated by the fact that the most common answer about supplemental income came from the 39% who named retirement income (Church of the Brethren 2022).

Multiple sources estimate bivocational pastors are serving about 30% of churches in the United States. There is some debate about whether, in the current context, the numbers and proportions are remaining relatively stable or growing. Often, differences in numbers and interpretation depend on how bivocational pastors are defined and counted. One strength of this book is that it accounts for much of the diversity of bivocational ministry. Personal and congregational circumstances vary so greatly that, while there are some similar and common dimensions of bivocational ministry, it may not be wise to make too many generalizations or make assumptions about commonalities.

The three-fold structure of the book—landscape, leadership, and learning—offers a comprehensive analysis of bivocational ministry that is badly needed. The blending of researchers and practitioners gives this volume a substantive discussion of bivocational ministry we have not had before. The absence of such literature points to another dilemma: for denominational traditions in which churches having a full-time pastor has been the assumption, almost no provisions are made in planning events, training, and education for bivocational pastors who will have commitments and limitations quite unlike full-time pastors. Even in denominations in which half or more of churches are served part-time, there are limited resources and training available for bivocational pastors.

Bivocational ministry can be a frightening possibility for some clergy and congregations. It need not be. However, neither party can continue to function as if their situation has not changed. If the roles and responsibilities can be shaped properly, both pastor and laity can feel new life for their respective ministries. The future is just as likely to feature growth as decline, though most churches will remain relatively stable. But simply coming to an agreement about changes in hours worked by the pastor and the budget allocations for clergy will not make for a healthy future without the faithful work of visioning for shared ministry. There must be discernment, sharing of hopes and dreams, and hearing each other in order to navigate a future with hope. Such an arrangement is a covenant of shared leadership to accomplish God's will, not a contract for services rendered.

Bivocational pastors, laity in congregations with or considering a bivocational pastor, judicatory leaders, and seminary faculty and administrators have much to learn from the impressive contributions of the authors of this book. All of us are in situations where a rethinking of assumptions about pastoral leadership is occurring. Bivocational ministry is one lane in the pathway to the future that needs careful and sustained attention. Make full use of this resource to learn and assess clues for your future!

LOVETT H. WEEMS JR.

Distinguished Professor of Church Leadership and Founding Director/Senior Consultant of the G. Douglass Lewis Center for Church Leadership, Wesley Theological Seminary

January 2022

Works Cited

Church of the Brethren. 2022. “Part-Time Pastor, Full-Time Church. Church of the Brethren Office of Ministry.” *brethren.org/ministryoffice/part-time-pastor.*

Kubichek, Amy. 2021. “Pastoral Leadership in the Church of the Nazarene, 2000–2019: A Preliminary Report.” Religious Workforce Project. The Lewis Center for Church Leadership of Wesley Theological Seminary in Washington, DC. *religiousworkforce.com/nazarene-demo-v-1#num-churches-attendance-2019.*

Preface and Acknowledgments

> *Now there are varieties of gifts, but the same Spirit; and there are varieties of services, but the same Lord; and there are varieties of activities, but it is the same God who activates all of them in everyone.*
>
> 1 Cor. 12:4–6, NRSV

In 2020, shortly before the onslaught of COVID-19, I embarked on a journey of discovery that led to this book. My academic dean at Lancaster Theological Seminary, Vanessa Lovelace, asked me to write a grant proposal and lead the seminary in a study of bivocational ministry. Awarded a matching grant from the In Trust Center for Theological Schools, our seminary community became a laboratory for learning about the varieties of gifts, services, and activities of persons called to ministry and how best to prepare our students to thrive as bivocational ministers.

With new insight, I began to see the variety of vocational identities as both the experience of individuals and an expression of the Body of Christ. As a theological educator, I have taught seminarians for more than 15 years, in a variety of schools. My students have prepared themselves for ministries as pastors, chaplains, lay leaders, educators, and not-for-profit leadership, to name only a few of the vocations to which they were called. And I have taught hundreds of laypersons in local congregations in Texas, Georgia, Illinois, and Pennsylvania, each time learning something new from the wisdom of the *laos*—the people of God. For years, I have also taught local pastors in the United Methodist Course of Study, a non-degree program of pastoral preparation—what those in the United Church of Christ would identify as one of the "multiple pathways" to theological education. Many, if not most, local pastors find themselves in the margins of church polity: theologically trained but not seminary educated, licensed but not ordained, pastoring but not itinerant, no longer laity but not fully clergy.

This in-between place is where bivocational and multivocational ministry thrives. With the assistance of many people, this is where I discovered anew the same Spirit at work within, among, and beyond the church.

I would like to thank the people who inspired, accompanied, and supported me on this journey. Thanks to Vanessa Lovelace for entrusting me with this project and to the In Trust Center for its matching grant. Thank you to Phil Baisley, whose prior research and connections provided the seed for creating an informal network of researchers, writers, educators, and reflective practitioners, over two dozen of whom gathered virtually on November 16, 2020, for an international consultation on bivocational ministry. Thank you to these and other collaborators, particularly those who took time to communicate and meet with me individually: Hartness Samushonga, Amy Bratton, Wanda Malcolm, Ross Bartlett, David Abbott, Dave King, and Linda Kuhn. A special thanks goes to Packard Brown, principal of Theology Careers Initiative, who shared his experience and wisdom as a consultant and taught a "Job-Hunting Field Guide" class for bivocational ministers through the Pennsylvania Academy of Ministry at Lancaster Theological Seminary.

A debt of gratitude goes to the many students, staff, and faculty who volunteered their time and energy teaching me and others about bivocational ministry and its challenges. Thank you to the student focus group participants: Mwat Dominic Asedeh, Eric M. Chase, Equilla Curry, Robert Garvey, Derrick Gutierrez, Bambi Hamby, Martha Harris, Cynthia Layton, Chynaah Maryoung-Cooke, Neil D. Reeves, and Rick Wrisley. Mwat deserves double thanks for his extensive bibliographic work as student researcher. A special word of thanks goes to my colleague Nilda Roman, who served as researcher and facilitator of the focus group over six sessions and who provided her own insights as a bivocational chaplain. Thank you also to Melvin Baber for sharing his pastoral insights.

I benefited from many interlocutors and colleagues who encouraged this project through the Engage ATS forum and personal communications. I am particularly grateful to colleagues who provided detailed feedback on my thoughts on theological education: Andy Keck, Kristina Lizardy-Hajbi, and Pete Gathje. Thank you also to Jo Ann Deasy and Deborah H. C. Gin for their encouragement and expertise at crucial junctures of my research and writing.

This journey of discovery was greatly enriched by the many alums and friends of Lancaster Theological Seminary who shared their experience, passion, and wisdom about bivocational ministry. In particular, I would like to thank the following persons for presentations to our student body: Barry Chambers, G. Jeffrey MacDonald, Connie Mentzer, Karen Monk, Marvin A. Moss, Amelia Price, Barbara Rowlett, and Gerald Simmons. There are too many others to name here who supported the creation of this book. Thank you for your prayers and encouragement.

This book would not be what it is without the leadership and support of Christine Fruin of Atla and James Estes of the editorial board of Books@Atla Open Press. Thank you for your confidence in this project, attention to detail, and persistent nudging. I am grateful that this book will be published in an open access format for readers throughout the world.

Finally, thank you to my immediate family members, each of whom assisted with this project in their own unique way, truly exemplifying the varieties of gifts promised by the Spirit.

DARRYL W. STEPHENS

Director of United Methodist Studies at Lancaster Theological Seminary and Director of the Pennsylvania Academy of Ministry

January 2022

Introduction

DARRYL W. STEPHENS

Bivocational ministry is a topic intimately related to congregational vitality and the future of the church in North America. Also called multivocational, covocational, dual career, partially funded, or tentmaking, bivocational ministry is a way of offering one's whole self in service to church and world. Bivocational ministry is generally defined as a combination of employment (paid or unpaid) within and beyond the local congregation by someone called to pastoral ministry. It is contrasted with univocational (full-time, fully funded) ministry as well as part-time ministry not accompanied by other significant employment or volunteer work. The term *bivocational* is widely connoted with Christian ministry, though the word multivocational more accurately describes the situations of many (Watson et al. 2020). While persons who serve and earn in multiple ways simultaneously are often marginalized in church and academy, there is much to be learned from intentional bivocationality as a missional, vocational, and faithful way of responding to God's call to all the baptized.

Bivocational ministry is gaining attention among North American seminarians, schools of theology, and the churches they serve. Over one-third of US congregations are served by a bivocational pastor (Chaves et al. 2020, 22), and 30% of seminary graduates in North America plan to be bivocational (Deasy 2018, 66). Some claim that the ecclesial landscape has experienced an increase in bivocationality in recent decades. However, this is a claim voiced more loudly than warranted by available data. An equally strong case can be made that the numbers are holding steady. The reality is complex and difficult to measure, given diverse definitions and practices of bivocationality. Undisputable though is the increased visibility of bivocational ministry among North American churches in the past 20 years. A heightened awareness of this reality is due to a combination of many factors, including the publication of Dennis W. Bickers's *The Tentmaking Pastor: The Joy of Bivocational Ministry* (2000), the rise of the "gig economy," a blurring of traditional notions of sacred and secular, missional innovation at the end of modern Christendom, and greater attention by White-majority institutions to the experiences of BIPOC students and pastors.

Many traditions of Christian faith consider bivocational ministry the norm. "We've always done it that way," declared Melvin Baber, a ministerial colleague in the Missionary Baptist Church (personal communication, August 6, 2021). In his experience, "Pastors held several jobs in order to do ministry. A lot of times, the pastor and pastor's family put more in than they were earning from the church." For pastors in the Black church tradition, holding a secular job is an expected part of the ministry. In fact, ministry in many congregations is not possible without an outside source of income. However, bivocationality is not simply a means for the have-nots to make do.

Additional jobs enable and extend the ministry into the community. For example, Raphael Warnock famously serves both as pastor of Ebenezer Baptist Church in Atlanta, Georgia, and as a US senator. What a loss to church and society it would be if Warnock's scholarly writing (2014), political action, public service, and preaching were considered incompatible! We are fortunate that he serves in a tradition that recognizes, values, and affirms multivocational ministry. The same is true for other faith leaders. Even after earning a Doctor of Ministry degree, Baber still holds multiple employments, including his pastorate and teaching and administrative roles at Lancaster Theological Seminary. “In our tradition, we don’t have ‘part-time’ pastors,” Baber observed. “Ministry is full-time. It’s not about the money or the benefits.” This arrangement is so much the norm that it does not have a special name. Baber explained, “We don’t call it bivocational. It’s just ministry.”

Yet bivocational ministry runs counter to expectations in more privileged communities of faith. Traditions accustomed to overly spiritualizing the pastoral office have difficulty bridging the divide between sacred and secular in the person of their pastor. Embracing the idea of a plumber as preacher, for example, may require a conceptual shift for some congregations. (Ironically, many of these same congregations have no qualms about expecting the pastor to fix a leaky toilet in the parsonage or church building!) Even those congregations that have learned to adapt to bivocational ministry by necessity often measure themselves against the perceived ideal of a fully compensated, full-time, univocational pastor. Imagining and valuing different ways of being church is a particular challenge for majority-White, mainline congregations, though Christian faith communities of all demographics, denominational traditions, and geographic locations would do well to reflect theologically on the meaning and implications of bivocational ministry.

The idea of intentional bivocationality presents many challenges to perceived and inherited ways of pastoring and educating pastors. Bivocational pastors are challenged to integrate diverse expressions of their calling, balance personal and professional obligations, overcome stigma, and achieve financial stability. Bivocational congregations are challenged to adapt to new leadership styles and expectations of both clergy and laity. Changing demographics and ecclesial situations are forcing institutions of theological education, many of which were designed for full-time students preparing for fully funded pastoral ministry, to reassess curricular programs, schedules, and content in light of multivocational realities. This book addresses these challenges as an opportunity for theological educators and church leaders alike to reimagine the church and its ministry.

This framing of the subject and this book is admittedly peculiar to (though not limited to) North American Protestantism, and readers are encouraged to augment this text with other resources. For an in-depth treatment of self-supporting ministry in the Church of England (also called non-stipendiary, volunteer, supplementary, or auxiliary ministry), readers are referred to *Tentmaking: Perspectives on Self-Supporting Ministry* (Francis and Francis 1998). This edited volume stands out as the most comprehensive, scholarly treatment on the topic in English, and its breadth expands ecumenically and geographically beyond the Church of England. Chapter two of the present volume engages these British perspectives, contributing to the conversations in both North America and the United Kingdom. The present volume also complements discussions of diaconia, worker priests in France, lay ecclesial ministry in Roman Catholic parishes in the United States, and Indigenous ministry (especially in relation to missiology). Additionally, books by Bickers (2007), Edington (2018), and MacDonald (2020) provide accessible guides for congregations and their leaders in the United States. The present volume distinguishes itself with a combination of scholarly and practical writings addressing the contemporary church and graduate theological education in North America.

Bivocational and Beyond: Educating for Thriving Multivocational Ministry is an attempt to make sense of this common, though misunderstood and under-researched, form of pastoral ministry. This book is intended to shift the scholarly and ecclesial conversation about bivocational ministry. It is intended to equip pastors, judicatory leaders, and theological educators to thrive in their understanding of multivocational ministry. In this volume, researchers, educators, and practitioners in bivocational ministries provide contemporary analyses and reflections on diverse issues facing bivocational pastors, congregations, and those persons who resource and teach them. This book is intended as a scholarly and professional resource for college, university, and seminary educators as well as graduate students, pastors, judicatory personnel, and lay leaders in congregations.

Contributors include researchers, reflective practitioners, denominational leaders, and academics working in multiple disciplines and from diverse perspectives. Eight chapters present the findings of empirical research based on surveys and interviews with bivocational and multivocational pastors, another is based on ethnographic research, and most are informed by the authors' personal experiences of bivocationality. Among the contributors, twelve traditions are represented, including the Christian Church (Disciples of Christ), United Church of Christ, Religious Society of Friends (Quakers), the United Methodist Church, Salvation Army, Presbyterian Church (U.S.A.), American Baptist Churches USA, Evangelical Covenant Church, the Episcopal Church (US), and several non-denominational churches of pentecostal and evangelical persuasion. Geographically, sixteen contributors are located in the United States, two in Canada, and one in the United Kingdom. Six chapters were written by women and thirteen by men. Fourteen chapters were written by White persons and five by BIPOC authors. Yet, this book barely touches the wide diversity of bivocational ministry in North America. It is my hope that this volume will serve as a catalyst for further research and wider conversation, inclusive of Latinx voices, Asian communities, Roman Catholic contexts, perspectives from immigrant congregations, and many others.

Bivocational and Beyond is arranged in three parts: landscape, leadership, and learning. The book begins more descriptively in part I, combines descriptive and constructive modes in part II, and leans more prescriptively in part III. Practitioners may be initially drawn to the chapters on leadership and educators to the chapters on learning. Judicatory personnel may be drawn to both. However, all parts of the book are intended to benefit and challenge persons regardless of their role in relation to bivocational and multivocational ministry. Readers are encouraged to begin reading chapters in any order, seeking first the voices and topics most relevant to their context and role and proceeding in a more exploratory fashion thereafter.

Part I, landscape, provides contextual viewpoints for understanding the nature of bivocational ministry. The section includes two overview essays—one from the United States and one from the United Kingdom—a personal retrospective by a bivocational pastor, and two empirical studies—one focused on the experiences of Black bivocational ministers and the other on perspectives and expectations of Black seminary students, particularly around issues of finances.

In chapter 1, "Bivocational Ministry as the Congregation's Curriculum," Darryl W. Stephens views ambiguities and uncertainties about defining bivocational ministry as an opportunity for theological reflection and religious education. Acknowledging a context of anxiety about congregational vitality in North American mainline denominations, Stephens utilizes Boyung Lee's communal approach to religious education to imagine new ways of being church, especially for White-majority congregations, which seem to have difficulty coming to terms with bivocational ministry. This chapter proceeds descriptively, exploring the breadth of definitions of bivocational ministry and related terms, organized around several themes: vocation and ministry, jobs and finances, and commitment. Constructively, this chapter presents intentional bivocational ministry as the congregation's curriculum, a practice of the entire faith community, and concludes with a call for theological educators to assist in this endeavor.

In chapter 2, "British Perspectives on Bivocational Ministry," Hartness M. Samushonga presents a history of the concept of bivocational ministry in Britain and explores contemporary challenges. Terms peculiar to the Church of England, such as *non-stipendiary ministers, ministers in secular employment,* and *self-supporting ministers,* describe the phenomenon in varied forms, though the term *bivocational ministry* is predominant among Pentecostals and other Protestants in the United Kingdom. Tracing the history of bivocational ministry in Britain from the sixteenth century forward, Samushonga highlights the ministry of Baptist, Catholic, and Church of England missionaries, the advocacy of Herbert Kelly and Roland Allen, and the influences of the French and Belgian Catholic worker-priest movement. The chapter then explores contemporary challenges for bivocational ministry in Britain, including a lack of statistical data and a need for focused programs of theological education. Samushonga observes that the momentum for bivocational ministry as a means of stimulating church growth in Britain is intensifying in the Church of England and beyond.

In chapter 3, "Changes in Ministry and Bivocational Ministry Since the 1960s," Ralph B. Wright Jr. presents personal reflections based on 45 years in bivocational ministries in the United States as well as overseas. He observes a crisis of decline among White, mainline churches within a context of increased secularization in North America and suggests that bivocational pastors—offering a broader set of skills and talents than traditional, univocational pastors—are often well positioned to meet the changing needs of congregations in the twenty-first century. Addressing issues of racism, ethnocentrism, classism, and patriarchy, Wright draws on his own experience to show how bivocationality can provide new opportunities for ministry within the larger community. Bivocational ministry can be an opportunity to revitalize the church in mission to the community at large, particularly majority-White congregations that have lost touch with the changing communities around them. He concludes with a plea for increased collegial and judicatory support for bivocational pastors, especially women in ministry.

In chapter 4, "Black and Bivocational," Jessica Young Brown provides deep insight into bivocational ministry based on empirical research with Black pastors and ministers. Noting that Black pastors have been engaged in this ministerial dynamic for a long time, she asks, Why are we not looking to Black bivocational ministers to inform our understanding about what it means to thrive in this context? Thus, this chapter looks to Black bivocational clergy as exemplars for navigating bivocational ministry. Based on survey and interview data, Brown explores issues of gifts and call, finances, self-care, professional responsibilities and boundaries, as well as challenges, such as patriarchy. She observes, among other things, that women may need additional resources and sources of support compared to men in bivocational ministry. She concludes that the Black church must reckon with the expectations that are placed on ministers in general and bivocational ministers in particular, and suggests a scaling back of the functional expectations placed on ministers to hold sacred space, allowing for their human limitations and sense of wellness.

In chapter 5, "Black Student Perspectives," Jo Ann Deasy examines the perspectives of Black seminarians on debt and finances in order to improve the support offered by graduate theological schools. The author draws on qualitative data she and co-researchers collected during a 2019 study on Black student debt by the Association of Theological Schools (ATS). Though not originally designed to inquire about multivocational ministry, the data revealed many challenges for multivocational clergy and the seminaries they attend. Few of the students interviewed expected to make a living wage in ministry after graduation. Most recognized that the congregations they came from and the congregations they planned to serve would not be able to support them financially. Many Black students considered educational debt and multivocational ministry as intentional strategies to assist them in answering their call, pursuing theological education not for financial success or security but in order to minister to their communities. This chapter concludes with implications for graduate theological education.

Part II, leadership, explores multiple perspectives on the opportunities and challenges of bivocational leadership for both pastors and the congregations they serve. This section addresses wide-ranging issues pertaining to bivocational ministry, including calling, perceptions, vocation, mission, spiritual growth, and mentorship. Authors provide important conceptual tools for leadership, including the ideas of unique fit, narrative wisdom, distributive ministry, incarnational ministry, personal growth in sanctification, the bivocational congregation, and shadowing as a mentoring method. These chapters provide numerous case studies and examples of bivocational ministers and congregations across North America, including the results of four empirical studies.

In chapter 6, "Calling in Multivocational Ministry," Mark D. Chapman and James W. Watson draw on data from the Canadian Multivocational Ministry Project to examine the ways in which multivocational leaders understand, frame, articulate, and apply their calling. They observe that that calling includes a general biblical mandate towards certain beliefs and actions and is highly individualized and contextual. They conclude that that calling can be understood as a conversation about the unique fit of the different elements of the multivocational life. To support this understanding of calling, theological educators can encourage self-awareness of how this unique fit contributes to clarity of action, minister health, and passion for what God has asked of the individual. Trainers should help multivocational ministers embrace the complexity and discern the spiritual significance of their calling, supporting integration between spiritual calling, non-traditional careers, and daily life.

In chapter 7, "Pitching Our Tent with Bivocational Ministry," Kristen Plinke Bentley compares Paul's model of self-supporting ministry with narratives of bivocational ministry today. Based on surveys and interviews with Christian Church (Disciples of Christ) ministers serving congregations in Kentucky, Bentley observed three primary narratives about bivocational ministry. Some leaders pointed to economic challenges for congregations, seeing the model as "a sign of the times." Others perceived the missional potential of bivocational ministry, describing it as "on the cutting edge." Others, particularly those in African American and Hispanic/Latinx contexts as well as those in rural communities, saw bivocational ministry as "the way we've always done ministry." These narratives reveal the varied experiences for congregations and ministers related to bivocational ministry. They also demonstrate that some congregations have long-term experience with bivocational pastors that could help others build capacity for well-being and thriving in ministry.

In chapter 8, "Exploring Distributive Ministry," Kwasi Kena argues that bivocational congregations are well positioned to offer the gospel to people in an ever-changing environment. Congregations in the midst of change have an opportunity to re-imagine their ministry configurations as bivocational, allowing non-ordained followers of Christ to participate fully in leadership. For these churches, the shift to bivocational ministry includes a shared-ministry framework the author calls "distributive ministry." Distributive ministry employs a team approach to leadership in which all persons in the congregation function as ministers, sharing pastoral responsibilities. This understanding of distributive ministry is derived from four schools of thought: the priesthood of all believers depicted in Scripture and Martin Luther's writings, missional ecclesiology as articulated by Lesslie Newbigin and others, distributive leadership theory, and the distributed pastorate model described by Geoffrey MacDonald.

In chapter 9, "Incarnating Christ through Bivocational Ministry," Steven C. Van Ostran encourages the church to reframe its understanding of bivocational ministry as a positive way of incarnating Christ. First, he offers the "incarnational church," based on 1 Corinthians 12 and Luke 10, as a model of holistic mission. Then, he presents four benefits of bivocational ministry that might lead churches and pastors to engage in bivocational ministry even when a full-time ministry is possible. The incarnational benefits of bivocational ministry include breaking down the sacred-secular divide, creating community and relationships outside the local congregation, uncovering new opportunities for ministry and mission outside the walls of the church, and reducing the dependencies of the pastor that hinder authentic leadership and prophetic action both in the church and in the community. This chapter draws on Ostran's experience as a pastor and as an executive minister in the American Baptist Churches, as well as experiences of the many bivocational pastors he knows personally.

In chapter 10, "Bivocational Ministry as a Path of Unexpected Spiritual Growth," Ben Connelly shares results and insights from a survey he administered to bivocational ministers regarding their motives and outcomes related to ministry. Motives were grouped in three categories: finances, mission, and convictions. Reported outcomes of bivocational ministry revealed several themes: growth in humility and dependence, a deepened need for a team, and growth in sanctification. Connelly's own experience in bivocational ministry and working with other bivocational ministers in various contexts revealed a pattern of unexpected personal spiritual growth within the bivocational minister. This pattern was supported by the research. Those surveyed entered bivocational ministry for one or multiple reasons, rarely related to their personal spiritual growth. Yet, nearly every minister surveyed shared personal spiritual growth as an outcome, which they did not expect but which came through this unique form of ministry. Regardless of motives, bivocational ministers often find this a path of personal, spiritual growth.

In chapter 11, "The Bivocational Congregation," Anthony Pappas, Ed Pease, and Norm Faramelli address the question: What is the shape of tomorrow's church? The authors answer this question by offering ethnographic case studies of five very different churches to illustrate certain qualities of bivocational congregations: healthy team functioning; a high commitment to being a ministering presence in a particular place; a willingness to die to self, if need be, in the cause of serving others; an acceptance of bivocationality as a full expression of the church, not a second-rate, temporary, expedient form of the church; and a willingness to experiment and trust that a higher power has something wonderful in store for tomorrow. The authors conclude that a congregation does not necessarily have to have a bivocational pastor to exhibit the positive qualities of a bivocational congregation. More important is the dual calling of the congregation to fresh understandings of mission and function. In an epilogue, Pease offers advice on how to prepare a congregation for bivocational ministry.

In chapter 12, "The Bivocational Pastor as Mentor," Herbert Fain shows how Paul's mentorship of Timothy and Titus offers a methodology for shadowing. The shadow methodology, sometimes called pastoral formation, is a specific type of apprenticeship relationship requiring modeling and imitation. Shadowing specifically addresses how to engage in an effective mentor-mentee relationship—a process that is mutually beneficial, providing leadership opportunities for both the mentor and mentee. The shadowing methodology of mentoring is rooted in the Hebrew apprenticeship process, illustrated in the New Testament, and adapted in a contemporary way by many popular leadership authors, such as John C. Maxwell and Harley Atkinson. Bivocational ministers can mentor successfully, despite apparent obstacles such as money and time. When a bivocational minister accepts the call to mentor, this action not only enhances the well-being of the mentor and mentee but also benefits the community.

Part III, learning, addresses the tasks of preparing, equipping, and resourcing persons for successful bivocational ministry. Among these seven chapters are three empirical studies and several discussions of the challenges multivocational ministry poses to traditional graduate theological education. Each of these chapters emphasizes that the task and responsibility of learning are shared by pastors, congregations, judicatories, seminaries, and non-degree programs alike.

In chapter 13, "Empowering the Full Body of Christ," Kathleen Owens aims to equip the full body of Christ for ministry using the variety of gifts, or charisms, found in all members. She employs the image of the Body of Christ, as developed by Paul in the early church and invoked by Luther during the Reformation, to guide the church through times of great technological and societal shifts, such as today. The church still needs people trained for various forms of ministry; changing, argues Owens, is the need for all these skills to be found primarily in one person. She proposes a new model of theological education, empowering the full Body of Christ through discernment of gifts, education and training, and ongoing support and accountability. The transition from full-time to part-time, or bivocational, pastorates offers the church an opportunity to utilize existing educational resources to empower and equip members with specific gifts for ministry. Bivocational pastors need the partnership and support of seminaries and middle-judicatory leaders in this effort.

In chapter 14, "Preparing to Educate for a Thriving Bivocational Ministry," Darryl W. Stephens investigates how institutions of higher learning in theological education can respond to an increasing need for bivocational ministry preparation, training, and support. This chapter presents data from surveys of students, staff, faculty, and trustees at a US, mainline Protestant seminary and learnings from a six-session student focus group. Explored are questions of perception and relevance of bivocational ministry, distinct stressors of bivocational ministry, opinions about current educational programs at the seminary, and opinions about institutional changes designed to better support and prepare seminarians for bivocational ministry. The chapter concludes with a discussion of challenges and opportunities facing institutions of theological education when developing strategic efforts to educate for a thriving bivocational ministry.

In chapter 15, "The Multivocational Plans of Students in Graduate Theological Education," Jo Ann Deasy challenges seminaries to respond to the reality of multivocational ministry, based on data from student questionnaires. Since 2013, the Association of Theological Schools in the United States and Canada (ATS) has tracked the bivocational plans of entering and graduating students among member schools. In 2019, ATS revised the questionnaires to better understand the nature and scope of bivocational ministry, expanding the idea of bivocational ministry beyond paid ministry. The ATS data reveals a complex landscape of multivocational students and graduates navigating work, ministry, vocation, and education in a wide variety of ways. In response, theological schools have the opportunity to rethink current educational models to focus more on integration and life-long learning, to attend to the broad financial ecology of ministry, and to create a more just system designed to equip and support those preparing to serve in multivocational and volunteer ministry roles.

In chapter 16, "Preparing to Teach a Bivocational Ministry Seminary Course," Phil Baisley shares the research behind his seminary course syllabus in bivocational ministry, informed by his own bivocational experience as well as empirical research. As part of a larger grant-funded project, the author spent much of 2015 driving across the United States, from Pennsylvania to Oregon, interviewing bivocational pastors and members of their congregations. He discovered a wide variety of ways of being bivocational as well as many commonalities among bivocational pastors and congregations. Interviewees also shared their ideas about what seminaries should teach about bivocational ministry. The author provides a succinct list of topics to be covered in a bivocational ministry course, along with suggested resources. He concludes by noting continuing challenges to teaching about bivocational ministry.

In chapter 17, "A Mentored Practice Approach to Bivocational Ministry Education," Ronald W. Baard discusses some of the strengths of a mentored practice approach to the formation and education of bivocational ministers. Mentored practice is a type of field education integrating classroom work with the practice of embodied ministry in a particular context. The author draws on his experience as the Dean of the Maine School of Ministry—a non-degree program of the United Church of Christ. Two extended case studies illustrate the mutual benefit to pastoral interns and congregations. For bivocational ministry students, this approach to formation provides deep personal and professional integration through service in the church as a parish pastor. For teaching congregations, mentored practice provides an opportunity to grow in faith along with the pastoral intern. The mentored practice approach to forming ministers provides an alternative to the still-dominant residential seminary-based model.

In chapter 18, "Seeking Information Mastery in Multivocational Ministry," Susan J. Ebertz adopts a model by Hubert Dreyfus to frame the importance of continual learning to achieve mastery in multivocational ministry. This chapter focuses on learning about information rather than learning specific facts: how to determine what information is needed, where to find it, and how to evaluate it. The author then walks through challenges, such as finding time for learning, countering algorithmic bias in internet search engines, and discerning trustworthy and knowledgeable sources. The author concludes by inviting the reader to share what is learned with their congregations, ministry colleagues, and community. Such collaboration brings one in contact with diverse voices, promoting innovation and allowing for creativity in thought and practice. Through careful and efficient research and collaboration with others, multivocational ministers can continue their learning in ways that support effective ministry.

The book concludes with chapter 19, "Reimagining Theological Education with a Multivocational Mindset." Darryl W. Stephens argues that a multivocational mindset is a helpful—perhaps necessary—way to reimagine graduate theological education in North America. The need to educate for intentional bivocational ministry arises from the context of the church in North America. Yet, common attitudes, perceptions, and experiences of bivocational ministry also present challenges to educating for bivocational ministry, and professional theological educators do not often address this topic. Intentional bivocational ministry preparation occurs primarily outside of accredited degree programs. Engaging the work of Justo González on the history of theological education and Daniel Aleshire on the future of theological education, the author reimagines theological education in light of bivocational and multivocational ministry, revealing obstacles to and implications for change. Noting both its necessity and insufficiency, the author argues that a multivocational mindset must be combined with antiracist and other justice-oriented commitments in order to reimagine and accomplish life-giving change within graduate theological education.

Works Cited

Bickers, Dennis W. 2000. *The Tentmaking Pastor: The Joy of Bivocational Ministry*. Grand Rapids, MI: Baker.

———. 2007. *The Work of the Bivocational Pastor*. Valley Forge, PA: Judson.

Chaves, Mark, Joseph Roso, Anna Holleman, and Mary Hawkins. 2020. "National Congregations Study: Waves I–IV Summary Tables." Duke University Department of Sociology, Durham, NC. Last modified January 11, 2021. *sites.duke.edu/ncsweb/files/2021/01/NCS-IV_Summary-Tables_For-Posting.pdf.*

Deasy, Jo Ann. 2018. "Shifting Vocational Identity in Theological Education: Insights from the ATS Student Questionnaires." *Theological Education* 52:63–78. *ats.edu/files/galleries/2018-theological-education-v52-n1.pdf.*

Edington, Mark D. W. 2018. *Bivocational: Returning to the Roots of Ministry.* New York: Church Publishing. *bivocational.church.*

Francis, James M. M., and Leslie J. Francis, eds. 1998. *Tentmaking: Perspectives on Self-Supporting Ministry.* Leominster, Herefordshire: Gracewing.

MacDonald, G. Jeffrey. 2020. *Part-Time is Plenty: Thriving without Full-Time Clergy.* Louisville: Westminster John Knox.

Warnock, Raphael G. 2014. *The Divided Mind of the Black Church: Theology, Piety, and Public Witness.* Religion, Race, and Ethnicity. New York: New York University Press.

Watson, James W., Wanda M. Malcolm, Mark D. Chapman, Elizabeth A. Fisher, Marilyn Draper, Narry F. Santos, Jared Siebert, and Amy Bratton. 2020. "Canadian Multivocational Ministry Project: Research Report." *canadianmultivocationalministry.ca/master-report.*

Landscape

CHAPTER 1

Bivocational Ministry as the Congregation's Curriculum

DARRYL W. STEPHENS

The term bivocational ministry connotes different things to different people.[1] For persons in non-White or immigrant communities, it may be the usual way ministry is done (Bentley 2018, 148; Christian Reformed Church in North America 2020, 13; Deasy 2018, 66, MacDonald 2020, 8–9). For persons in White-majority settings, it may indicate falling short of a goal—namely, the model of a full-time pastorate. For others, it may represent the cutting edge of leadership for the missional church, reaching out into the world in creative, entrepreneurial ways. For many, it begs definition. The range of possible meanings and connotations of this term provide an opportunity for theological education, leading Christian congregations to imagine new ways of being church.

Many congregations in the United States and Canada employ a bivocational pastor. According to a 2018–2019 survey of US congregations, 35% were served by a "head clergyperson" who "also holds another job" (Chaves et al. 2021, 22). Nearly 46% of Episcopal congregations in the United States had no full-time priest in 2014 (Episcopal Church 2014). Preparing pastors for this reality is only one part of the picture. Based on a 2015–2018 study of the economic implications of bi-vocational ministry on Disciples of Christ clergy and congregations in Kentucky, Bentley concluded, "successful bi-vocational ministry relies on more than a minister with a second job that helps pay the bills. It also involves collaboration within congregations and the formation of a sense of ministry that is shared" (Bentley 2018, 147). In other words, the success of bivocational pastorates hinges, in large part, on the ability of the congregation to embrace an understanding of ministry that differs from what they may have been taught to expect, at least in predominantly White, mainline Protestant traditions in North America (MacDonald 2020, 8–9).

This chapter views the ambiguities and uncertainties about defining bivocational ministry as an opportunity for theological reflection and religious education. It begins by acknowledging a context of mainline anxiety about congregational vitality in North America and utilizes Boyung Lee's communal approach to religious education to facilitate imagining new ways of being church. White-majority mainline Protestant denominations in North America are in particular need of coming to terms with bivocational ministry. The central sections of this chapter proceed descriptively, exploring the breadth of definitions of bivocational ministry and related terms, organized around several loci: vocation and ministry, jobs and finances, and commitment. Drawing on a definition of practice by Dorothy Bass, this chapter proposes intentional bivocational ministry as a practice of the entire faith community; bivocational ministry becomes the congregation's curriculum. This chapter concludes with a call for theological educators to assist in this endeavor.

Congregational Vitality and Religious Education

Every White-majority, mainline denomination in the United States and Canada faces anxiety about declining numerical indicators of congregational vitality (Stephens 2020, 2).[2] Cahalan (2005, 63) observed that many of the questions raised in response to North American mainline decline were practical in nature, spurring a turn to practical theology for answers. In response, she suggested moving beyond the problematic "clerical paradigm" identified by Edward

Farley by asserting, "practical theology is first and foremost about wisdom-seeking for all Christians" (64, 93). While Cahalan did not venture into a conversation about bivocational ministry, the questions and concerns are similar. The focus on vital congregations—how to achieve them and how to measure them—coincides with an emerging awareness of bivocational ministry as an alternative to the way many declining congregations have conceived of and structured their ministry since their founding.

The professional model of a full-time, seminary-trained pastor captures and confines the imagination of many congregations. MacDonald (2020, 23) termed this "the full-time bias." According to Edington (2018, 5), this "standard model" of ministry "has shaped not just the economic arrangements that underlie what we think of as 'church'; it has shaped much of what we understand to be involved in the practice of ministry and congregational leadership." At issue is not merely a financial strategy to accommodate declining church budgets but a different approach to ministry entirely. Thus, bivocational ministry can seem counter to the received wisdom of what counts as "church." Edington pressed further: "the question many congregations face today is whether this professional model of ministry is consistent with their future, or with them having a future" (6).

The traditional, full-time pastorate is yielding to other models of ministry, many of them bivocational. Many congregations find themselves seeking a bivocational pastor out of financial necessity. They simply cannot afford to pay a full-time salary—unless the pastor happens to be a married male in the US South or Midwest regions (Perry and Schleifer 2019). The Church Pension Group of the Episcopal Church (US) reported "that only 52% of all priests are in single full-time parochial calls in churches," described as "the model of years ago," and that, disproportionately, a greater share of the fully compensated priests are men (Episcopal Church 2018). This reality is not lost on seminary students preparing to enter the job market. "In 2017, 30% of all graduates reported plans to serve in bivocational ministry," according to the Graduating Student Questionnaire administered by members of the Association of Theological Schools (Deasy 2018, 66). In the face of financial pressures, bivocational ministry, also called multivocational, dual career, nonstipendiary, or tentmaking ministry (a reference to the example of Paul in Acts 18:3), offers another path for the future of congregational ministry.

There are barriers to this path. Lee (2013, viii) identified individualism as "the fundamental problem in our [US] society as well as in theological education and ministry of the mainline" and presented a communal model of pedagogy in response.

> Christian education seeks to lead one out to new and imaginative ways of being in relationship with God and others. The root meaning of education and Christian education challenges us as mainline Christians to think differently and broadly. We need to move to holistic ways of imagining and being the church. (Lee 2013, 49)

Transforming congregations requires imagination enabled by a process of religious education. The heart of her argument is, "if the mainline rethinks its ministry through pedagogical reformation, a healthy community can be created and promoted" (ix). Thus, Lee provided a holistic way of integrating education and reflection:

> education is to help people find a truth that is already within them . . . helping learners, regardless of their age, to remember what they know and to critically reflect on this in their present life contexts; it is to develop something new for the future. (Lee 2013, 47)

Lee's emphasis on theological reflection as an essential part of education grounds religious education in practical theology, understood here as critical reflection on the practices of the church for the sake of improving those practices. In order to improve the practice of ministry, however, congregations must be educated to imagine ministry in new ways.

Vocation and Ministry

Generally, the term *bivocational* describes the work life of a pastor (paid or unpaid) who also holds another job (paid or unpaid). This definition begs significant theological questions, however. For example, what does it mean to have a vocation or more than one vocation, and what does that imply about what counts as ministry?

In common usage, the term *bivocational* (or *bi-vocational*) refers almost exclusively to persons in ministry, as easily confirmed by any internet search engine. One does not typically refer to a teacher as bivocational, even if they simultaneously hold another job unrelated to teaching—unless, of course, the "other" job is leading a Christian congregation. The term *bivocational* implies pastoral ministry as being among one's vocations. While the word *bivocational* is more common, the word *multivocational* more accurately describes the actual situation of some pastors. Seeking to discover a wide diversity of secondary employment among pastors, the team of researchers behind what was originally called the Canadian Bivocational Ministry Project found that it was not uncommon for a bivocational minister to have more than one job or significant volunteer commitment in addition to "a congregational leadership role" (Watson et al. 2020, 5). Thus, they renamed their study the Canadian Multivocational Ministry Project.

Vocation can mean job, profession, or calling. In the context of ministry, vocation is often laden with an understanding of God's design, directive, or nudging. For example, to be "called" into ministry implies some kind of divine prompt, traditionally requiring a response along the lines of, "Here I am!" (Gen. 22:1; Exod. 3:4; 1 Sam. 3:4; Isa. 6:8, etc.). There is some intentionality and purpose behind vocation. The term *bivocational* could imply either the existence of more than one divine call on a person's life or simply more than one understanding of the word *vocation*—one sacred and one secular. Often implied is the latter (without any critical exploration of the supposed sacred/secular distinction): a bivocational minister is a person called to pastoral leadership who also earns money doing something else. Must the "ministry" in bivocational ministry necessarily be pastoral, though?

On the one hand, *bivocational* accurately describes many non-pastoral forms of ministry, expressed in diverse contexts and often combined with other careers. "In some ways the idea that ministry is bivocational may seem like a statement of the obvious; each of us who shares in the ministry of the baptized is meant to carry out that ministry in the world, and not merely in the church" (Edington 2018, 2). The ministry of all Christians—the priesthood of all believers—is premised on the idea that Christians are called to many different jobs in combination with living out their discipleship. This form of ministry is called *diakonia*—"Christian service to which all the baptized are called and which is part of the mission of Christ's church in the world" (DIAKONIA World Federation Executive Committee 1998). Persons called to representative *diakonia*—the diaconate[3]—are ordained as permanent deacons in some traditions and work in a variety of capacities within and without the church. For example, the Episcopal Church (US) reported, "The majority of the church's 3000 permanent deacons are by nature bivocational in that they are generally non-stipendiary, at least in parochial positions" (Episcopal Church 2018). Ironically, because the work of *diakonia*, including that of persons set apart for the diaconate, essentially involves multiple expressions of ministry and employment, these folks are generally not described as bivocational.

On the other hand, the word *bivocational* tends to be reserved for those persons in a ministerial role considered by many to be incommensurate with holding a job outside of the church: pastoral leaders. For example, Watson et al. (2020, 3) observed, "Tentmaking, bivocational, and multivocational are all terms currently used to describe how people who are involved in congregational leadership and work outside the congregation can combine those worlds." Here, "congregational leadership" implies the work of a pastor as distinct from other expressions of ministry. The normative valence of the congregational context for ministry is also evident in the post-2013 Association of Theological Schools Graduating Student Questionnaire, in which "ministry positions were divided into two categories: ministry in a congregation/parish or ministry in an 'other' setting" (Deasy 2018, 64). For example, Watson et al. (2020, 5) included "chaplain" in their list of "other occupations" held by bivocational pastors. Thus, persons primarily engaged in ministries located outside the congregation are not usually considered under the umbrella of bivocational ministry even if they also hold other forms of employment.

Univocational ministry, termed the "traditional pastoral model" (Woods 2013) or "the standard model" (Edington 2018, 5), paradoxically points both to the larger context in which bivocational ministry makes sense and to the paradigm of ministry that intentional bivocational ministry transcends. A spectrum of congregational employment arrangements vary from the standard model: bi-ministry involves "sharing a pastor with another ministry setting," bi-congregational involves "sharing a pastor with another congregation," and bivocational involves "sharing a pastor with a business or company" (Woods 2013). Bi-congregational arrangements are familiar in Methodism, for example, in which a pastor may be appointed to multiple congregational settings known as "charges." In the United Church of Christ in the United States, yoking parishes is becoming a more common arrangement. When both jobs are the same vocation (i.e., pastoral ministry), however, is the arrangement still considered bivocational (MacDonald 2020, 99)? Regardless, the fully funded pastor of a single congregation is both the reference point and the departure point for developing a robust theology of intentional bivocational ministry.

Jobs and Finances

At the most basic level, the word *bivocational* implies having more than one job and source of income. A bivocational pastor typically earns money through non-ministerial activities outside of the congregation they serve. Unpaid work can also be considered a part of the mix. For example, the research team for the Canadian Multivocational Ministry Project interviewed people who had "more than one job or serious volunteer commitment in addition to a congregational leadership role" (Watson et al. 2020, 5). Some claimed volunteer positions as their second vocation. Conversely, some bivocational pastors do not receive a salary from the church they serve. Brown brought attention to the large numbers of unpaid ministerial staff in the Black church context who are necessarily bivocational (chapter 4 in this volume). Drawing on the activities of Paul, Kruger (2020, 163) defined tentmaking as an intentional "missiological method of complete self-support," in which the pastor refuses remuneration from the congregation they are serving. "Volunteer ministers" and "non-stipendiary clergy" engage in what is termed "self-supporting ministry" in the Church of England context (Lees 2018; Samushonga 2020, 4; Samushonga, chapter 2 in this volume). Thus, Samushonga (2019, 69) advocated a broad definition of bivocational minister: "one who has a ministry vocation and another vocation that is not ministry oriented" and was quick to note that "even this definition is open to further interrogation due to the uniqueness and diversity of ministry practice." In actuality, the proportion of time spent in pastoral ministry and pay received from the congregation varies from case to case. Many bivocational pastors work a full-time job outside of the church, for example. Whatever the configuration, multiple responsibilities of employment and finances are integral to understanding bivocational ministry.

The bivocational pastor is more than a lay volunteer, even if unpaid. Bentley (2018, 118), the lead researcher at Lexington Theological Seminary, emphasized: "Bi-vocational ministers are individuals who are licensed, commissioned, or ordained ministers serving in a congregation who also receive income through employment outside the congregation." The bivocational minister is set apart for the task; some form of credentialing is often implied or assumed. The boundary-blurring feature of bivocational ministry is that the pastor also crosses back over, employing themselves in what is often considered the "secular" realm through activities beyond the scope of their ministerial credentialing.

Multiple jobs can mean multiple loyalties. One judicatory task force specifically pointed out the connection between finances and accountability: "Bivocationality is the arrangement in which a pastor spends time and energy working for compensation and is accountable to another in addition to the setting in which s/he has been called to minister" (Christian Reformed Church in North America 2020, 11). Emphasizing multiple accountabilities, this definition raises the question of divided loyalties and commitments. Perhaps to prevent unnecessary conflicts of interests, some church polities require judicatory oversight of such arrangements. For example, in the Episcopal Church (US), "it is canonically required that a priest get permission from the bishop to accept another part-time or full-time secular job" (Episcopal Church 2018). The same expectation is present in other denominations. United Methodist polity dictates, "full-time service shall be the norm for ordained elders," and defines "full-time service [to] mean that the person's entire vocational time . . . is devoted to the work of ministry in the field of labor to which one is appointed by the bishop" (United Methodist Church 2016, para. 338.1). Transgressing the boundary between a traditional pastorate and other means of making money creates no small degree of institutional anxiety.

Commitment

The presence of other commitments in the bivocational pastor's life should not be mistaken for a half-hearted commitment to the church. Bivocational ministry is not just the result of receiving an insufficient congregational paycheck—a depiction feeding the stigma that the bivocational pastor is "judged 'not good enough' to draw in the people needed to pay that full-time salary" (McDougall 2016, 3; see also MacDonald 2020, 6). A singular focus on remuneration can unwittingly play into cultural evaluations of worth measured in dollars. Samushonga (2019, 72) identified two common criticisms of bivocational ministry, both tied to money: "the conceptualising of [bivocational ministry] as serving two masters (God and money)" and "the consideration of bivocational ministers as those 'lacking faith' to trust God for provision." Both criticisms call into question the bivocational minister's commitment to ministry.

"Don't call us part-time!" This sentiment is prevalent among bivocational pastors. "[M]any bivocational ministers do not describe themselves as part-time because they consider their entire lives as full-time ministry" (Samushonga 2019, 68). Edington (2018, 2) noted that while "many pastors are part-time," it would be more accurate to call them "partially compensated." Bivocational ministers in Kentucky "made the case that even though bi-vocational ministers have employment outside the congregation and are not paid what others would call a full-time salary by congregations, they are fully engaged in ministry in ways not communicated by the term, 'part-time'" (Bentley 2018, 118). The task force of the Christian Reformed Church in North America asserted: "Every pastor in a nontraditional arrangement is fully and at all times the pastor of the community they have been called to serve. Thus we discourage any reference in any context to a part-time pastor" (Christian Reformed Church in North America 2020, 12). Taking a different tack, MacDonald (2020, 28) argued for removing the stigma from the term: "Just as America has embraced working mothers, mainline churches need to embrace part-time [pastoring] as a legitimate, holy, every-bit-as-dedicated calling." MacDonald's implication is clear: bivocational pastors are fully committed to ministry.

Specifically, many pastors are fully committed to bivocational ministry. "[T]here is an emerging concept of intentional bivocationalism," observed Samushonga (2019, 77). This understanding of ministry is distinct from part-time and shared pastoral ministries that exist as extensions of the professional model of ministry (Edington 2018, 7). Done intentionally, "bivocational ministry begins with a different set of assumptions, and ends with a different understanding of how the church can be structured to do its work of ministry" (8). Rainer (2016) made a distinction between "a traditional bivocational pastor" as a matter of necessity because the congregation cannot afford a full-time pastor and "a marketplace pastor" who serves in a church that could offer full-time compensation but, by mutual decision, chooses not to. Some intentional bivocational ministers reported that their financial independence from the congregation empowered their ministry, allowing them "to engage with the congregation on equal footing" (Bentley 2018, 129). Not beholden to the congregation as their sole employer, bivocational ministers can afford to take risks and innovate new ministries—a testament to their vocational commitment.

Bivocational ministry can be an intentional missional and vocational strategy. The incarnational aspect of ministry by a pastor and congregation engaged in work outside the walls of the church allows them to reach folks they would not otherwise be able to reach (Christian Reformed Church in North America 2020, 17; Edington 2018, 14; Watson et al. 2020, 15). In some contexts, such as extreme secularization (Watson and Santos 2019, 139) or in countries that restrict evangelism (Forum for World Evangelization 2004, sec. 3.1; Global Connections 2008), working a secular job is a cross-cultural missional strategy, though "overseas" tentmaking is sometimes distinguished from other forms of bivocational ministry (Samushonga 2020, 2). This option is of particular importance to church planters, who cannot count on a salary from a fledgling congregation. The term *covocational* is sometimes used to identify a situation in which "the pastor's calling and ministry occur in a traditionally nonpastoral setting," such as a church planter running a coffee shop as a ministry (Christian Reformed Church in North America 2020, 11–12). For these and other bivocational ministers, the secular job is also ministry: "Tentmakers witness with their whole lives and their jobs are integral to their work for the Kingdom of God" (Forum for World Evangelization 2004, sec. 3.1). This whole-life witness evidences integration of one's multiple vocations.

Integration can contribute to successful and healthy bivocational ministry. Edington (2018, 6) argued that the bivocational pastor's "spiritual health depends on how well [they] can integrate [multiple] aspects of [their] working life." The importance of vocational integration arose as one of the main findings of the Canadian Multivocational Ministry Project: "Multivocational work is integrated when there is a synergistic relationship between congregational leadership and other work" (Watson et al. 2020, 16). Regarding "other work" in relation to pastoral ministry, Watson and colleagues (2020, 17) found successful examples along a spectrum: "contributing to ministry (integrated), providing a personal benefit (complementary), or worth the money (lucrative)." Done well and intentionally, however, any of these relationships between multiple vocations would seem to fit Edington's understanding of integration toward spiritual health of the bivocational pastor.

Bivocational Ministry as the Congregation's Curriculum

In light of the foregoing discussion of vocation and ministry, jobs and finances, and commitment, it should be clear that bivocational ministry is more than a money-saving strategy for dwindling congregations. While church finances are an important consideration, intentional bivocational ministry requires much more than a part-time employment contract. "Financial necessity just happens to be the catalyst" for re-imagining pastoral ministry (MacDonald 2020, 29). Put more forcefully by Kirkpatrick (2014)—also writing from a US context—"Now is the time for creativity, innovation and experimentation to adjust to what is increasingly the new normal for congregations around the country." Theological reflection on intentional bivocational ministry as a practice involving both clergy and laity provides opportunity for transforming congregational life. Bivocational ministry can become the congregation's curriculum.

Bivocational ministry can be imagined as an intentional practice of an entire faith community. "Practices are those shared activities that address fundamental human needs and that, woven together, form a way of life" (Bass 1997, xi). Ministry is such a shared activity, and the practice of ministry is and should be "a way of life" for the congregation. Practicing ministry, though, is not sufficient for transforming congregations. Disciplined, theological reflection on this practice is also needed.

> Reflecting on practices as they have been shaped in the context of Christian faith leads us to encounter the possibility of a faithful way of life, one that is both attuned to present-day needs and taught by ancient wisdom. And here is the really important point: this encounter can change how we live each day (Bass 1997, xi).

Exploring various definitions of bivocational ministry is one means of attending to present-day needs and learning from the wisdom of those who have blazed this trail. To press this learning even further, theological reflection within a process of religious education can help this encounter become transformative.

Ministry has many facets, offering a full curriculum for learning a faithful way of life. Building on the work of Maria Harris, Lee proposed,

> a church's entire ministry of worship, fellowship, teaching, mission, and proclamation can serve as its curriculum. Even without participating in an educational event, people teach and learn how to be a member of the community through the church's basic forms of ministry. (Lee 2013, ix)

Bivocational ministry, of course, encompasses this entire range of activities. This process can be transformative: "the mainline can create a healthy community by approaching its entire ministry as an educational endeavor" (Lee 2013, ix). For bivocational ministry to become the congregation's curriculum, though, it must be embraced as the practice of the entire faith community.

As a congregational curriculum, intentional bivocational ministry is a shared practice of laity and clergy. The congregation and the pastor must be equally committed to bivocational ministry (Bickers 2007, 6; Edington 2018, 8; MacDonald 2020, 65). One of the limitations of the standard model of ministry is its almost-exclusive focus on the role of clergy. Many definitions of bivocational ministry share this limitation, parsing what kind of "other" employment qualifies the pastor as bivocational. Without a robust understanding of the priesthood of all believers, bivocational ministry cannot take root within a congregation. A successful and healthy bivocational pastorate requires an understanding of shared ministry and mission between the pastor and the entire congregation. Members of the congregation cannot engage in bivocational ministry as passive recipients of a professionalized ministry. Thus, a congregation must enter into an intentional process of Christian education, in which all members are challenged to embrace "holistic ways of imagining and being the church" (Lee 2013, 49). For the practice of bivocational ministry to become the congregation's curriculum, the entire congregation must become bivocational.

Becoming a bivocational congregation requires moving beyond the received model of "clericalism" centered on the seminary-trained, ordained pastor. Edington (2018, 5) observed, "congregations that are relatively more 'group centered' than 'pastor centered' will likely find themselves better suited to a bivocational pastorate." The pastor in a bivocational congregation becomes part of a team of leaders—and perhaps not the starring role (MacDonald 2020, 63). Pappas and colleagues (chapter 11 in this volume) even suggested that a congregation does not necessarily need "a bivocational pastor to exhibit the positive qualities of a bivocational congregation." Their point was that bivocational ministry characterizes the congregation, not only its leader. Thus, they identified "healthy team functioning" at the top of their list of attributes of an effective bivocational congregation. They were not alone in identifying shared leadership as essential to the bivocational congregation (see for example, Watson et al. 2020, 19). MacDonald (2020, 69) offered three models for pastors in bivocational congregations: equipper, ambassador, and multistaff team member. Each of these options de-centers the pastor and spreads responsibility and authority among the laity. Edington (2018, 6) offered a concise account: "A bivocational ministry is a work of the entire congregation; it is not merely a way of describing the working life of one person who happens to be ordained." Bivocational ministry prioritizes the identification of each member's particular gifts and graces and enables them to contribute to the overall ministry of the congregation.

The transformative potential of intentional bivocational ministry depends, for many, on a change in perception of what counts as church and ministry. MacDonald (2020, 7) emphasized: "this is a different breed of congregation." A bivocational congregation includes laypersons who express "a willingness to experiment and take responsibility for [their] congregation" (Pappas et al., chapter 11 in this volume). Church members and leaders might benefit from studying what has been termed *mutual ministry, collaborative ministry, every-member ministry,* and *total ministry* (Fenhagen 1977; Pickard 2009; Tiller 1998, 384; Zabriskie 1995). Each of these models emphasizes the role of the laity in the ministry of the congregation. Laity must learn how to bear one another's burdens, lead each other in prayer, reclaim the liturgy as the work of the people, share the faith, and support ongoing Christian education for all ages. For example, Stephen Ministries provides a model for equipping laity to serve in roles of pastoral care, complementing the role of the pastor (Stephen Ministries St. Louis n.d.). The specific ways in which laity and clergy partner in ministry must be worked out in the context of each congregation and in light of the gifts that each member brings to the community.[4] Bivocational congregations require an expansive understanding of Christian vocation, bridging lay and clergy, sacred and secular (see for example, Cahalan 2017).

This understanding of bivocational ministry as the practice of a congregation clearly differs from forms of tentmaking ministry undertaken by individuals outside of or prior to an anticipated congregational context. Covocational ministry, "overseas" tentmaking, and early stages of church planting are important missional strategies undertaken by pastors, often with a source of income beyond the church. These ministries, however, can only become the curriculum of the faith community when there is a congregation to share in the bivocational endeavor. It does not take many: only two or three gathered in Jesus's name (Matt. 18:20).

Conclusions

Bivocational ministry is a topic of increasing relevance within conversations about the future of the church and congregational vitality. Imagining new ways of being church is a particular challenge for White-majority, mainline congregations in North America, though Christian faith communities of all demographics, denominational traditions, and geographic locations are being challenged to reflect theologically on the meanings and implications of bivocational ministry. Theological educators can guide congregations in imagining and being the church in ways that transcend the model of a fully funded, professionally trained pastor of a single congregation. As an intentional practice, bivocational ministry can become the congregation's curriculum.

Theological educators can assist congregations in this task. A bivocational congregation transgresses inherited divisions between clergy and laity, sacred and secular, pastoring and mission. Each of these developments presents an opportunity for re-imagining the church and its ministry. Further research on bivocational congregations, building on existing research on the missional church, vital congregations, and ecclesiology, is needed. Furthermore, there is a lot that White-majority, mainline congregations can learn from Christians outside their immediate demographic, many of whom have been engaged in faithful bivocational ministry for generations.

Works Cited

Bass, Dorothy C. 1997. "Preface." In *Practicing Our Faith: A Way of Life for a Searching People*, edited by Dorothy C. Bass, ix–xv. San Francisco: Jossey-Bass.

Bentley, Kristen Plinke. 2018. "Perspectives of Bi-Vocational Ministry: Emerging Themes in Bi-Vocational Ministry Research at Lexington Theological Seminary." *Lexington Theological Quarterly* 48:115–51. *lextheo.edu/wp-content/uploads/2021/09/j-4-Perspectives-of-Bi-Vocational-Ministry.pdf.*

Bickers, Dennis W. 2007. *The Work of the Bivocational Minister.* Valley Forge, PA: Judson.

Cahalan, Kathleen A. 2005. "Three Approaches to Practical Theology, Theological Education, and the Church's Ministry." *International Journal of Practical Theology* 9:63–94. *doi.org/10.1515/IJPT.2005.005.*

———. 2017. *The Stories We Live: Finding God's Calling All around Us.* Grand Rapids, MI: Eerdmans.

Chaves, Mark, Joseph Roso, Anna Holleman, and Mary Hawkins. 2020. "National Congregations Study: Waves I–IV Summary Tables." Duke University Department of Sociology, Durham, NC. Last modified January 11, 2021. *sites.duke.edu/ncsweb/files/2021/01/NCS-IV_Summary-Tables_For-Posting.pdf.*

Christian Reformed Church in North America. 2020. "Study of Bivocationality Task Force." October 30. *faithaliveresources.org/Products/830135/study-of-bivocationality-task-force.aspx.*

Deasy, Jo Ann. 2018. "Shifting Vocational Identity in Theological Education: Insights from the ATS Student Questionnaires." *Theological Education* 52, no. 1: 63–78. *ats.edu/files/galleries/2018-theological-education-v52-n1.pdf.*

DIAKONIA World Federation Executive Committee. 1998. "Diaconal Reflections: How We Experience Our Diaconal Calling in Our Diversity." *diakonia-world.org/files/theologiepapier98english.pdf.*

Edington, Mark D. W. 2018. *Bivocational: Returning to the Roots of Ministry.* New York: Church Publishing. *bivocational.church.*

Episcopal Church. 2014. "Episcopal Domestic Fast Facts: 2014." *episcopalchurch.org/files/documents/2014 _fast_facts.pdf.*

———. 2018. "Bivocational Clerics." *Title IV Website. titleiv.org/general-education-and-best-practices/priest-and-deacons/bivocational-clerics.*

Fenhagen, James C. 1977. *Mutual Ministry: New Vitality for the Local Church.* New York: Seabury.

Forum for World Evangelization. 2004. "The Local Church in Mission, Lausanne Occasional Paper No. 39." *lausanne.org/content/lop/local-church-mission-lop-39#cpb.*

Global Connections. 2008. "The Challenge of Tentmaking, Serving God through One's Profession and Business Overseas." *globalconnections.org.uk/papers/the-challenge-of-tentmaking.*

Kirkpatrick, Nathan. 2014. "It's Time to Recalibrate Expectations for Clergy." *Faith & Leadership,* August 5. *faithandleadership.com/it%e2%80%99s-time-recalibrate-expectations-clergy.*

Kruger, Kurt T. 2020. *Tentmaking: A Misunderstood Missiological Method.* Eugene, OR: Wipf & Stock.

Lee, Boyung. 2013. *Transforming Congregations through Community: Faith Formation from the Seminary to the Church.* Louisville: Westminster John Knox.

Lees, John. 2018. *Self-Supporting Ministry: A Practical Guide.* London: SPCK.

MacDonald, G. Jeffrey. 2020. *Part-Time is Plenty: Thriving without Full-Time Clergy.* Louisville: Westminster John Knox.

McDougall, Diane J. 2016. "The Many-Layered Lives of Bivocational Pastors." *EFCA Today* 91: 3–5. *efcatoday.org/sites/default/files/downloads/printable/EFCA_Spring2016_PDF-4.pdf.*

Perry, Samuel L., and Cyrus Schleifer. 2019. "Are Bivocational Clergy Becoming the New Normal? An Analysis of the Current Population Survey, 1996–2017." *Journal for the Scientific Study of Religion* 58: 513–25. *doi.org/10.1111/jssr.12593.*

Pickard, Stephen K. 2009. *Theological Foundations for Collaborative Ministry.* Explorations in Practical, Pastoral, and Empirical Theology. Farnham: Ashgate.

Rainer, Thom. 2016. "The New Marketplace Pastor. Church Answers Featuring Thom Rainer." January 26. Audio. *churchanswers.com/podcasts/rainer-on-leadership/the-new-marketplace-pastor-rainer-on-leadership-193.*

Samushonga, Hartness M. 2019. "A Theological Reflection of Bivocational Pastoral Ministry: A Personal Reflective Account of a Decade of Bivocational Ministry Practice Experience." *Practical Theology* 12: 66–80. *doi.org/10.1080/1756073X.2019.1575040.*

———. 2020. "On Bivocational Ministry-focused Training in British Theological Schools: Dialoguing with British Theological Educationalists." *Practical Theology* 13: 385–99. *doi.org/10.1080/1756073X.2020.1787006.*

Stephen Ministries St. Louis. n.d. "History of Stephen Ministries." Accessed January 11, 2021. *www.stephenministries.org/aboutus/default.cfm/721.*

Stephens, Darryl W. 2020. "Healing Congregations: A Corrective to the Metrics of Congregational Vitality." *Witness: The Journal of the Academy for Evangelism in Theological Education* 34: 1–13. *journals.sfu.ca/witness/index.php/witness/article/view/59.*

Tiller, John. 1998. "Towards a Theology of a Local Ordained Ministry." In *Tentmaking: Perspectives on Self-Supporting Ministry*, edited by James M. M. Francis and Leslie J. Francis, 382–88. Herefordshire: Gracewing.

United Methodist Church. 2016. *The Book of Discipline of The United Methodist Church 2016*. Nashville: United Methodist Publishing House.

Watson, James W., and Narry F. Santos. 2019. "Tentmaking: Creative Mission Opportunities within a Secularizing Canadian Society." In *Mission and Evangelism in a Secularizing World: Academy, Agency, and Assembly Perspectives from Canada*, edited by Narry F. Santos and Mark Naylor, 131–48. Evangelical Missiological Society Monograph Series 2. Eugene, OR: Pickwick.

Watson, James W., Wanda M. Malcolm, Mark D. Chapman, Elizabeth A. Fisher, Marilyn Draper, Narry F. Santos, Jared Siebert, and Amy Bratton. 2020. "Canadian Multivocational Ministry Project:

Research Report." *canadianmultivocationalministry.ca/master-report.*

Woods, C. Jeff. 2013. "Alternative Pastoral Models." *Alban at Duke Divinity School.* January 9. *alban.org/archive/alternative-pastoral-models.*

Zabriskie, Stewart C. 1995. *Total Ministry: Reclaiming the Ministry of All God's People.* Herndon, VA: Alban Institute.

Notes

1 This research was funded by Lancaster Theological Seminary and a matching grant from the In Trust Center for Theological Schools. An earlier version of this chapter, published under a CC-BY license, appeared as: Stephens, Darryl W. 2021. "Bivocational Ministry as the Congregation's Curriculum." *Religions* 12, no. 1: 56. Special Issue: Practical Theology & Theological Education — An Overview. *doi.org/10.3390/rel12010056.*

2 Discussion of this anxiety is well beyond the scope of this chapter. Many factors contribute to the White-majority, mainline church's difficulty embracing bivocational ministry as a legitimate, faithful, and equally valuable alternative to fully funded ministry. Factors include racism, ethnocentrism, nationalism, exceptionalism, colonialism, Christendom, patriarchy, individualism, materialism, and an obsession with numerical success. There is much that the White mainline could learn from non-White and immigrant communities about diverse ways of being church and about bivocational ministry, in particular.

3 According to the DIAKONIA World Federation, the diaconate consists of "those called, identified, prepared, set apart and/or commissioned [or ordained] for 'public' ministry of diakonia, sometimes doing diakonia in the name of the church, sometimes encouraging greater involvement of all the baptized in diakonia, and sometimes serving as a sign and reminder that Christ has called the whole church to diakonia" (DIAKONIA World Federation Executive Committee 1998).

4 In this light, *bivocational* could also refer to the partnered vocations of laity and clergy. It is beyond the scope of this chapter to pursue this new, innovative use of the term.

CHAPTER 2

British Perspectives on Bivocational Ministry

HARTNESS M. SAMUSHONGA

The notion of bivocational ministry, in which ministers have another vocation outside of ministry, is not new. Bivocational ministry is considered the original model for ministry in the New Testament. From the time of the apostle Paul, many ministers have taken this approach to participate in the *missio dei* (Samushonga 2020a, 144). In fact, in recent years, bivocational ministry (or multivocational ministry) is increasingly becoming a subject of interest and dialogue in a variety of locations and contexts, including churches, denominations, and theological schools. Recently, the quest to understand and develop bivocational ministry has taken an international approach. The year 2020 saw the establishment of an international consultation among practitioners, researchers, writers, and educators, mainly from the United States and Canada, to collaborate on research pertaining to bivocational ministry. This initiative was spearheaded by Darryl Stephens, the editor of this volume, as part of the Educating for a Thriving Bivocational Ministry Project at his institution, Lancaster Theological Seminary.[1]

Stephens's international approach to bivocational ministry stimulated me, as a participant in the consultation, to write this chapter with the focus of offering insights on bivocational ministry from a British perspective. I am a British practical theologian with research interest in bivocational ministry practice. Although my interests in the phenomenon are wide-ranging, I have paid particular attention to exploring and researching the notion of bivocational ministry from the context of Britain (Samushonga 2020b). Through my research, I found that although Britain has one of the wealthiest legacies of bivocational ministry (Allen 1923; Francis and Francis 1998; Lees 2018; Samushonga 2019; Vaughan 1987) and a sizable literature on self-supporting ministry (Francis and Francis 1998; Fuller and Vaughan 1986; Lees 2018), academic literature on this phenomenon in the context of Britain is obscure. It is important for practitioners, researchers, writers, and educators to be aware of how these approaches to ministry are described in order to inform a broader understanding of this phenomena. With Britain having a wealth of the phenomenon (as will emerge in this chapter), an exploration of British bivocational ministry constitutes an important contribution to a global picture of bivocational ministry. This chapter hence offers insights on bivocational ministry in the context of Britain to complement other perspectives presented in this volume.

Statistics on the incidence of bivocational ministry are scarce. Many countries, church denominations, and ministries do not widely publish statistics of how many of their clergy also hold another job out of ministry. The Church of England (CoE), also known as the Anglican Church, is one of the oldest and historically largest church establishments in Britain. CoE publishes annual data of self-supporting ministers—a concept associated with the notion of bivocational ministry. In 2019, 37% of ministers in the CoE were self-supporting (Church of England 2021). This mirrors the 35% of US churches served by a bivocational pastor (Chaves et al. 2020, 22). However, the label "self-supporting ministers" largely refers to ministers with another vocation (or vocations) that supports their livelihood without depending on the ministry. In the context of the Church of England, this category also includes retired ministers who have returned to ministry practice supported on their pension rather than another job. Nevertheless, some forms of self-supporting ministry fit the definition of bivocational ministry proffered above.

In this chapter, I discuss the following broad questions on bivocational ministry from a British perspective: (1) How is bivocational ministry described in British literature? (2) What is the history of bivocational ministry in Britain? (3) What are the current and predicted states of play of bivocational ministry in Britain? In responding to these questions, I present the reader with the opportunity to evaluate how the scope of bivocational ministry in Britain measures against that of other parts of the world.

Describing Bivocational Ministry in Britain

Although bivocational ministry is prevalent, the term "connotes different things to different people" (Stephens, chapter 1 in this volume). Bivocationalism is described in a variety of ways in different geographical and ministry contexts. In defining bivocational ministry, I have advocated for a definition that moves away from the traditional description based on how ministers are remunerated (or not). I proffered that "a bivocational minister [is] one who has a ministry vocation and another vocation that is not ministry oriented" (Samushonga 2019, 69). In proffering this definition, I acknowledge the diversity of Christian ministry, which is not restricted to ecclesial ministry. Therefore, bivocational ministry can be carried out in non-congregational settings.

While the labels *bivocational ministry* and *bivocational pastor* are widely used in US practice and literature to describe the ministry of pastors who receive part of their salary from another role outside of church ministry (Bickers 2010), this label is a rarity in British literature. The majority of British literature on bivocational ministry, as defined above, is in the context of the CoE. The phenomenon has been described in different ways in the CoE throughout the generations using labels such as *voluntary clergy, auxiliary priests, honorary ministers, working* or *worker-priests, priest-workers, tentmaking ministers* (from the Apostle Paul's example), *dual-role pastors* or *priests, non-stipendiary ministers*, and *self-supporting ministers, priests*, or *pastors* (outside of CoE) (Francis and Francis 1998, xv).

From a broader perspective, bivocational ministers are described as clergy who have two vocations—one that is ministry-oriented and another that is outside the church. This contrasts with the description of a bivocational minister as one who serves in a paid ministry position and has income from another source. Although using different labels, the Church of England generally follows this salary or wage-based approach to describe members of clergy who serve in a bivocational capacity. In the CoE literature, a *non-stipendiary minister*, a term introduced by Bishop Russell Barry in 1935 (Lees 2018, 22), is defined in contrast to a stipendiary minister—one who is fully supported financially by the church.

According to both CoE official literature and other CoE-focused research, the notion of non-stipendiary ministers has a broad application, which includes retirees (ministers) who return to serve in ministry without receiving a stipend (wage), ministers who serve in the church but receive their income from another ministry outside of church, such as hospital chaplains, and ministers who continue work in secular employment while undertaking ministry in a non-stipendiary capacity. Although the CoE largely uses the label *non-stipendiary ministers*, scholars have sought to differentiate between the various forms of non-stipendiary ministers and favor the term *ministry* (or *ministers*) *in secular employment*. It is reported that this title originated from the ministers themselves "and appeared in the title of the First National Conference of Ministers in Secular Employment held at Nottingham in 1984" (Fuller and Vaughan 1986).

Yet the use of the term *secular* to describe the non-ministry-oriented vocation is a cause of debate in bivocational literature. The Cape Town Commitment described the use of the term *secular* as "the falsehood of a sacred-secular divide" (Lausanne Movement 2011). However, ministry and non-ministry vocations are distinct from one another; for example ministry-focused vocations such as teaching (in non-theological school or subjects), engineering, accounting, nursing, and so on, do not require ministry awareness, ministry calling, or ministerial skills and competency. I therefore find no concern in making the distinction in order to give a clearer definition of the concept of bivocational ministry. The term *bivocational ministers*, as described in this chapter, is one way of responding to this secular versus ministry debate.

Although the term *bivocational ministry* is not widely used in UK literature, which is largely focused on or is mostly written by scholars from CoE, others are more familiar with the term. A recent study consisting of twenty-two ministers and theology scholars of the European Pentecostal Theological Association showed that eleven respondents from Belgium, Burma, Ecuador, Germany, Netherlands, Russia, United States, United Kingdom, Finland, and Sweden were more familiar with the *bivocational ministry* label than the other labels, and three of these respondents were from the United Kingdom (Samushonga 2020a). This finding indicates that, while the common descriptions of the phenomenon (for example, *self-supporting ministry, non-stipendiary ministry*, and *ministers in secular employment*) in the United Kingdom are located within the CoE context, some UK-based Pentecostal theologians, unlike their CoE counterparts, are more familiar with the *bivocational ministry* label. The term *multivocational ministry* is, however, rarely used in the British context.

History of Bivocational Ministry in Britain

While there appear to be more focus, support structures, and resources on bivocational ministry in the United States, the British Church and the CoE in particular have a wealth of bivocational history. In this section, I discuss the history of bivocational ministry in Britain, from the sixteenth century to the present. The documented history of bivocational ministry in Britain is predominantly in the context of the CoE. The CoE historically restricted what is often described as "secular employment" for ministers. In spite of this position, some early British missionaries in the CoE and other denominations became bivocational ministers, thereby laying a foundation for this approach to ministry in Britain. Now, bivocational ministry in its various forms is flourishing in the contemporary CoE, due in part to the influence of the French and Belgian Catholic "worker priest" model. I conclude this section by showing that bivocational ministry is becoming increasingly prominent across Britain today.

Many "colonial" ministers of the CoE in the 1600s supported themselves by means of the parson's glebe—a piece of land set aside for the minister's use to support themselves (Dorr 1988). Historically, there have been three kinds of authority that have controlled or limited secular employment of Anglican clergy: namely statute law, canon law, and the ordinal. Statute law—for example, the 1529 Parliament Act (21 Hen. VIII, cap. 13)—is believed to be a part of King Henry's strategy to use Parliament to restrict the power of the Church. This law consequently restricted clergy from holding several "benefices in plurality." Canons (or church law) have also contained phrases or notions mitigating against the legal development of "non-stipendiary ministry." The ordinal, containing ecclesiastical services for ordination, stated that all priests ordained into the CoE between 1550 and 1979 were admitted to their office with the charge to give themselves wholly to their ministry office and to forsake and set aside as much as possible all worldly cares and studies (Vaughan 1987). The ordinal has historically constituted the ethos of, and defined the office of, clergy and pastors for many churches, ministries, and denominations.

In spite of some reservations and challenges to clergy having gainful employment outside of ministry to protect them from distractions of financial need (Lees 2018), others have passionately advanced bivocationalism in Great Britain. William Carey (1761–1834), an English Baptist missionary to India and one of the greatest missionaries of modern times, served as a bivocational minister for most of his life. He started his ministry as a bivocational pastor in England and later migrated to India, where he spent an active forty-one years of Christian ministry, which included translating the scriptures—while also working as an entrepreneur in various fields, including agriculture (Carey and Masters 1993). Missionary Herbert Kelly (1860–1950), a Catholic in the CoE and founder of the Society of the Sacred Mission and of the Theological College at Kelham, was a notable early proponent of bivocational ministry. Kelly was involved in setting up churches in Anglican provinces. After encountering practical challenges to establishing traditional diocesan structures, due to the shortage of clergy in overseas missions, he advocated for an alternative model (Jones 1971; Vaughan 1987). In Kelly's view, the working class became "an untapped source of energy and power" for the CoE (Jones 1971, 13). Kelly transcended the church tradition and envisaged a mixed ministry of professional and non-professional clergy.

Another key proponent of bivocational ministry in Great Britain was Roland Allen (1868–1947), an English missionary to China known as "the effective prophet of non-stipendiary ministry" (Vaughan 1987, 69; see also Allen and Paton [1968] 2002; Francis and Francis 1998). Like Kelly, he followed personal experiences and a recognition of the need to provide clergy for the church overseas. Allen went further by publishing his ideas for addressing the lack of clergy for the church abroad and proposed that the principle of "voluntary clergy" could be extended to the local church (1923; 1928; 1930). Allen based his views on Paul's tentmaking practice in the New Testament. He held the view that the model of "stipendiary professional" contrasted Paul's tentmaking model (Allen and Paton [1968] 2002, 22). Allen, however, aptly acknowledged that voluntary clergy would only be suitable in some situations, as there was need for the church to support ministers "who can give all their time to the care of parishes and to study, and [who] should not be engaged in business" (Vaughan 1987, 79). Allen also challenged the view that ordained ministers with other vocations would necessarily be part-time ministers (Vaughan 1987, 82). After resigning a parochial position in reaction to a debate on baptism policy, Allen "spent the rest of his career as an unauthorised non-stipendiary" minister (Lees 2018, 25). He put his idea in *Voluntary Clergy*, one of the earliest British publications to discuss the notion of bivocational ministry (Allen 1923).

Allen's definition of voluntary clergy is akin to the definitions of bivocational ministry, in their various versions, offered by many scholars and popular literature today. By defining voluntary clergy, Allen contributed to one of the common themes of bivocational ministry discourse—definitions. On voluntary clergy, Allen stated:

> I mean men in Full Orders, exercising their ministry but not dependent upon it for their livelihood. I mean men with the qualifications laid down by the Apostle, but not necessarily those added by us. It is such men that I think we ought to ordain. We ought to ordain these men not because there is a dearth of candidates for ordination of the type to which we are accustomed, but because it is in itself right and wise to do so . . . I have rested my argument for Voluntary Clergy not upon the dearth, but upon Divine Truth. (Allen 1923, 73–4)

Allen's thesis is based on his view that the shortage of stipendiary ministers in his time, whom he referred to as professional clergy, was designed by God in order for the church to learn that professional ministry is not the only type.

For Allen, the category of voluntary clergy applied both to foreign missions and the local church. Allen considered the incorporation of voluntary clergy in the church necessary for ensuring that the sacrament would be regularly available to small groups of Christians in remote locations. Allen argued that the prevailing view of considering stipendiary (salaried) ministry as the only way to do ministry was to restrict the "Divine vocation" (1923, 2). He also challenged the prevailing order of his day that only young, educated men were qualified to enter ministry. He sought to differentiate this practice from the selection of ministers in 1 Tim. 3:2–7 and Titus 1:6–9 that focused on mature, married, and respected men who had proved to be good leaders and teachers. Allen, like most bivocational ministry scholars and writers, demonstrated the views that voluntary clergy are not half-time ministers and that stipendiary clergy continue to be necessary. Although there are divergent views in bivocational ministry and associated literature on whether the non-ministry vocation of bivocational ministry is to be regarded as necessarily secular, Allen proffered that "there is no such thing as secular business for Christian men" (84). Allen thus contributed to the development of a form of what we understand as bivocational ministry in the British context.

It is important to note that the notion of bivocational ministry in Britain was also fuelled by experiences of other countries and denominations. Particularly influential was the French and Belgian Catholic "worker priest" model, in which hundreds of French and Belgian priests entered factories to take up manual labor as an essential aspect of their ministry to the industrial workforce (Arnal 1986). According to Arnal, this model influenced other countries, and "the Anglican Church (CoE) in Britain has pushed forward with its own forms both in urban missions and on the high seas" (172). British worker-priests in the early 1950s and 1960s comprised a movement of a handful of British Anglican priests (following a similar movement of French Catholics), who with their families and some lay ministers, went out to work in factories and mines after World War II. Some of them continued into retirement (Lawson 2000).

Factors Shaping the Growth of Non-stipendiary Ministry

The effect of Kelly and Allen's dream of non-stipendiary clergy took time to be realized within the CoE, as in other denominations. For centuries, the ordained ministry of the CoE was generally considered a sacred office consuming the minister's whole attention on ministerial tasks; benefits included a house and a stipend or allowance to support the physical needs of the minister. By the late nineteenth century, parochial ministry in particular was regarded as a "full-time" occupation. However, insufficient ministry income drove many poor clergy to supplement their incomes with other employment. The CoE officially accepted non-stipendiary ministry into its institutional structures in 1970. Vaughan (1987) identified four key aspects influencing this revolutionization of the office of ordained ministry in the CoE, factors that continue to influence bivocational ministry and are also mirrored in other denominations and ministry persuasions outside of the CoE.

First is the continued pressure for local communities to be self-sufficient in ministry and sacraments. This self-sufficiency is achieved through the training and ordaining of local candidates to serve their own home parish (Francis and Francis 1998). Some of the pressure arises from the fact that membership in the CoE is declining (Lees 2018), particularly in smaller and rural churches (Gill [2003] 2018). As a result, the capacity for the church to support a stipendiary minister has diminished, making it more difficult for churches to attract and support ministers from outside their locality. There is, therefore, focus on having local parishioners taking on ministerial responsibilities in their home or local church. These self-supporting individuals become bivocational ministers. This approach is increasingly being considered in the CoE and is likely to be considered beyond the CoE.

Second, there is pressure for the church to offer ministry in a style and expression congruent with working-class culture. The relevance of the church in contemporary society has been a subject of theological interest in recent years. The church has been accused of being insular and not relevant to contemporary society by some quarters. Theologians and ministry practitioners have thus, over the years, made efforts to address this situation and to demonstrate that the church can be relevant for today's society. Ministers in secular employment, as they are described in the CoE context, are considered to be more in touch with working-class culture, as they are part of it.

Third is the continued pressure for the removal of the divide between clergy and laity. The divide emanates from how lay ministers are described in CoE official literature:

> Readers (also called Licensed Lay Ministers) have a leadership role serving alongside clergy to support people in faith and enable mission. They are lay people who are trained and licensed by their bishop. Reader / LLM ministry looks different in different places depending on the local context. Many Readers / LLMs teach, preach, lead worship and are involved in mission. Some also take funerals after additional training. Many Readers carry out their church ministry at the same time as having another job. (Church of England n.d.)

Although lay ministers or readers preach, lead worship, and are involved in mission, they are largely described as ones serving alongside clergy. This description diminishes the ministry of lay ministers and portays the sense that their ministry is validated by their serving alongside clergy. It should, however, be noted that there is a distinction between lay leaders/ministers and bivocational ministers. Lay leaders serve under a trained or ordained minister. On the contrary, while a bivocational minister will have another vocation outside of ministry, they usually are the lead pastor or minister of a congregation—unlike the lay leaders who ordinarily serve under an ordained senior minister.

Fourth is the continued pressure for the church to offer meaningful witness in the contemporary world of work. It is becoming increasingly recognised that in today's world of secularisation, the church has the duty to take the gospel to the workplace. Bivocational ministers, particularly ministers in secular employment, are positioned to present Christian witness in the workplace (Fuller and Vaughan 1986). This missiological argument does not, however, mean that bivocational ministers should engage people in the workplace on the subject of faith (or the gospel) "willy-nilly." In fact, in parts of the United Kingdom, the law prohibits subjecting another person to "harassment" at work on the grounds of religion or belief or by engaging in unwanted conduct that has the purpose of violating their dignity or creating an intimidating, hostile, degrading, humiliating, or offensive environment (Employment Equality [Religion or Belief] Regulations 2003). Nonetheless, even within the confines of the laws, bivocational ministers have opportunities to share their faith with others in the world of work.

Bivocational Ministry in Britain Today

The need for bivocational ministry that is increasingly being acknowledged in our world today is also recognised in Britain. Within the CoE, "many English dioceses are planning increased dependency on SSMs [self-supporting ministers]" due to projected dwindling church attendance and resources (Lees 2018, 7). In fact, 25–40% of CoE clergy are self-supporting ministers, serving 60% of CoE dioceses (Morgan 2010). Self-supporting ministry (which manifests as bivocational ministry in many cases) is seen as a solution and response to dwindling attendance and resources in the CoE. Furthermore, other denominations in Britain, such as Pentecostals and "new churches" consider bivocational ministry instrumental and necessary for church planting and growth.

It is interesting to note the differences in approaches taken in Britain for incorporating bivocational ministry. On one hand, churches like the CoE are seemingly adopting bivocational ministry to sustain or preserve their existing churches, whereas other churches are adopting bivocational ministry to plant new churches. For example, the concept of bivocational ministry is increasingly becoming a subject of discussion in the UK Baptist Movement (King 2013). Like the US Southern Baptist Convention, the UK Baptist movement is beginning to consider bivocational ministry more seriously (Haward 2013). Similarly, the Newfrontiers Broadcast Network, Church Planting (UK) published an insightful article highlighting the need for bivocational ministry in church planting (Newfrontiers 2016). Although data pertaining to the incidence and prevalence of bivocational ministry in UK churches is limited, there are strong indications that bivocational ministry is both common and on the increase in Britain and the wider United Kingdom.

Another area of interest is theological training. There is a gap between the prevalence of bivocational ministry and the availability of bivocational ministry-focused theological education in Britain. In 2019, I interviewed four educationalists about their views. Although the research involved only four British theological schools, these schools had been established for over 70 years. The research concluded that: (1) the educationalists were well versed with the concept of bivocational ministry; (2) a significant number of current and former students at the four institutions practiced bivocational ministry, (3) the current educational curricula at the four institutions did not incorporate bivocational ministry training; and (4) there were mixed views on whether there should be specific training for bivocational ministry or if the institutions should consider this pathway (Samushonga 2020b). This research shows that the subject of bivocational ministry training is still developing in Britain and needs further attention (see also Lees 2018).

Conclusion

This chapter explored the notion of bivocational ministry in the context of Britain, highlighting the diversity of the concept. The phenomenon of bivocational ministry was described in a variety of ways peculiar to the CoE, such as *non-stipendiary ministers, ministers in secular employment*, and *self-supporting ministers*. The chapter also revealed that, outside of the CoE, the term *bivocational ministry* is used in Britain. The lack of a firmer definition for bivocational ministry presents problems for exploring the phenomenon. Nevertheless, it is clear that the notion of bivocationalism in Britain, in its various forms, points to the ministry of men and women involved in ministry who also have other vocations outside of ministry.

Another challenge for bivocational ministry in Britain presented in this chapter is the lack of statistical data on the numbers or proportion of ministers in Britain serving as bivocational ministers. Much of what is available are estimates. Although the CoE publishes official ministry statistics yearly, reporting the number of ministers who support themselves financially, the number also includes pensioners with no other jobs. As a result, the CoE statistics of non-stipendiary ministers are not true statistics of bivocational ministers in the CoE. It therefore remains that the number and or proportion of bivocational ministers in the CoE and wider Britain remains unknown. This missing data is crucial for giving context and more understanding of bivocational ministry and providing an evidence base for research that focuses on bivocational ministry in Britain.

This chapter crucially highlighted that, while the notion of bivocational ministry is established and predicted to grow in the future, there is little focus on bivocational ministry training in Britain. This gap is not unique to Britain. However, discourse about theological education in the United States has intensified in the last few years, with denominations like the Southern Baptist Convention and theological seminaries like Lancaster exploring training and educational programs aimed at equipping candidates with bivocational ministry knowledge and skills.

This chapter also showed that the momentum for bivocational ministry (or forms of it) in Britain is intensifying in the CoE and beyond as a means of preserving the local church and stimulating church growth. Thus, there is need for further research on bivocational ministry to focus on other churches beyond the CoE.

Works Cited

Allen, Roland. 1923. *Voluntary Clergy*. London: SPCK.

———. 1928. *Voluntary Clergy Overseas*. Self-published, Beaconsfield.

———. 1930. *The Case for Voluntary Clergy*. London: Eyre and Spottiswoode.

——— and David M. Paton. (1968) 2002. *The Reform of the Ministry: A Study in the Work of Roland Allen*. Cambridge: Lutterworth Press.

Arnal, Oscar L. 1986. *Priests in Working Class Blue: The History of the Worker-Priests (1943–1954)*. New York: Paulist.

Bickers, Dennis Wayne. 2010. "Coaching Bivocational Ministers for Greater Ministry Effectiveness." DMin diss., Liberty Baptist Theological Seminary. *Doctoral Dissertations and Projects* 345. *digitalcommons.liberty.edu/doctoral/345*.

———. 2013. *The Art and Practice of Bivocational Ministry: A Pastor's Guide*. Kansas City: Beacon Hill.

Carey, S. Pearce. 1993. *William Carey*. 3rd ed. London: Wakeman Trust.

Chaves, Mark, Joseph Roso, Anna Holleman, and Mary Hawkins. 2020. "National Congregations Study: Waves I–IV Summary Tables." Duke University Department of Sociology, Durham, NC. Last modified January 11, 2021. *sites.duke.edu/ncsweb/files/2021/01/NCS-IV_Summary-Tables_For-Posting.pdf*.

Church of England. n.d. "No Ordinary Ministry." Accessed January 3, 2022. *www.churchofengland.org/life-events/vocations/no-ordinary-ministry#na*.

———. 2021. "Ministry Statistics 2020." *churchofengland.org/sites/default/files/2021-07/Ministry%20Statistics%202020%20report%20FINAL.pdf*.

Dorr, Luther M. 1988. *The Bivocational Pastor*. Nashville: Broadman.

Employment Equality (Religion or Belief) Regulations. 2003. *legislation.gov.uk/uksi/2003/1660/regulation/5/made.*

Francis, James M. M., and Leslie J. Francis, eds. 1998. *Tentmaking: Perspectives on Self-Supporting Ministry.* Leominster: Gracewing.

Fuller, John, and Patrick Vaughan, eds. 1986. *Working for the Kingdom: The Story of Ministers in Secular Employment.* London: SPCK.

Gill, Robin. (2003) 2018. *The 'Empty' Church Revisited.* Explorations in Practical, Pastoral and Empirical Theology. New York: Routledge.

Hacking, Rod. 1990. *On the Boundary: A Vision for Non-Stipendiary Ministry.* Norwich: Canterbury.

Haward, Joe. 2013. "Being a Minister and 'Doing Stuff.'" *Baptists Together.* October 30. *www.baptist.org.uk/Articles/376820/Being_a_Minister.aspx.*

Jones, Alan William. 1971. "Herbert Hamilton Kelly S. S. M., 1860–1950: A Study in Failure: A Contribution to the Search for a Credible Catholicism." PhD diss., University of Nottingham. *eprints.nottingham.ac.uk/27617.*

King, Ivan. 2013. "What Kind of Ministers Do We Need for the Next 20 Years? How do We Prepare Them for this Ministry?" *Baptists Together.* December 20. *baptist.org.uk/Articles/386948/What_kind_of.aspx.*

Lausanne Movement. 2011. "Cape Town Commitment." *lausanne.org/content/ctc/ctcommitment#capetown.*

Lawson, Kevin E. 2000. *How to Thrive in Associate Staff Ministry.* Herndon, VA: Alban Institute.

Lees, John. 2018. *Self-Supporting Ministry: A Practical Guide.* London: SPCK.

Morgan, Teresa. 2010. *Self-supporting Ministry in the Church of England and the Anglican Churches of Wales Scotland and Ireland: Report of the National Survey 2010.* Oxford: Teresa Morgan. *workerpriest.uk/uploads/1/6/5/7/16572376/2010_morgan-ssm-report.pdf.*

Newfrontiers. 2016. "The Bivocational Question." November 30. *newfrontierstogether.org/words/184/the-bivocational-question.*

Rayner, Keith. 1998. "Reflection on the Theology of Ordained Ministry in Secular Employment." In *Tentmaking: Perspectives On Self-Supporting Ministry*, edited by James M. M. Francis and Leslie J. Francis, 287–95. Leominster, Herefordshire: Gracewing.

Samushonga, Hartness M. 2019. "A Theological Reflection of Bivocational Pastoral Ministry: A Personal Reflective Account of a Decade of Bivocational Ministry Practice Experience." *Practical Theology* 12, no. 1: 66–80. *doi.org/10.1080/1756073X.2019.1575040.*

———. 2020a. "A European Theological Pentecostal Perspective to Bivocational Ministry." *Journal of the European Pentecostal Theological Association* 40, no. 2: 144–59. *doi.org/10.1080/18124461.2020.1795421.*

———. 2020b. "On Bivocational Ministry-focused Training in British Theological Schools: Dialoguing with British Theological Educationalists." *Practical Theology* 13, no. 4: 385–99. *doi.org/10.1080/1756073X.2020.1787006.*

Vaughan, Peter. 1987. "Non-Stipendiary Ministry in the Church of England: A History of the Development of an Idea." PhD diss., University of Nottingham.

Endnotes

1 The project, "Educating for a thriving Bivocational Ministry," was funded by Lancaster Theological Seminary and a matching grant from the In Trust Center for Theological Schools.

CHAPTER 3

Changes in Ministry and Bivocational Ministry since the 1960s

RALPH B. WRIGHT JR.

There is nothing like being a student chaplain from Brooklyn, New York, leading a summer worship service facing a once-active volcano with steam still coming out of its vents. Each Saturday evening, I visited campgrounds in Lassen Volcanic National Park in California, inviting campers to come to church the next morning in the amphitheater. The next day, I led campers, park employees, and visitors in worship from a pulpit in the shadow of the volcano with a ten-foot-high cross hanging from the stage rafters. It was a summer ministry, and I did it for two years.

That was my introduction to being a bivocational pastor. To raise sufficient funds to return to seminary each year, I worked for the park company. Early on weekday mornings, I drove the garbage truck as part of the maintenance crew. Then in the afternoons (after taking a shower on company time), I led tours of the park for visitors from all over the Western United States. Who would have guessed that this experience would help me understand and address the current crisis in US churches?

Today, many churches providing valuable ministries in their communities would not survive without bivocational ministers. Small member congregations are being pressured to close their buildings or adapt by combining church parishes, sharing a full-time pastor, or hiring a bivocational pastor. These changes may be prompted by financial necessity, but bivocational pastors are more than simply an answer to decreased congregational budgets. Bivocational ministry can be an opportunity to revitalize the church in mission to the community at large, including ministries with young people, the elderly, and shut-in members of the parish.

When I began my ministerial career in 1965, I encountered the "traditional," White Presbyterian structure of full-time, male pastors serving churches that had been in existence since at least the post-World War II era, if not before. However, during the preceding centuries, parishes were served by circuit-riding preachers who not only rode horses between the various services on a Sunday but also carried in one saddle bag the Bible and in the other saddle bag medications that could be used to heal the sick. This kind of bivocationality ceased as preachers hung up their saddlebags and medicine bottles in favor of settled pastorates.[1]

In a sense, we have come back to needing circuit-riding pastors in the twenty-first century. Some pastors again have more than one parish to serve each Sunday. Many Presbyterian congregations are being served by commissioned ruling elders (laity) rather than teaching elders (clergy).[2] Also serving this changing church scene are bivocational pastors.

Bivocational pastors are the circuit riders of the twenty-first century. Instead of carrying medicine bottles, they are expected to perform CPR (cardiopulmonary resuscitation) on dying churches. In a metaphorical sense, many churches today need spiritual and financial resuscitation. Pastors with a background in psychology and counseling, accounting, and finance, or experience as a teacher or contractor may benefit a church as much or more than a pastor whose knowledge of Greek and Hebrew or archaeological sites in the Middle East is unaccompanied by other life skills. While no person can have all the skills and knowledge needed to meet the needs of a vibrant congregation, bivocational pastors, due to their other professions, are able to bridge gaps in the operations of a church's ministry. Since pastoral ministry is a collegial enterprise that provides and receives support from various individuals and religious entities both within and outside the congregation, a broader set of skills and talents is often available to churches with bivocational ministers.

Oftentimes, a bivocational pastor is better positioned than a pastor supported solely by a congregation to meet the changing needs of the church in the twenty-first century. There is no one-size-fits-all when it comes to church leadership, be it a full-time pastor or a bivocational pastor. Both types of clergy may have appropriate theological education. The issue is whether the pastor has a diverse lifestyle that is both solidly grounded in the Christian faith and in the lifestyle and professions of the community surrounding the congregation. The crisis of White, mainline congregations, despite many who have worked to evangelize and overcome the lack of religious faith of many persons in the United States, is the secularization of church and society. Mission and support, when confined to a church's own members, provides minimal outreach to the community at large. Bivocational ministry can reach a much broader community. This chapter presents my personal reflections based on forty-five years in bivocational ministries, serving many localities in the United States as well as overseas. This variety of employment and church service has benefited my own vision of what church service is and, specifically, how bivocational ministry can benefit the church universal.

Becoming Bivocational

I did not set out to become a bivocational pastor. After serving four happy years as a full-time youth pastor at the thousand-plus-member Lafayette-Orinda Presbyterian Church in the San Francisco Bay area, I moved back to Los Angeles and served as an assistant pastor for youth and community outreach. I must admit I struggled in that position because I could not reconcile the teachings of Jesus from the pulpit with attitudes in the congregation. Some long-time members did not see the needs of newly arriving residents, who in many instances were poor and in some instances were homeless, as a ministry of the church. Fortunately, I was able to set up a meals program for seniors in cooperation with the city and county welfare offices. The program was supported by volunteer cooks, helpers, and the small amounts of money requested from those attending. With the mutual consent of the congregation and the Presbytery, I left my full-time position to become bivocational, helping those needing social service assistance during the day and working in the evenings and weekends with churches in need of pastor.

At that time, most of the White Presbyterian churches in Southern California had full-time pastors. However, the poorer and racially and ethnically diverse congregations did not. The leadership of the Presbytery was happy for me to assist these parishes serving ethnically diverse populations, including African Americans, Hispanic, Native American, Asian, and European people. My zeal for civil rights and humanitarian assistance was greatly supported by the diverse parishioners I served and kept me from uncomfortable debates with homogeneously White church boards and trustees. With that, my life and style of ministry were set for the next forty years.

Racism and ethnocentrism are difficult issues for most churches, even those that claim to have no racial bias. Because bivocational ministers are out in the community on a daily basis, these issues may be confronted more regularly. At one time in California, I was criticized by the mother of a young high school-age daughter for featuring the work of Dr. Martin Luther King Jr. during a church program and sharing my own experience in and providing support for the Selma to Montgomery march. From that time on, I did not see her daughter very much. The ministry of the church, however, initiated a biracial nursery school, working with an African American community some twenty miles away.

When working with a high school youth group in another White suburban church, I at times referred to my roots in Brooklyn. The Brooklyn church in which I was baptized closed some years later and sold the building to an African American congregation. The White leaders used the money to pay off debts and transferred the remaining funds to a suburban White church in the name of extending Christ's ministry to the young families moving out of the city. In light of today's environment of political and race relations, this action highlights the need for clergy to understand race and cultural issues more deeply.

New Opportunities for Ministry

Bivocational pastors minister not only in the parish but also in the world, encountering the needs of a much broader community. An issue I have found in churches, not only fifty years ago but also today, is the idea of "separation of church and state." Many White churches want to keep their pastors out of the politics of the community. In my bivocational ministry, I tried to be non-partisan while addressing the many social issues encountered by the members of the parish and the community at large. We should be able to work together, both church and state. Church people can support food banks that help the needy, provide medical care for those in need, and work with governmental leaders to address problems as diverse as building codes, traffic congestion, and housing of the homeless. As a bivocational minister with two career tracks, ministry and accounting, I learned how to address government paperwork, bureaucracy, and political and civil servant leadership.

As a bivocational minister, I was able to serve a much larger population than that of a local parish in the middle of the city. My dual role in the community afforded me new opportunities for ministry. I was able to converse and work with various governmental units including the mayor's office, the city council, and various legislators in the area. Serving on a variety of community projects, such as addressing the earthquake issues of California, created a symbiotic union between the churches I served and the governmental and nonprofit units with which I was involved.

For example, my position at the American Red Cross Southern California Region created good relations with government bodies, particularly in Los Angeles. Consequently, I received an invitation from a member of the City Council to join, at his office's expense, an Earthquake Exploratory Commission to China. The purpose of the trip was to study the response of China to the 1976 Tangshan earthquake, one of the deadliest of the twentieth century. The City Council and the Building Department wanted to determine what could be learned to improve the building codes and disaster response in the City of Los Angeles, particularly in light of the devastating 1971 San Fernando Valley (Sylmar) Earthquake, which destroyed five Presbyterian churches in addition to other buildings in Los Angeles.

We attended an International Seismic Conference in Beijing and traveled north to Tangshan to visit the destruction and observe its rebuilding. Los Angeles Building Department engineers on the Commission gleaned valuable information from this visit. This visit resulted in building code revisions and safer buildings in the city of Los Angeles. The need to update sanctuaries and fellowship halls to the new, higher standards was an expensive and contentious issue for churches. Being a bivocational minister put me in the middle of a debate of earthquake safety versus church financial capabilities. My experience on the Commission helped me to explain to the religious community the reasons for the stronger earthquake building codes. This is a good example of how being bivocational can benefit both the community and the church.

My training as an accountant also helped me bridge church and community. I worked with non-profit and other organizations as well as churches and their staff with financial and tax reporting systems. My secular employment led to international ministry opportunities. In 1984, I traveled and worked in Ethiopia with the "We are the World" response of US and international outpouring of support in response to the Ethiopian famine. Eventually, I was asked to move with my family to Geneva, Switzerland, to work for the International Federation of Red Cross and Red Crescent Societies. During this decade of international service, I worshiped in and supported local churches as a congregant rather than as a pastor. In Geneva our family attended the American Church, which was a part of the Episcopal Church (US). Due to my ordination, I was allowed to teach the communicants class and to lead services and celebrate the eucharist when the rector was not available.

In 1994 my family and I returned to the United States and settled in Long Island. I once again became a full-time worker-priest (the New York Catholic way of saying bivocational). This time I worked for the tax accounting firm of my family and, with the encouragement of the General Presbyter, served part-time as pastor of a small historic church in Yaphank, New York. (This town gained acclaim in 1918 when a young Army recruit by the name of Irving Berlin wrote songs to raise money for a community building at nearby Camp Upton. This ultimately led after the war to the Broadway musical *Yip, Yip, Yaphank*, out of which one later-released song, "God Bless America," became an American classic.) By serving the community, we were able to build additional educational facilities, which housed various programs, such as a nursery school, and various community groups, including scouts, Alcoholics Anonymous (AA), and theatrical productions. Most importantly, these facilities helped the church to interface with the local community.

As a bivocational pastor, I not only preached in the Yaphank Presbyterian Church on Sundays but also became involved in numerous community activities, including the creation of a self-sustaining summer camp for children and youth that grew to one hundred campers per week for the summer. Needing events to excite the campers, we involved the Yaphank Fire Department, who drove their various fire trucks to demonstrate their usage to the campers. In the process, I was invited to be the chaplain of the department.

On September 11, 2001, my chaplaincy changed my ministry. I became a minister to a grieving community, and the Presbyterian Church became a center for community support. Members of the Long Island Fire Departments died in the collapse of the World Trade Center. Friends and relatives also died as the buildings collapsed. In Yaphank, we held prayer vigils and services in the fire house for the community. This relationship with the community led to more children attending the pre-school nursery at the church, as well as the summer camp. Other activities, including a Halloween Walk fundraiser and special services and events at Christmas and Easter, increased in attendance. Requests for the pastor to officiate at weddings and funerals also increased. To this day, even in retirement, I have continued as the chaplain of the Yaphank Fire Department at their request and with the approval of the Presbytery of Long Island.

Ten years ago, I retired from the Yaphank church to begin a decade of suburban "tent making." Whereas in previous years bivocational ministers were not needed in the suburbs, now, due to lower memberships and budgets, these congregations can no longer afford a full-time pastor. The annual total salary and support package exceeds $100,000; a Sunday honorarium for a pulpit supply pastor is only $150 plus mileage. Hiring a bivocational pastor allows these congregations to reallocate monies to children and youth ministries. Needed today are not just more Sunday school and confirmation classes but also after-school tutoring programs, service projects to help those in need, and summer youth programming, which includes opportunities for travel and meeting other young people of various cultures and religious backgrounds. I continue as a bivocational minister since I still own and manage the family accounting business. Many of our clients are pastors or church members and their families. Additionally, the firm does the books and the annual audits for a number of churches and pre-school nurseries. I also continue to be a member of presbytery committees, including the board of trustees, budget committee, and Presbyterian disaster relief committee.

A Shifting Religious Landscape

When I was young, the Presbyterian Church was a major religious institution on Long Island. With a history going back to 1640, hardly a hamlet on the island was without a Presbyterian or Congregational Church. This was true up to the end of World War II, when the rush of city residents moved to the suburbs. With the migration of Irish, Italians, Hispanics, and Eastern Europeans, the Roman Catholic Church became the major Christian denomination. Additionally, the movement of Jewish citizens from Europe and New York City led to a more diverse population. Instead of being the church of the politically and wealthy elite as well as the blue-collar workers, Presbyterians are now just one of many religious groups in the community. Congregations are now either closing or merging due to the smaller number of parishioners.

During the coronavirus pandemic, congregations across the United States had to rethink their worship services and their ministries. The ability to meet and worship online requires ministry and lay staff who can broadcast services to their at-home members and friends. Ministry in the cyberspace world requires an understanding of computers and cameras, which few pastors have, either from their seminary training or their ministerial interests. Into this void, bivocational ministers occupy a crucial role. Given the small size of many Protestant parishes, we need to train bivocational ministers to provide this assistance.

Another difficult issue is finances. With the contraction of churches and church ministries in the last two decades, judicatories have been forced to cut back in all areas. This affects the ability to provide scholarships for students in seminary. It also affects budgets for small church ministries. It also affects support for the work and fellowship of bivocational ministers. In the Presbyterian Church (U.S.A.), financial support for the Association of Presbyterian Tentmakers has been eliminated, and the association no longer meets. The need to fellowship and share ministries is still there but is not adequately addressed.

Finding Collegial Support

By attending the bi-annual General Assembly of the Presbyterian Church (U.S.A.), I met other bivocational ministers, called tentmakers after St. Paul's example. I learned of their lifestyle and ministries. Many were from either rural or urban parishes. Few were from suburban areas. An organization had been set up with the title the Association of Presbyterian Tentmakers. We met annually, often on the campus of one of the seminaries. During that time of fellowship, we also met tentmakers from other denominations and countries. For me, these were always exciting and productive times. To find out that bivocational ministries in Europe had a wider footprint in the church than in the United States was quite valuable to my understanding of the nature of my own ministry. I was particularly impressed by conversations I had with Phil Aspinall of the United Kingdom over the years and with *Ministers-at-Work*, a journal for Christians in secular ministry published periodically by CHRISM (CHRistians In Secular Ministry).

These meetings were also good for my religious mental health. There were times when I felt I did not have what it took to be a minister of Jesus Christ. The institutional church was looking for full-time pastors and preachers, not social workers who held together a small congregation off of the main church row. At times, I felt I was more appreciated by my friends and contacts in the community, governmental, and secular world than by my own church, for which I had spent five years beyond college studying Greek and Hebrew, biblical exegesis, church history, pastoral counseling, and so on, in seminary. My church background as a young person had challenged me "to evangelize the world for Jesus Christ." To preach the gospel was my calling. By meeting with other bivocational ministers, I discovered that there are other good Christians who preach the gospel where they work. They had regular contacts not only with their church parishioners but also with persons who were unchurched and who would find it difficult to come to a church, though they had spiritual needs. In many ways, these modern-day, bivocational Christians were more akin to the evangelists and leaders of the early Church than some of the full-time pastors in the high pulpits of mainline churches.

I need also to reflect on the role of women in the church. When I attended seminary in the 1960s, women were allowed to attend seminary classes, but they could not graduate with a divinity degree, even after attending and passing the required courses. Today that is not the situation, and I welcome all my female colleagues into the leadership of the church. However, I am also aware that a number of Christian denominations do not allow ordination of women. Furthermore, many families still prefer a male clergy person when it comes time for a baptism, wedding, or funeral. Providing opportunities for women to speak and preach from the pulpit, as well as to hold Bible studies for the entire congregation and to serve on church boards, is a way to help broaden a congregation's understanding of the changing role of women—not only in society but also in our congregations. These are issues that we, as bivocational ministers, need to address and be aware of.

Conclusion

We need more compassion in our ministries, in our churches, and in our communities. The financial bottom line is not the most important part of a successful business, church, or society. As I read the scriptures and live in the world, I find the real need is a theology and ministry of caring, loving, and compassion. I learned this from being a bivocational minister out in the world—not in seminary.

Since 1960, the role of bivocational pastors has shifted from a more rural ministry to one that deals with both suburban and urban life in the United States. This demands not only a good theological foundation but also a knowledge of both urban issues and the onslaught of digital technology. The disparity between the poor and the wealthy is a challenge for the United States as for many other nations. Likewise, the needs of the mission field are great. But, where is the mission field? Yes, it is international, and it is also right here at home. The church needs leadership that understands not only the scriptures but also the world in which we live as well as the communities in which we minister. The challenge is great—definitely more difficult than for the church of the 1960s. We can learn a lot from St. Paul—not only his writings but also his tentmaker's way of life. God is with us. We just need to follow God's directions. Shalom!

Works Cited

Holifield, E. Brooks. 2007. *God's Ambassadors: A History of the Christian Clergy in America*. Grand Rapids, MI: Eerdmans.

Vacek, Heather H. 2015. *Madness: American Protestant Responses to Mental Illness*. Waco, TX: Baylor University Press.

Endnotes

1 Editor's note: For a discussion of the medical ministries of clergy in the colonial era and early United States, see Vacek (2015). For mention of post-Civil War clergy working other jobs, see Holifield (2007, 149–53).

2 In the Presbyterian Church (U.S.A.), a commissioned ruling elder is an ordained lay person with leadership and other responsibilities who has not had the three years of seminary education required of teaching elders but has taken sufficient coursework to administer the sacraments.

CHAPTER 4

Black and Bivocational

JESSICA YOUNG BROWN

Research on the ministerial profession for the past twenty years indicates an increasing reliance on bivocational ministers in parish ministry. Congregational finances are a significant contributing factor. In the United States, fewer people are identifying with organized religion, and this translates to fewer members at churches and fewer monetary resources to make those churches run. This shift has resulted in much-deserved attention to a variety of topics related to bivocational ministry, including how seminaries can train clergy for bivocational ministry, the financial implications of this shift, and ways to support clergy in mental, emotional, and spiritual wellness.

Bivocational ministry is clearly a specialized way of doing ministry. The example of Paul as a bivocational minister balancing his tentmaking with his church planting has become a foundational framework for theological discussions of bivocational ministry (Dorr

1988, 1). Dorr's discussion of the financial and cultural realities that necessitated this balancing act mirrors some of the same realities we see today. Simply put, some people are in bivocational ministry because they must be for financial reasons. Still, this does not mean they are not called to and cannot thrive in a multifaceted ministry context. Ferris (2001, 82) acknowledged that bivocational ministry necessitates an ability to be professional and effective in multiple domains—often simultaneously. To call it a juggling act is an understatement. These ministers must be able to prioritize time, organize their tasks, and be efficient in their professional lives.

Deasy (2018), Stephens (chapter 1 in this volume), and others have stressed the need for seminaries to educate clergy about the realities of bivocational ministry. Stephens made the argument that it is the project of the whole congregation to envision and imagine the ways bivocational ministry can be practiced. Bickers (2007, 14) acknowledged that there is a call to bivocational ministry and a choice that can be made about embarking on this kind of vocation. Thus, there is a need not only for traditional seminary education but also continuing education, which can be a challenge due to the busy schedules of bivocational ministers. The truth is that much of the formal education ministers receive imagines a life committed to parish ministry as the sole vocation. This is an incomplete vision for multiple reasons. As mentioned, a large segment of ministers who are bivocational will need to balance ministry demands with other paid employment. Second, as a part of the same dynamics that yield increasing numbers of bivocational ministers, we must acknowledge that parish ministry is not the only place ministers engage their call. Ministers serve in nonprofit organizations, policy positions, and education, while still holding other paid professional responsibilities. Thus, the true educational mandate is one that allows for a more expansive view of what ministry is, one that fully incorporates work inside and outside the church.

Sometimes lost in the larger discussion of bivocational ministry is the impact of culture, particularly race. A 2017 survey by the Association of Theological Schools revealed that about 30% of graduating seminarians anticipated bivocational ministry (Deasy 2018). However, when these numbers were broken down by race, people of color were much more likely to anticipate this track: almost 60% of Black seminarians and over 40% of Hispanic/Latinx seminarians were preparing for bivocational ministry. There is a clear trend that people of color are more likely to be involved in bivocational ministry

(Young Brown 2017). In many Black church communities, there may even be an expectation of bivocational ministry (Crawford 2012). From the inception of the Black church in the United States, pastoral leaders have engaged in other professions simultaneously, including education, politics, and other forms of civil service. In addition, Black pastors are more likely to serve in part-time pastoral positions, less likely to serve in fully funded ministry positions, and more likely to identify as bivocational than their White and Latinx counterparts (Crawford 2012, 20). This dynamic is likely even more pronounced for licensed and ordained ministers who do not serve in a primary pastoral role, such as unpaid associate ministers. In a Black church context, the inclusion of unpaid ministerial staff is critical because unpaid associate ministers, in conjunction with bivocational and partially funded pastoral leaders, are heavily involved in the everyday functioning of the church and are active and visible ministerial leaders. It is safe to say that bivocational ministers probably make up the majority of the vocation.

While a large segment of Black ministers is bivocational, there is a dearth of research about the experiences of these clergy. Perry and Schleifer (2019, 2) acknowledged that, while bivocational ministry has become more of a trend in the past twenty years for the church at large, Black pastors have been engaged in this ministerial dynamic for longer (see also Crawford 2012, 24). This reality begs the question: why are we not looking to Black bivocational ministers to inform our understanding about what it means to thrive in this context? In any professional context, the people who have been engaging in a practice longer and more extensively naturally become the experts. Thus, this chapter looks to Black bivocational clergy as exemplars for navigating bivocational ministry. The goal of this qualitative exploration is to explore the practices and strategies these clergy use to thrive.

Methodology

Through email listservs and social media invitations, Black ministers who self-identified as bivocational were invited to participate in a brief survey about their experiences as bivocational or multivocational ministers. In addition to free response items, participants were asked survey questions on a five-point Likert scale to assess their experiences in bivocational ministry, where a score of one would indicate they have not had that experience, and a score of five would indicate they have had that experience very often (figure 1).

Figure 1: Likert scale response.

After completing the survey, participants were invited to participate in a 30–40-minute individual interview to share their experiences in more detail. Survey data was collected from March 2021 to August 2021, with interviews held in June and July 2021.

Of twenty-eight survey participants, sixteen indicated interest in completing the interview, and seven interviews were successfully scheduled. It should be noted that the difference between those who expressed interest in the interview and those who were able to complete the interview is likely telling of a common dynamic in bivocational ministry—full schedules and very little free time.

Survey Results

The 28 survey participants were 64% male and 36% female. Almost half (46%) were married, 28% percent identified as single, 14% indicated being in long-term romantic relationships, and 10% were divorced.

Clergy who responded to the survey had been in ministry an average of 14.6 years, with an average of 11 of those years serving bivocationally. In addition, almost 68% reported that their ministry work was unpaid. Yet 61% of this sample reported having an official position in a parish context.

Participants were asked a variety of questions, which sought to explore experiences in bivocational ministry that might be seen as positive or helpful. Over 80% of respondents stated they are able to use their "secular" skills in their ministry work often or very often. Slightly over 78% stated that they are able to explore gifts and passions that they would not have been able to with just one job. Eighty-two percent of participants endorsed that they are often able to find opportunities to see God in different ways (see figure 2).

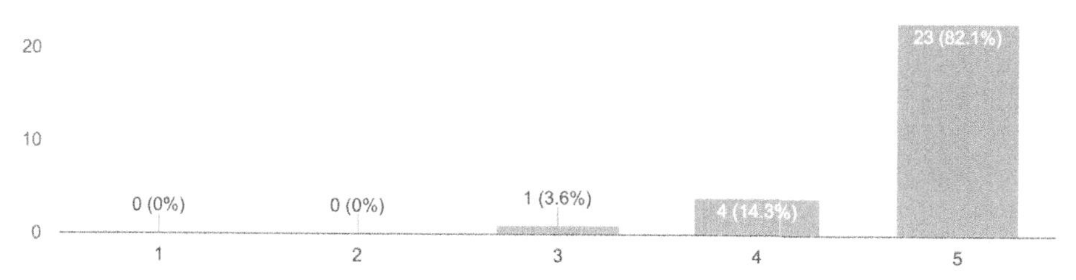

Figure 2: Finding opportunities to see God in different ways.

When asked about finances, results were more mixed. One of the purported benefits of bivocational ministry is increased financial security. However, in this sample, about 35% provided neutral or negative responses, while the other 65% stated they have more financial security due to bivocational ministry.

Unsurprisingly, results were mixed when asked about spending time with family and making time for self-care (figures 3 and 4). While some ministers felt they are able to respond to these demands appropriately, others did not see opportunities for self-care or family in their lives. The most common response to a question about the ability to have work/life balance was neutral (figure 5). Likewise, most participants (60%) provided neutral or negative responses when asked about their ability to engage in leisure activities (figure 6). This is consistent with the literature on the challenges associated with ministry in general and bivocational ministry in particular (for example, Ferguson et al. 2014; Wells et al. 2012). These results suggest that, while some clergy are finding a flow between personal life, ministry responsibilities, and caring for themselves well, this balance is not happening for all.

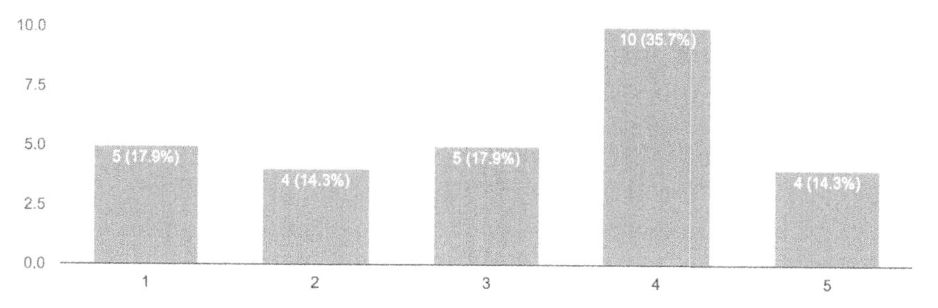

Figure 3: Spending time with family.

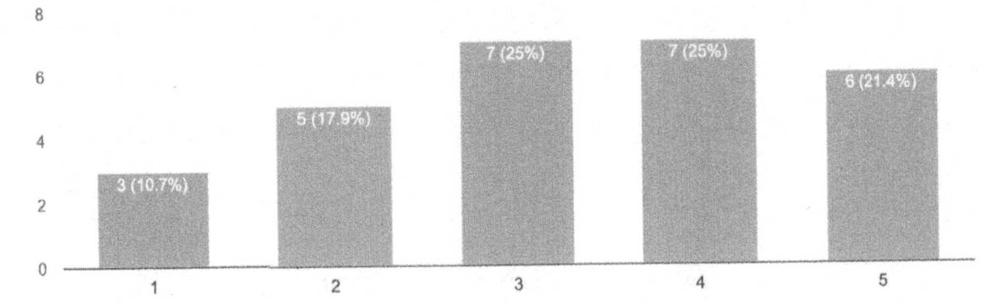

Figure 4: Making time for self-care.

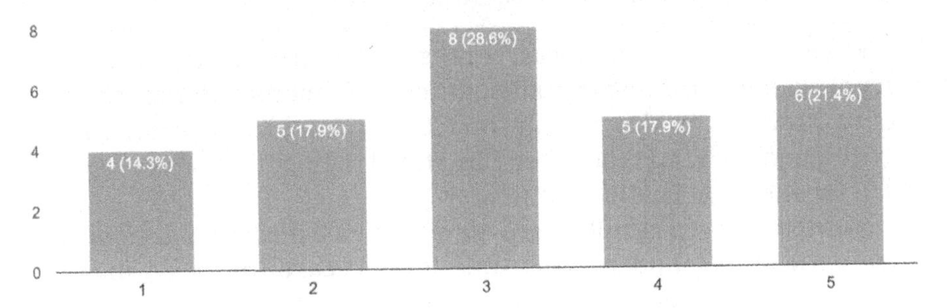

Figure 5: Work-life balance.

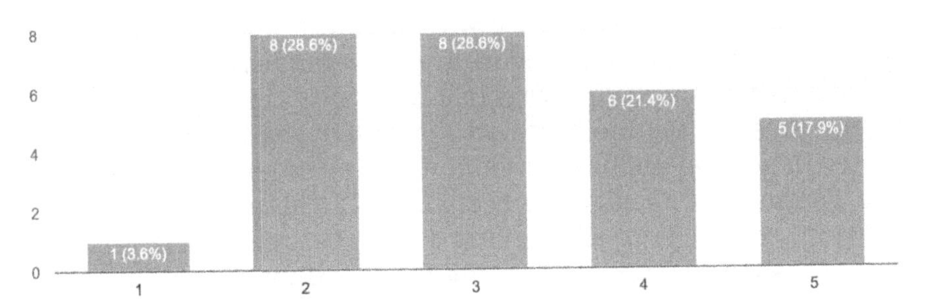

Figure 6: Time for leisure activities.

The last set of survey questions asked about how participants navigate their professional responsibilities. Responses were mostly in the affirmative when participants were asked about whether they had opportunity to be creative professionally, with 79% stating that they can do so often or very often. Most participants (70%) stated that they are able to meet the needs of their parishioners or community members often or very often. In addition, most (60%) answered that they feel professionally fulfilled often or very often. However, it should be noted that about one-third of respondents provided a neutral or negative response to this prompt. Likewise, while most (64%) reported having appropriate boundaries often or very often, the rest responded in the negative or neutral. A final question asked about ministers' ability to learn and develop new skills, which most (75%) indicated they could do often or very often.

Survey respondents were given an opportunity to provide open-ended responses to what they see as the opportunities and challenges of bivocational ministry. Two main themes arose from this question: money and flexibility. Respondents noted both the necessity and gift of having additional income outside the church. Others noted that this provides a flexibility to take risks in ministry and affords the opportunity to minister to a wide variety of people and exercise a larger set of skills. When asked about challenges in bivocational ministry, the overwhelming response was related to difficulty with time management. Many shared the sentiment of not having enough time, constantly juggling multiple demands, and shared concerns about how this could lead to burnout or difficulties in some other domain of life. Some ministers also expressed frustration that their work is not valued at the same level as fully compensated pastors, in terms of influence and in terms of finance, due to their bivocational status.

Overall, the survey results confirm what previous research suggests about both the gifts and challenges of bivocational ministry (Scroggins and Wright 2013; Smith 2014). Of particular note in this population of Black ministers is the volume of unpaid ministers who are actively involved in ministry work on a regular basis. Often, the study of bivocational ministry focuses on clergy with two paid positions, one of which is in ministry. However, in the Black church context and in small or rural ministries, it may be more common to have unpaid leaders in official roles. It is important to hear and respond to the experiences of these leaders as they are running churches alongside pastors who may be bivocational as well. Though this sample is small, pastors, assistant pastors, Christian educators, youth ministers, executive or administrative pastors, and chaplains were all represented. Regardless of pay level or number of contracted hours, congregations likely expect ministers in these roles to operate in ways that mimic a full-time minister. This sentiment was confirmed by the reflections provided in interviews. These expectations present a serious challenge when attempting to also make time for self and family.

Also of note in the survey responses are the ways bivocational ministers seem to find the good in their bivocational status. The overwhelming majority of this population identified transferable skills that can be used across contexts, the ability to use different gifts or passions, and the ability to see God in multiple and varied ways. There are clearly opportunities in bivocational ministry that will be supported and enhanced by shifting church and denominational systems to recognize and respond to the particularities of bivocational ministry.

Interview Results

Seven clergy were interviewed about their bivocational experiences. There were three men and four women. Of this group, two were senior pastors, three were in paid part-time ministerial positions, and two were in unpaid part-time ministerial positions. The interviews focused on understanding the practices and strategies that help clergy to sustain bivocational ministry, the challenges they face in executing their vocation, and their hopes for how churches and denominations would support bivocational clergy.

A primary theme expressed by these clergy was a continuity of their sense of vocation and calling both in the context of their ministry work and in their other professional activities. For some, this was exemplified in the form of transferable skills that they use in various contexts. For others, it was the sense that being called in a "secular" context provides an opportunity to minister to people who might be uninterested in or disconnected from the church. Every participant rejected a stark distinction between their call as a minister and their other professional work. One interviewee stated, "I don't have a secular vocation," when describing her non-church work. "I get to see God at work everywhere." Each minister could identify a common thread that connects the work they do across environments. One participant said he feels his main paid position equips him to do ministry more effectively because he has a sense of how organizations run and is able to put processes in place. Another pastor stated it this way: "In every part of my life, I'm pastoring . . . It's all building relationships with people." Yet another interviewee described her vocation as "multifaceted, multi-layered, complex, [and] intersectional."

Related to the concept of an all-encompassing vocational thread, four interviewees acknowledged that one of the things they enjoy about being bivocational is the ability to connect with people and do ministry outside of the traditional church context and with people who may not be connected with God or the church. Of those four interviewees, three specifically mentioned that this sense of doing ministry is not necessarily connected to whether people know they are ministers or even if they identify as Christian. They noted enjoying opportunities to listen, respond, and attend to the needs of others, seeing it as "God-work" regardless of whether it is labeled that way. There was a sense that bivocational ministry broadens the scope of possible ministry.

Respondents shared that spiritual disciplines are crucial to their functioning in ministry. Several participants noted that in addition to more formal spiritual disciplines and time set aside for devotional activities, they commit to a constant prayer life centered on praying throughout the day that helps them to navigate the choices they make and opportunities to do ministry in and out of church. Two ministers distinguished study and devotion for their own personal spiritual enrichment from preparation for sermons or bible study. Others talked about maintaining a sense of deep connection to their personal call—their sense of why God called them as individuals (see Chapman and Watson, chapter 6 in this volume).

Five participants shared that one of the ways they manage competing demands is to have firm boundaries. Several talked about setting up boundaries around their time so that certain tasks and times are protected—for example, having certain days for family or personal time or dedicating certain evenings to sermon preparation. Additionally, participants talked about communicating these boundaries to parishioners. One participant shared his frustrations that parishioners seem to have expectations of him that do not take into account that he has a full-time job outside his ministry work. Another stated that she finds herself reminding her pastor that she works, and this might mean that her pace in how she moves through ministry "elevations" might be different. One pastor said it simply: "I refuse to be burnt out . . . you have to have a balance." This pastor also noted that delegating is an important practice in her ministry work. Four participants also shared that committing to mental health therapy has been crucial for them in maintaining a sense of balance. Two of these four also noted that sharing with others about their mental health journey has been helpful in setting and maintaining appropriate boundaries.

All female interviewees identified bivocational ministry as a way to do ministry in resistance to the patriarchal frameworks in the Black church that present barriers to being in full-time ministry, being compensated ethically, or being seen as a viable church leader. Though the bivocational role does not present an escape, they noted that they are able to access opportunities to exercise their gifts when those doors are not open in the church. As one participant noted: "I never dealt with sexism until I got baptized. The sin of the Black church is sexism." For these women, the challenges they face as bivocational ministers are connected to and exacerbated by the struggle of being a woman in a patriarchal system. This oppressive framework impacted their understanding of how they are compensated (or not), people's perceptions of their ability and fitness to lead, and their sense of place in their congregations. One interviewee noted her influence in the community is not mirrored in the church, due to the challenges of Black patriarchy in the church. She also noted that while the expectation for men in ministry is to be in a pastoral role, the expectation for women is to be in a teaching or auxiliary role. The dual challenge of being a woman and bivocational also elongates and presents barriers to moving through denominational credentialing processes. Two women talked about how their educational process and consequently their dates of ordination were delayed; there was a sense that this delay then led others in the community to question their abilities and status as a minister. Another noted that she does not get the same respect as male ministers in her church, despite being credentialed in two different denominations and having more education than her male counterparts. The female pastor noted a desire for female mentorship in addition to the positive relationships she had with male pastors, noting the particular experiences of women in ministry.

In addition to the dynamic of patriarchy in the Black church, all seven participants noted the way the particularities of Black church culture complicate a bivocational identity. Crawford's (2012, 21) review of the Black church as an institution highlights the way Black clergy have historically been pillars of the Black community, intrinsically connected to the nuclear family and engaged in community life. This salient cultural reality does not discriminate based on full-time or bivocational status, and congregational expectations do not calibrate with the amount of compensation. Several participants noted that they feel the pressure of expectations to live into this all-encompassing historical and cultural role. One pastor put it this way: "Pastoring a church is a 24-hour job . . . being available, taking calls in the middle of the night, visiting nursing homes." The necessity of the changes needed in response to the COVID-19 pandemic seemed to heighten these expectations. One participant shared that trying to live into this cultural norm was costly for him: "Before I took a vacation in June 2021, I had preached 63 straight Sundays, because I didn't want to take time off during COVID. . . . I was ready to stop pastoring." Another interviewee stated a desire to push back against a "transactional" view of bivocational ministers that conceptualizes their worth and status in ministry to what they are paid, declaring "I am not your prostitute!"

Of course, money is a primary theme for these ministers. Two interviewees talked about a sense of financial freedom that comes with being bivocational. They acknowledged that because Black churches are typically less equipped to provide ethical salaries and comprehensive benefits, having another job allowed them to have a sense of financial security and not be concerned about their livelihood while doing ministry. One participant noted: "The blessing is, there was an opportunity to serve. I wasn't going to make money, because my money comes from elsewhere. I'm not basing my livelihood on it, and I'm ok with that. It changes the stress level." Two even noted that after being suddenly let go from ministry jobs, their other professions helped them to stay afloat financially. For others, there was a sense of frustration that their ministry work could not provide a living and that their other work, even when they enjoy it, is simply a necessity. Several expressed desires that they would be compensated more fairly for the work they do in ministry.

Time is another common theme for bivocational clergy. As one of the pastors in the group noted, "It never seems that there are enough hours in a day." Several noted that time presents a serious challenge and that their faith and sense of commitment to their call keeps them motivated and committed. Almost all of the interviewees talked about being engaged in community activities in addition to their ministry work and their other job responsibilities. Their passion and desire to serve fueled them even in the midst of limited time and personal resources. This theme seemed to be intrinsically connected to the common vocational thread that connects various activities. Time management seems to be viewed through this lens of an overall call that guides life activities. One interviewee stated, "It's all one big ball. I'm not inclined to compartmentalize those identities unless I'm forced to."

Two interviewees—one who is a senior pastor and another who is in an unpaid ministry position—shared that they have a desire to engage in various continuing education opportunities but feel there is neither enough time to do these things nor sufficient opportunities for people who are working full-time. The pastor acknowledged that if it had not been for the COVID-19 pandemic and conferences shifting to virtual platforms where session recordings can be viewed later, he would have had to take leave from his full-time job to get any continuing education in ministry.

Interviewees had various suggestions for how Black churches and denominations can support and equip bivocational clergy. One participant stressed the need for Black churches to convene conversations and disseminate research about bivocational ministry. According to him, we should "let people know that it's possible and realistic. We have that thought that 'if I'm not full-time, I'm not successful' . . . but that's not realistic. . . . I think how we present ministry for our culture needs to change. . . . It just means you're skillful at more than one thing. I don't think people look at it like that."

A significant challenge highlighted in this sample is that because bivocational clergy often do not have full-time status, they are not afforded some of the benefits afforded to full-time clergy, such as paid leave, insurance and retirement benefits, or sabbatical time. Both senior pastors noted the need to have sacred spaces for pastors to talk with each other and receive support. Others noted specific needs, such as having practical ways to take time off without being financially burdened and a fund to support educational endeavors. As one minister in an unpaid position shared, "I can go to my sorority and get a scholarship . . . I should be able to get support from my denomination."

Conclusions

The Black ministers in this study reported some of the same gifts and challenges as non-Black bivocational ministers, affirming that much of the research on bivocational ministry is applicable to Black populations. They also described some cultural experiences particular to the Black church that intersect with the realities of being bivocational. Historically, most Black churches have not been equipped to provide a full-time salary. Bivocational ministry has, in some ways, been the norm, even when it was not labeled that way. Black pastors have developed practices to make it work and are often doing well. However, this does not save them from the stresses and challenges of bivocational ministry. Due to their vast lived experience, these clergy have also provided some key insights into the experience of being Black and bivocational.

As a start, the Black church must reckon with the expectations that are placed on ministers in general and bivocational ministers in particular—expectations that are reflective of a historical and cultural reality that may be outdated in some ways. This reckoning speaks directly to Stephens's encouragement that the congregation envision and co-create intentional bivocational ministry (chapter 1 in this volume). This re-envisioning does not mean a loss of the role of minister as vital to the community. It does, however, require a scaling back of the functional expectations placed on ministers to hold sacred space, allowing for their human limitations and sense of wellness. It also requires that bivocational clergy be seen as information-sharers and ambassadors who provide a diverse set of skills to the church and serve a vital role in the functioning of the church—rather than being seen as less-than. Embedded in the hierarchical models embodied by some Black churches are oppressive systems such as patriarchy, homophobia, and elitism. Because they do not hold full-time ministry status, bivocational ministers are especially vulnerable to these barriers. Unsurprisingly, the women in this study seemed to readily identify the way these oppressive systems have impacted their lives and their ministries. If bivocational ministry is the new norm, as many have argued, the Black church must find a way to make this arrangement more just and equitable by working to dismantle these oppressive systems in the context of ministry life. A just and equitable system of bivocational ministry demands more consistent compensation, financial and functional support for educational engagement, and clear pathways for advancement and credentialing. A bivocational status should not present a barrier to active engagement in ministry life.

In this research sample, clergy clearly felt a sense of passion about their call. Despite the challenges, they reported excitement about ministry, a deep sense of connection to their parishioners and community members, and a wonder at their engagement with God in their life and work. This passion is a gift that undoubtedly keeps them going and provides a sense of motivation. This passion can also act as a double-edged sword as it might make it difficult to pull back or say no and might put ministers at greater risk for overwork and burnout. This intrapsychic dynamic, combined with a Black church culture that prioritizes accessibility and availability of its pastoral leadership, is a recipe for an overworked and overextended minister. As we seek to shift church culture to more reasonable expectations, we also open up space for bivocational ministers to honor and communicate their own limits without sacrificing their sense of call.

The most salient sustaining factor for these clergy is a clear sense of ministerial identity active in all their professional activities, regardless of whether this was in the context of the church or not. This identity seems to be the driving force that helped these clergy to transfer skills from one domain to another, to remain connected to their understanding of God in their lives, and to prioritize tasks on a daily basis. This identity was fueled and sustained by a commitment to spiritual disciplines and practices that helped clergy to maintain a sense of connection with the divine. For these Black clergy, this sense of connection helps them navigate this commitment to family and self as it sets the standard for prioritizing competing tasks and setting appropriate boundaries. Several interviewees talked about this connectivity as also being encompassed in their understanding of call: they viewed themselves as being called to church work and their other professional responsibilities—not one or the other. Integration is crucial to a healthy sense of flow.

Survey results suggested wide variability in the extent to which ministers are able to enjoy leisure time, make time for family, and dedicate energy for balance and self-care. The feedback from interviewees suggests that a clear and coherent set of boundaries is a key practice for meeting these goals. Boundaries include internal commitments to certain priorities and external communication with others about how those priorities will impact interpersonal engagement. In the context of the powerful Black church culture mentioned earlier, this communication process is crucial and must be taught as a sustaining practice.

This research yielded fruitful insights into the experiences of Black bivocational clergy, and there is still much more work to do. Because time availability is a challenge, this sample was small. Larger groups of Black bivocational clergy need to be accessed to create a fuller picture of the diversity of experiences within the Black community. Observing the distinctions between men and women, between seminary-trained and those less formally trained, and between diverse ministerial positions is likely to provide a more nuanced understanding of how churches and denominations can help these clergy thrive. It is clear from this small sample that women may need additional resources and sources of support compared to men. It is also clear that the pathways for thriving might be different for pastoral leaders than those who hold associate positions. What is clear is that any solutions and resources for Black bivocational clergy must take into account the nuances of the Black church experience.

Works Cited

Bickers, Dennis W. 2007. *The Work of the Bivocational Minister.* Valley Forge, PA: Judson.

Crawford, Erika D. 2012. "Serving Them is Killing Me: Using Technology as a Vehicle for Self-Care for Bi-Vocational Pastors in the Black Church" DMin diss., Fordham University. *proquest.com/docview/1316905977.*

Deasy, Jo Ann. 2018. "Shifting Vocational Identity in Theological Education: Insights from the ATS Student Questionnaires." *Theological Education* 52, no. 1: 63–78. *ats.edu/files/galleries/2018-theological-education-v52-n1.pdf.*

Dorr, Luther M. 1988. *The Bivocational Pastor.* Nashville: Broadman.

Ferguson, Todd W., Brita Andercheck, Joshua C. Tom, Brandon C. Martinez, and Samuel Stroope. 2014. "Occupational Conditions, Self-Care, and Obesity among Clergy in the United States." *Social Science Research* 49: 249–63. *doi.org/10.1016/j.ssresearch.2014.08.014.*

Ferris, Robert W. 2001. "Of Tents and Taxonomies." *Christian Education Journal* 5, no. 1: 79–82.

Perry, Samuel L., and Cyrus Schleifer. 2019. "Are Bivocational Clergy Becoming the New Normal? An Analysis of the Current Population Survey, 1996–2017." *Journal for the Scientific Study of Religion* 58, no. 2: 513–25. *doi.org/10.1111/jssr.12593.*

Scroggins, Jimmy, and Steven Wright. 2013. "The Math Doesn't Work: Why the Future of Church Planting is Bi-Vocational." *9 Marks*, January 3. *9marks.org/article/journalmath-doesnt-work-why-future-church-planting-bi-vocational.*

Smith, Gregory Harris. 2014. "Effective Strategies for Bi-vocational Ministry." DMin diss., Talbot School of Theology, Biola University. *proquest.com/docview/1525999370/4BEC2D3FD6F348A2PQ/1.*

Wells, Carl R., Janice Probst, Robert McKeown, Stephanie Mitchem, and Han Whiejong. 2012. "The Relationship Between Work-Related Stress and Boundary-Related Stress Within the Clerical Profession." *Journal of Religion and Health* 51, no. 1: 215–30. *doi.org/10.1007/s10943-011-9501-9.*

Young Brown, Jessica. 2017. "Don't Be Afraid of a Future with More Bivocational Ministers." *Duke Leadership Education*. November 12. *thrivinginministry.org/dont-be-afraid-of-a-future-with-more-bivocational-ministers.*

CHAPTER 5

Black Student Perspectives

JO ANN DEASY

In 2019, the Association of Theological Schools (ATS) launched a qualitative research project to study Black student debt. This research helped ATS better understand how Black seminary students understand the connection between money and their call to vocational ministry. Respondents emphasized multivocational ministry as a way to address financial challenges. This chapter examines this qualitative data to explore how multivocational ministry impacts the calling and education of Black ministers.

While there are many reasons that people serve in multivocational ministry, for Black graduates, multivocational ministry often reflects the financial challenges faced by these graduates and their communities. According to the 2021 ATS Graduating Student Questionnaire, 30% of theological school graduates reported plans to serve in multiple paid positions after graduation. Half of them (15% of theological school graduates) were planning on at least one of those positions being in ministry. Of all racial groups, Black/African American/African Canadian graduates had the highest percentage with 43% planning to serve in multiple positions, and just over half of those planning on multivocational ministry. Black graduates were more likely to have educational debt at graduation (65% versus 39% overall), and they borrowed at higher levels, averaging $42,500 in debt, approximately $10,000 higher than the overall average among all racial groups. Black graduates were also slightly more likely to still be seeking a job when they graduated from seminary (ATS 2021). Despite these financial challenges, ATS member schools have continued to see an increase in enrollment among Black students even as overall enrollment has declined (ATS 2020).

It is one of the ironies of graduate theological education that those students who are least likely to benefit financially from a theological degree continue to enter graduate theological education in increasing numbers. What drives these students to gain graduate theological degrees, and what can we learn from them about what it means to pursue multivocational ministry? Though not originally designed to inquire about multivocational ministry, data from the 2019 ATS qualitative research project on Black student debt help shed some light on these questions. This chapter interprets these findings, originally released by ATS in February 2021, through the lens of multivocational ministry (Deasy and Love 2021).

Overview of the Project

In 2019, ATS launched the Black Student Debt Research Project—a qualitative study designed to privilege the voices of Black students and their experiences in order to expand our understanding of the factors contributing to educational debt and to help us imagine possible solutions. The project invited students at ten ATS member schools to complete money autobiographies, in which they reflected on their family background and current experiences with money. Forty-six students responded to this invitation and participated in focus groups. A majority (80%) of the respondents were Master of Divinity students. They were evenly divided by gender, marital status, and age. They represented a wide range of educational debt levels, and almost all (90%) currently had educational debt incurred before or during seminary. Six of the participants owed over $140,000 each in educational debt before they ever started their seminary program.

Using a grounded theory approach, the research team (including this author) analyzed the money autobiographies to identify key themes emerging from the responses. From the initial analysis, we developed a series of themes to be further discussed by the students in focus groups at each participating school. Themes included: "the connection between God's provision, vocational calling, and sacrifice; the financial intersection of Black students, congregations, and denominations; and how theological schools are addressing the financial ecology of Black students" (Deasy and Love 2021, 13). Multivocational ministry emerged as both an expected future of Black seminarians and an intentional strategy to meet the needs of their communities. Voices of respondents quoted in this chapter are drawn from the final research report by Deasy and Love (2021, 15–23).

Multivocational Ministry as an Expected Future

In the focus groups and interviews, it became clear that few of these students expected to make a living wage in ministry after graduation. Black students pursued theological education not for financial success or financial security but rather as a form of preparation, service, and sacrifice in order to fulfill their vocation to minister to their communities.

Most of the students recognized that the congregations they came from and the congregations they planned to serve would not be able to support them financially. Representative statements included:

> My future work will not offer a living wage, but the salary at the VA is above average.

> If I become a pastor, I will most likely serve those that are not financially aware. . . . Funds will be a challenge.

> Congregations are struggling with the same economic issues people are struggling with, so I don't know that Black congregations as a whole have the ability to help pay for school.

Most were planning on working multiple jobs in order to provide financially for themselves and their families while also pursuing their call from God to ministry. Some planned to rely on their secular vocational skills to make money as a bivocational pastor, including working in retirement. Others were more entrepreneurial in their approaches, building consulting firms, starting companies, finding speaking engagements, or "developing multiple projects."

Did these students have realistic expectations regarding multivocational ministry? Data from a 2003 Pulpit & Pew study of Black pastors suggests that their expectations are fairly accurate. According to the study, apart from those who pastor megachurches and large, middle-class churches, Black clergy often struggle more than their White counterparts in similar church settings to meet their personal financial obligations, to satisfy denominational assessments, and to address the financial woes of congregants with limited resources. The Pulpit & Pew study found that 41% of Black pastors earned less than $13,000 per year and that Black clergy salaries were, on average, about two-thirds of White clergy salaries (McMillan and Price 2003, 14–15). The report went on to argue that, other than educational levels,

> most other factors that affect salaries would suggest African-American salaries should be more comparable to white salaries. African-American churches have slightly larger attendance . . . and the percent of African-American clergy who serve small churches is 56 percent versus 61 percent for white. The average percent of attendees who report they tithe is 57 percent in churches of African-American clergy, versus 38 percent in those of white clergy. And, despite the fact that African-American incomes are lower than those of whites in national averages, the distribution of self-reported income levels in the congregations where African-American clergy and white clergy serve are remarkably close. (McMillan and Price 2003, 15)

In addition to salaries, the Pulpit & Pew study found a large race gap in the provision of benefits. The authors referred to congregations where regulations around clergy salaries were somewhat or completely centralized within a larger denominational entity as connectional. Methodist, Lutheran, Presbyterian/Reformed, and Episcopalian congregations were all considered connectional. Congregations in which regulations around clergy salaries were decentralized and operated as a "free market" were labeled congregational. Congregational polities included Baptist, Pentecostal, United Church of Christ, and independent congregations (McMillan and Price 2003, 6). The Pulpit & Pew study found,

> In Connectional polities, 90 percent of the congregations of white clergy pay into a retirement benefits fund compared to less than half (42 percent) of the congregations African-American clergy serve. In the Congregational polity ... it is markedly worse for African-American clergy, at only 28 percent. (McMillan and Price 2003, 15)

They also found that, in connectional polities, Black clergy were less likely to have employer-sponsored health coverage (56%) than their White counterparts (93%), while in congregational polities health coverage for White and Black clergy was about the same at 68% (McMillan and Price 2003, 15).

Pulpit & Pew also highlighted the bivocational nature of Black clergy. In 2003, they found that 43% of all Black pastors were bivocational—the same percentage reported in 1990. However, the kinds of second jobs had changed. In 2003, most bivocational Black clergy (72%) worked in white-collar settings and only 3% in blue-collar or farm jobs. This was a significant shift from 1990, when 40% of Black bivocational clergy served in blue-collar or farm jobs (McMillan and Price 2003, 14).

The Pulpit & Pew study describes many of the financial challenges facing Black clergy but does little to explain why these differences exist. Jessica Young Brown, former associate professor of counseling and practical theology at Samuel DeWitt Proctor School of Theology, suggests that these differences may reflect significant differences between the ecclesiology of White and Black churches. She writes, "I wonder if this has to do with the cultural role that clergy have historically served in the Black church." She argues that Black clergy are often seen as community members rather than professionally trained staff members. As a result, in Black churches "there might be a tendency to decentralize budgets to focus on missions and church activities as opposed to equitable pay and benefits" (Young Brown, personal communication, January 5, 2022).

There has been little research on the financial challenges facing Black pastors since the 2003 Pulpit & Pew study (Deasy and Love 2021, 6–12). Through a Lilly Endowment-funded National Initiative on the Economic Challenges Facing Pastoral Leaders, several denominations recently began more general research on the financial challenges facing pastors. However, initial reports did not provide any specific data related to Black clergy. In addition, Young Brown's comments suggest a need for more research on how the culture of the Black church shapes its financial models and the implications for clergy salaries and theological education.

Educational Debt and Multivocational Ministry as Intentional Strategies

The Black students in the 2019 ATS study recognized the possible financial struggles of the congregations they will serve and the strong possibility that they will end up serving in multivocational ministry, described by one participant as "working another full-time job alongside my full-time commitment to the church." In response to these struggles, a majority of respondents had developed plans to work towards long-term financial health and stability. Several spoke of trying to avoid educational debt to pay for their undergraduate education. Other ways they were working towards long-term financial health included:

> I am financially sound and have money set aside for unexpected emergencies.
>
> I have taken the Dave Ramsey Debt Program.
>
> I have learned to budget my time and finances to maintain a healthy order of things for myself.
>
> I plan to own my own home in the next few years. I think home ownership is important to bring about stability for my family and generational wealth.

While most Black seminarians in the study had a plan to work towards long-term financial health, almost all of them (90%) also took out student loans to pay for their undergraduate and graduate education. For some, educational debt was a tool, "a means to accomplish God's plan," and necessary to follow God's path for their lives. They believed that if they were following God's call to ministry, God would provide the money needed to pay off their student loans.

This connection between God's provision in response to following a call to ministry applied not only to student loans but also to finances as a whole. Several students shared their belief that if they were following God's call, God would provide for them financially. One student put it this way: "If God has called me into this urban core, then God will provide for me to be a pastor to the cities." These students were not expecting God to provide them with a middle-class lifestyle. Many understood ministry as requiring financial sacrifice—a sacrifice pleasing to God. One student shared: "I am a tither who believes that God will bless those who are willing to make financial sacrifices to help others and the church."

While educational debt was a means to follow God's call, it was also a burden for these students to carry. They hoped that God would "lift the burden" or "provide the means for me to pay my bills, debts, and provide for my well-being." One student, responding to a question about whether their debt was manageable, put it this way:

> I mean "manageable" is relative. I have it and knew it was necessary to incur it to pursue the path God asked me to walk. So, I assume that means it's manageable. I think having prayed about and discerned each of my choices made me be conscious of getting into and seriously developing my ministry.

Several students mentioned the lack of people to talk to about paying for seminary, possibly due to the fact that Black students (59%) are more likely than White students (36%) to be the first in their family to attend college or graduate school (RTI International 2021). One student talked about their own ignorance and lack of planning when it came to student loans. Another admitted that they did not yet have any plan to pay for their debt. One student connected struggles with student debt to a lack of familiarity with the system:

> The debt for me as a Black scholar-theologian-minister is a means to accomplish God's plan. However, as a university administrator, I have seen the Black community is greatly lacking in education in terms of financial aid processes, scholarships, and the needed preparation in terms of academics. All of this directly determines debt.

While students were willing to make the sacrifice, a few reflected on how debt hindered their ability to be fully present to their call to ministry and the tension they felt between their calling and their responsibility to fulfill their financial obligations.

> Yes, I think for me in terms of my personal experience with student debt, I will say it has, at times, caused me to force my focus to be on things that I wouldn't or don't necessarily want to be thinking about. I desire freedom to be thinking about ministry creatively in ways that I desire. I will confess that there's been times where my creative side, in terms of some of the things I'm sensing in my heart for ministry, have not been pursued to the extent that I've had to focus on just the practicalities of dealing with my student debt. "How do you creatively free yourself up from those burdens?" is what I'm constantly thinking of.

While some students focused on debt as a burden, others focused on debt as an opportunity and a strategy to help someone else along:

> The debt is not a burden to us. The debt is an opportunity to get creative. An old-style example is this: it's like sharecropping. We know we aren't going to get this field, but God gave it to us to sustain us. He gave us this education to help someone else along, maybe they get this field. I will not be debt free, possibly, but I can help somebody else maybe make a better decision. But I would not even [have] been aware of how to work this field and teach them how to do it if I had not been willing to say, "I'll be underfoot for a little while. I'll do it because I have been a trailblazer my whole life."

Several students particularly named multivocational ministry as an intentional strategy—a choice they were making so that they would not be a financial burden to their congregations. They wanted their congregation's finances to be used for ministry, not their salaries. One student stated,

> I will not be a paid pastor of the church, but the resources the church gets will be what is used to take care and bless the people. The church will learn what it means to be empowered and to live in sacrificial ways to one another.

Another student said,

> My ultimate hope is to do congregational ministry for free because I believe that the cost "to do" church in America is ridiculous, unsustainable and out of touch with scripture. My wife and I hope to bring in enough money from our personal business and the other half of bi-vocational career to cover our expenses.

For many, long-term financial stability was tied to working multiple jobs, and for several it involved developing their own businesses.

> I am a working retiree who will use my salary to pay my debt.
>
> I have ministry jobs that assist to pay off the debt. . . . I am developing multiple projects and speaking engagements . . . as an entrepreneur.
>
> I . . . have been building my organizational systems consulting and editing company. My position as minister will not be my sole source of income.

Implications for Theological Education

The 2019 ATS qualitative study on Black Student Debt revealed many challenges for multivocational clergy and theological educators alike. This chapter concludes with observations presented by Deasy and Love (2021, 27–8), discussing implications for theological education.

Comments from the research participants about bivocational ministry and lack of adequate financial compensation in ministry suggest that these students have realistic expectations about the limited earning power of their professional ministerial degrees but are, nevertheless, committed to graduate theological education as a means of preparing them as they serve in low-wealth communities and congregations. These findings raise questions about the theological education curriculum and the apparent disconnect between educational cost and earning potential. Some of the important questions for consideration include the following:

- To what extent should theological education prepare pastors to serve as agents of change in the area of economic and community development?
- What core competencies would be needed?
- Is "community exegesis" just as important as "biblical exegesis" in the theological education curriculum? If so, what elements are included in "community exegesis"? Are there any existing models that theological schools can learn from?

- What new educational models could equip pastors to lead congregations in efforts to break cycles of generational poverty?
- How might theological education offer alternatives to the "self-sacrifice" models that pastors are currently embracing in order to be of service to low-wealth communities?

For theological schools interested in serving Black students, the development of curriculum must include considerations of helping to break cycles of generational poverty and skills that will best prepare students to serve in low-wealth communities. Theological schools must start with questions of the purpose and role of clergy, congregations, and Christian leaders in serving low-wealth communities, serving as agents of change, and providing prophetic voices against injustice and inequality.

How theological schools address these questions will differ depending on their own histories and traditions. In some theological schools, particularly Historically Black Theological Schools, "faculty are also pastors, and may have lower than average pay with both jobs." There can be "a cultural/historical tradition around how Black clergy serve which in some ways encourages and reinforces generational poverty. It is perpetuated by spiritual messages about having just enough, God's provision, 'making a way out of no way,' etc." (Young Brown, personal communication, January 5, 2022). Other theological schools will need to reflect on their own economic privilege and how their assumptions about educational models, clergy roles, and finances make theological education financially inaccessible for those coming from or planning to serve in low-wealth communities.

Such a rethinking of the curriculum might decenter the long dominant core areas of Bible, theology, and history and give more attention to areas of leadership, finance, administration, and community development. Learning goals would focus on the core competencies students need to succeed in real-world ministry, especially in under-resourced communities. In addition, learning goals would focus on rich theological reflection around issues such as poverty, injustice, and suffering that would equip students in two ways. First, such theological reflection would be needed to equip students to respond as theological leaders, preachers, and pastoral caregivers to individuals struggling deeply with these issues. Second, such theological reflection would be needed to equip students with a type of pastoral imagination that would allow them to critically reflect on resources and practices related to finances and leadership. Young Brown suggests that such a rethinking of curriculum might also decenter traditional models of pastoral ministry. She writes, "Black students know . . . that many of them won't be in parish positions, and so ministry is conceptualized more broadly . . . Maybe [theological education] looks like having a broader variety of certificate or concentration programs as well so that people can specialize in particular areas of ministry where they feel called" (Young Brown, personal communication, January 5, 2022).

The students in this research project also suggest a need to rethink both our educational and financial models. What does it mean to design a curriculum for students who will be working full-time while in theological school? How does one learn best when juggling multiple responsibilities? What types of assignments are most effective for learning part-time? For those who are serving in ministry settings while in theological school, how can assignments be designed in ways that benefit the students and the communities they serve? What would it mean to create a calendar and scheduling that is based on the church and not the academy? Many of these students, however, will not be paid a living wage for their work in the church. How do we support students who will be working full-time while completing their degree? How do we create programs that are more affordable and accessible?

In reflecting on this research, Young Brown asked, "at what point do we coach students *not* to do degree programs and acquire more debt? What are nontraditional/noninstitutionalized training models that can help clergy get the necessary skills for ministry without a $30k price tag?" (personal communication, January 5, 2022). Her questions are important. Is it ethical for theological schools, denominations, and congregations to encourage or require clergy to acquire expensive graduate theological degrees in order to receive a credential? Are there other forms of education that might provide clergy what they need at a lower cost? Is there a way to provide alternative forms of theological education that will be equally valued by churches and denominations, that will not create a second, lower class of clergy? Perhaps just as critical is the question of what it might mean for theological education if it only serves students who can afford a graduate degree? How would it diminish the ability of theological schools to serve the church and the world?

Very few of the Black students engaged in this research project expected to be paid a living wage while in ministry. For these students, a graduate theological degree had no financial benefit. In fact, it was a significant financial sacrifice made in order to follow God's call and to serve their communities. In order for theological schools to serve these students, the schools themselves may also need to hear a call to serve low-wealth communities.

Works Cited

Association of Theological Schools (ATS). 2020. "ATS Annual Report Enrollment Dataset, 1988–2020." *ats.edu/Data-Visualization.*

———. 2021. "ATS Entering and Graduating Student Questionnaires Total School Profile Dataset, Revision E. 2020–2021." Some of the data is available in the annual total school profile report available on *ats.edu.*

Deasy, Jo Ann, and Velma E. Love. 2021. "The ATS Black Student Debt Project: Final Report." Association of Theological Schools, the Commission on Accrediting. February. *ats.edu/files/galleries/ats-black-student-debt-project-report.pdf.*

McMillan, Becky R., and Matthew J. Price. 2003. "How Much Should We Pay the Pastor? A Fresh Look at Clergy Salaries in the 21st Century." *Pulpit & Pew Research Reports* 2 (Winter). *silo.tips/download/how-much-should-we-pay.*

RTI International. 2021. "First-generation College Graduates: Race/Ethnicity, Age, and Use of Career Planning Services." Washington, DC: NASPA. *firstgen.naspa.org/files/dmfile/FactSheet-011.pdf.*

Leadership

CHAPTER 6

Calling in Multivocational Ministry

MARK D. CHAPMAN AND JAMES W. WATSON

This chapter examines the ways in which multivocational leaders understand, frame, discern, and apply their calling. Multivocational calling should be understood as calling in conversation with both God and a social environment. There is no single model of multivocational leadership; rather, each individual has a unique fit in relation to self, family, congregation, and additional employment. Multivocational calling needs to be articulated in a meaningful way among these pieces, and we suggest that educators and others who resource and support multivocational leaders pay specific attention to this understanding of calling.

The Wellness Project @ Wycliffe defines vocational calling as "feeling called to the ministry life you are engaged in, the fit between your personal and ministry life, and your sense of God's direction and involvement as you move forward" (Watson et al. 2020, 29). To put it a different way, calling is not about the specific tasks ministers do or the schedules they keep, but rather calling is a testimony of the presence of God in any context and helping those present experience this reality (compare to Root 2019, 268). In a multivocational context, calling may encompass multiple occupations, roles, or places. That is, calling is highly individualized and contextual.

This chapter begins with an overview of the larger research project—the Canadian Multivocational Ministry Project—followed by a biblical reflection on calling that makes the case for a variety of understandings of the concept. Then, a review of the research shares what we have learned about calling from multivocational leaders; we argue that calling can be understood as a conversation about the unique fit of the different elements of the multivocational life. We end with a summary of what that tells us about the training and ongoing support of multivocational leaders. For example, specific attention to unique elements for a particular individual when exploring calling would be productive in equipping the multivocational leader to thrive in their complex life and livelihoods.

The Canadian Multivocational Ministry Project

The Canadian Multivocational Ministry Project used a mixed-methods research approach to exploring multivocational ministry. The primary methodologies were a quantitative clergy wellness survey and qualitative interviews. Quantitative data was provided through cooperation with the Wellness Project @ Wycliffe, which developed a pair of questionnaires to measure ministry-specific stress and satisfaction (Malcolm, Coetzee, and Fisher 2019). This chapter concentrates on the qualitative data. The research was conducted using a community-based research approach that involved practitioners in the development of the research and in the subsequent data analysis and knowledge mobilization. The qualitative interviews adopted a semi-structured approach to allow multivocational leaders to share what they thought was important.

The research project included 40 semi-structured qualitative interviews (Watson et al. 2020). Respondents included women (16) and men (24) in diverse combinations of work and ministry roles from a variety of denominations and ethnocultural backgrounds from across Canada. The focus of the study was exploratory rather than representative, with the intent of providing insight into some common themes in the Canadian tentmaking experience (Hagaman and Wutich 2017). Interviewers asked about patterns of work in congregational ministry and other settings, what these leaders found positive or negative about their other work, how they understood their theology of work, and their recommendations for those who train or resource multivocational leaders. The interview questions addressed issues of fit and theology of work but not specifically calling. The respondents' understanding, framing, discerning, and application of their calling and the role it plays in their lives provided an insider perspective, helping us understand the nature of a calling to multivocational ministry that can inform training and support of those leaders.

Biblical Reflection on Calling

While addressing the issue of calling in diverse ways, different Christian traditions generally agree that God provides direction for vocation. Understandings range from a specific emphasis on vocation as primarily focused on clergy to consideration of additional commitments. Broader motifs of communication and direction from God found within scripture support diverse interpretations of calling. The following short review of biblical perspectives on calling points to the variety of ways calling has been understood, framed, discerned, and applied as a way of identifying and following God's direction in partnership with the unfolding *missio Dei*.

God directed Abram and Sarai to take the initial steps beyond their country of origin and promised a blessing for all people (Gen. 12). This personal direction ties into God's salvation history, and the obedience to direction partners with what God is accomplishing in the world (Wright 2006). God's direction and recognition of purpose may be identified in hindsight. For example, it is at the end of the Joseph narrative where God's purpose is fully recognized (Gen. 45). For some leaders, such as Esther, the circumstances described in the text are driven by the necessity of the situation but are interpreted in terms of divine destiny. Some follow in their appointment from their mentor's designation, such as from Moses to Joshua and Elijah to Elisha. The tradition of establishing leaders (judges, priests, prophets, kings) recognized by God and/or chosen by people contains spiritual implications for the nature of calling and provides opportunity for theological reflection. Some of the narratives include very explicit calls from God, such as Moses responding to "I am who I am" in the desert (Exod. 3) or Eli assisting Samuel in identifying God's voice (1 Sam. 3).

We find parallels in Jesus's ministry. Jesus invited a disparate group to follow him. This call demanded a shift in personal obligations; he invited them to change their occupations metaphorically or metaphysically (become fishers of people). All were directed to realign their lives. After the resurrection, Paul's calling to be an apostle (Acts 9, 22, and 26) included a specific encounter with Jesus. Yet, Paul also provided a broader framework when he addressed the church in Rome and reminded them that they have all been called to be saints (Rom. 1). Furthermore, while there is no indication that Paul considered making tents (or leatherworking) a divine appointment, it was intertwined with his ministry of connecting with people in different communities and offering the gospel (Watson and Santos 2019). The biblical text shows there is no one way in which God calls.

Multivocational Leaders Discuss Calling

The way that multivocational leaders understood, framed, discerned, and applied calling as reported during the Canadian Multivocational Ministry Project shows all the diversity of the biblical record. Calling is very much related to the specifics of the context of the individual and the task(s) that God sets before them. Yet, in that diversity, multivocational ministers agreed on the importance of calling. Multivocational leaders' approach to their calling encompassed their understanding of what calling is, framed why calling is necessary, explained their discernment of how to find a calling, and articulated their application of what calling does.

Calling is not an optional part of ministry training and understanding. Rather, a clear understanding of vocational calling and continual discernment of the nature and application of that calling is a vital part of the ongoing effectiveness and sustainability of multivocational ministry. One multivocational leader provided the following advice for entering this kind of ministry:

> bivocational ministry is something that will only work if you have a very clear sense of call to the demands that you'll face. Because

> there's, you know, seasons and moments where bivocational / trivocational work, you're exhausted you're depleted and it's that sense of calling that you rely on, the trust that God by Spirit is going to enable you and empower you and that this is your reasonable act of service and love for God and for Jesus.[1]

This leader identified the close connection between thriving in multivocational ministry and having a clear calling. They also did not confine calling to one part of the multivocational life.

Passionate about their calling, these leaders often provided a personal story or a theological explanation for that passion. The leaders we interviewed rooted their understanding of calling in the larger picture of God's work in the world.

> I guess my theology of work is: starting in the Garden of Eden and God gave us work to do. . . . It wasn't a work-free zone. The expectation was that creation was to be tended and cared for, so I talked about vocation and calling and I think God created us to work; for rhythms of work and rest and meaningful work.

As opposed to compartmentalized lives, some leaders stressed a theological approach in which "nothing should be considered outside of divine oversight or our spiritual engagement" (Watson et al. 2020, 14). Many multivocational leaders had a concept of ministry that encompassed every aspect of their lives. While they did not always identify this as calling, it matches our definition because of the manner in which the different parts of their lives are addressed and the emphasis on God's direction and involvement. For these leaders, calling was typically not just to a church but also to other work within the community. Some leaders indicated that calling was necessary for effective multivocational ministry. Furthermore, some recognized that when both spouses are involved in multivocational ministry, they both have unique callings that need to be taken into account as they navigate their lives and ministries. However, not every multivocational leader included their non-congregational work as part of their understanding of ministry engagement. A few indicated the other work was primarily or solely a financial benefit.

Multivocational leaders understood the concept of calling in many different ways. Some individuals talked about a general biblical mandate for churches or individuals. Other individuals talked about an approach to living where all aspects of life are considered part of one's spiritual vocation. Others referred to taking a specific role or being part of a specific organization as calling. Holding these different understandings of calling together, sometimes within the same individual, is a sense of listening for and following God's direction.

Multivocational leaders agreed that God provides direction for living and that some of that direction is a general biblical calling to the church as a whole. Calling as an approach to living was sometimes understood as a biblical mandate for all Christians. One respondent referenced Matthew 28:16–20: "This includes doctrines like the Great Commission but also the importance of prayer and seeking God's guidance in ministry. It's just not pastors or the church as a whole. It's as individuals. We're all called to be disciples, so we all have work to do." This biblical conviction—that God directs—contributes to an understanding of calling as a general approach to life. Another way of describing it is one calling with a variety of different roles. One leader explained, "It's all spiritual. It doesn't matter what I'm doing. If I was serving doughnuts at Tim Hortons, it would be the same thing. So, I don't feel that; I don't see a huge divide between secular and holy work." In sum, multivocational leaders connected calling with communication from God about specific actions and ways of living, and they understood their calling as rooted in the mandates of scripture.

For most leaders, the opportunity to express one's calling in multiple roles is a privilege, but, for the occasional individual, multiple roles lead to a ministry life without boundaries, threatening its sustainability. This reality emphasizes the need for training multivocational leaders how to navigate the diverse roles that constitute their calling or to clarify their calling.

Even individuals who talked about calling as a constant vocation that applied to all areas of life saw calling as also applying to specific roles or organizations. Some individuals talked about a specific time in their life when they received a "call." Others talked about a call to a general ministry area, such as missions; a specific role in an organization, such as an officer in the Salvation Army; an occupation, such as pastor or farmer; or a location, such as a particular church. Some specifically identified being bivocational as part of their calling, "Where is your heart in, in doing ministry . . . how can you best accomplish God's call on your life? . . . for me [it] just happens to be ministry and, as well as . . . working this [Educational] Assistant job." One couple shared about a call to ministry that initially seemed to conflict with the business they were running, which, though independent of their denominational work, they also understood as part of their vocation. However, they explained that the apparent conflict was reconciled: "We felt like God opened up the heavens and created a way for us to still serve in the denomination."

An understanding of the integrated nature of different life responsibilities as calling can provide ministry opportunities. "Non-ministry" work provides contact with those outside the church and may provide opportunities to discuss the spiritual value of the work being done (Watson et al. 2020, 16). Such opportunities require intentionality and may be more prevalent among individuals whose secondary work is not seen as a break from ministry but rather an extension of their calling as a minister of the gospel.

Framing

Describing what calling is helps identify some of the reasons that calling is necessary: calling aligns people's lives with their biblical reflection or spiritual discernment and helps to focus or assign meaning to life directions. An understanding of calling provides a framework for discussing God's direction and one's response. This framework is manifest in both application and how multivocational leaders make decisions. A meaning-making frame helps to keep multivocational leaders healthy and gives them a passion for the hard work to which they are called. Issues of decision-making, minister health—particularly in tough times—and passion for ministry action were the most commonly identified reasons why calling is necessary.

Clarity of action and decision making can be seen most clearly in multivocational leaders' discussion of role discernment and their rationale for ministry engagement. One pastor explained: "There's no set approach for that, but I would absolutely ensure that anyone who wants to be bivocational or tri-anything and ministry, for that matter . . . have a clear, not mere, sense . . . there is absolute clarity in calling." Sometimes that clarity of role and action comes from general guidelines.

> So there are three kinds of phrases that are central to my sense of call and that were named at my ordination. And they are: feed my sheep, share my story and love my people . . . I don't find it particularly helpful health-wise to do things that are really not my calling. . . . And so when the opportunity to edit came up, it aligns so closely with what I feel it means to be able to share God's story more broadly . . .

This individual's general calling framework (that is, feed, share, love) might be widely shared with other ministry leaders, but they then apply it in a very specific manner to an editing job. For other individuals, calling to decision making was relatively specific:

> [we] spent a weekend fasting and praying and asking God for direction. And we both had this moment where she said, I'm really sensing God calling us to a smaller place, a place where there isn't a Christian counselor and a place where they have [struggled to] get a pastor and I said, "Yeah, that's exactly what I was hearing from God."

For this couple, decision making was not derived from general principles but rather from the specific skills they had and a time of discernment.

This sense that God has called one to something plays a key role in making life meaningful and thus in minister health. Over 90% of multivocational leaders rated vocational calling as a "core satisfier" in the wellness survey; those who did not "showed indices of burnout" (Watson et al. 2020, 9). Further, the interviews suggested that "calling appears to play a pivotal role in clarity and persistence" (19). This is not surprising given the challenges of multivocational ministry identified by respondents (for example, family organization, complicated scheduling, erratic support). Such challenges are easier to surmount if one is convinced that one is living a life to which one is called by God. If God has called one to a specific set of responsibilities, it is reasonable to assume that God will provide the necessary resources to fulfill them. One leader explained the dichotomy like this: "the things that God has asked us to do are hard, and there's that weird . . . juxtaposition where Jesus [says], 'Come, come walk with me, learn the unforced rhythms of grace . . . learn to live freely and lightly' but Jesus is talking about a yoke." For this individual, the hard things God asked them to do were made feasible by the specific call on their life and by the general scriptural description of the nature of God's calling.

However, calling is not just necessary for practical reasons like decision making and helping with hard times. Calling also brings energy and passion for what needs to be done. Explained one pastor, "my true passion is, the number one is, church planting. I'm definitely a pioneer . . . the centre of my purpose would be to be a pioneer and to plant churches and so many others." Passion came from being where God wanted them to be. Many multivocational leaders talked about calling as being connected to gifting, with gifting being something one is good at, either because of innate ability or because of God-given supernatural aptitude. Awareness of that gifting was part of hearing from God. If calling is hearing direction from God, passion would seem to be the resulting inner spiritual drive that results from clarity of calling.

Discernment

This discussion of gifting was closely connected with discerning the process of calling—how to articulate or find a call and the related theme of how God calls. Multivocational leaders had much to say about the discernment process with specific attention to hearing from God and attending to gifting.

Hearing from God and attending to gifting were the most-mentioned parts of the discernment process. Other means of discerning calling included fasting, discernment groups, family conversation (including with children), trusted advisors, circumstances, or self-assessment. Some multivocational leaders had a clearly thought-through process for discernment. This quote illustrates the degree to which some leaders have worked out their understanding of discernment and how to guide others through this process:

> I feel like I would need to have a conversation with them and find out some specifics of what they're feeling or thinking. And then, if the Holy Spirit would be guiding me, just give them some words at that moment, then I would deliver those words . . . I feel like I would just pray with them . . . I would ask them to explain to me the thoughts that are going on around the job. When and where that desire originated. What kind of tasks they would see themselves doing. How those tasks

> fit in with their spiritual gifting. I would ask them a bit about their home-work-life balance. I would ask them about their awareness of their emotional responses to the ideas of the job and if they were positive or negative and how just to get a reading of emotionally where they're at. I would encourage them. And I would encourage them to [also discuss] the ideas and possibilities with other godly people in their life.

This individual not only thinks working out one's calling is related to discernment but has thought through a process of discerning that includes spiritual, practical, and emotional elements. This further emphasizes the need for discussions of calling to take into account the entire life of the ministry leader. Not all respondents had a discernment process as elaborate as this one, but some approach to discernment was common and used to make many types of life decisions. Multivocational leaders discerned the role or location of their activity, as well as education and family choices that are less commonly considered in discussions of calling. Not only does multivocational calling encompass all of leaders' lives, but much of this discernment takes place in conversation with others with a specific focus on hearing from God.

Hearing from God is a fundamental part of the way multivocational leaders understood their calling. It is hearing from God that led these leaders to take up specific positions, move to certain cities, start certain organizations, and engage in multivocational ministry. That is not to say that listening to God was always easy. One leader explained, "Jesus is nuts, he calls us to do ridiculous things, things that are hard and terrible and difficult and dangerous and all of those things." This leader was not arguing that Jesus is unreasonable but rather that following Jesus can be challenging. They were not questioning what God was calling them to do but recognizing there can be a cost. Another participant made a similar point: "You know I have one plan for my life and God had another. And so I followed God into officership [pastoral leadership] kicking and screaming. And I'm thankful today that I did." This sense of the necessity of following God's direction was so strong that leaders would pursue it over the instructions of their organization if necessary: "if I'm going to listen to [church] or [denomination] or God, it's going to be God." While many leaders talked about these kinds of intense beliefs about how to hear from and pursue God's call, a lot of the discussion was about the mundane business of daily faithfulness: "we pray every day asking the direction of God through the Holy Spirit." Prayer was a constant presence in multivocational leaders' understanding of their responsibilities.

Almost as commonly mentioned as prayer was the need to attend to the gifting of the leader to figure out how to live the multivocational life. Sometimes this was a reference to a specific skill set (such as spiritual direction or marketing). At other times this was a reference to general aptitudes. There was some understanding that attending to gifting was important not only for discerning calling but also to maintain passion and keep the individual from burnout. Gifts needed to be identified and cultivated so that their value could be brought to the ministry. Some also argued that gifting was for a specific task and perhaps provided for a specific time.

Discernment, hearing from God, attending to gifting, and many other aspects of finding a calling are closely related to self-awareness. Multivocational leaders needed to know how to fit the many pieces of a complex life together in a way that allowed them to sustain their lives. One leader explained, "just really know the niche that you're wired for. And so that plays into boundaries too, if there's something that you're just not good at don't be a superhero." The large variety of ministries, other work, and life circumstances among our forty interviewees showed no one pattern of multivocational ministry. Self-awareness of how one is called was crucial for these leaders to identify the unique fit of the different elements that are part of their lives.

Application

Calling matters for multivocational ministry. An exploration of what calling is, why it is necessary, and how to find it already provides substantive detail about what calling does. Calling explains actions, makes ministry meaningful, and provides guidance by, among other things, helping to set priorities and developing gifting and leading people to the unique fit of their calling.

Calling provides a reason why certain actions are taken. This applies to the movement into ministry, and multivocational leaders also applied it to other life roles. For example, non-ministry jobs were considered for their compatibility with the ministry role. There were a variety of ways leaders understood compatibility, and there were several who lamented a lack of compatibility. This sense of a calling to certain action could also extend beyond work towards the daily business of living. One individual explained how they worked this out as a ministry couple: "As a pastor and a spiritual director together . . . we discern almost everything based on our sense of call, yeah. Even . . . how often we do things or . . . whether things are congruent with who we are and who we've been called to be in the world." This congruence or alignment of actions is clarified through reflection on calling.

Having a reason for action contributes to making ministry meaningful. This is not only about dealing with hard times but also about knowing one can draw on God's support and just enjoy the work to which one is called: "It's all my ministry, and it's what I get to do, so it's not work for me, you know." Many participants talked about a joy and passion for the ministry: "Ministry is my passion. When I say I feel fully alive when I'm writing a sermon or doing a visit or even preparing a funeral and that sort of thing—these are things that I love to do, and they give me life." However, multivocational leaders did not always agree on whether they had choice in the nature of the calling. For example, one couple we talked to disagreed with each other on this issue.

The understanding that calling provides a reason for action and makes ministry meaningful fits naturally with an understanding that God prepared the multivocational minister for the kind of work they are doing. God calls and guides them through situations and circumstances. God's guidance extended beyond the specific tasks of ministry to a calling towards appropriate life priorities: "I realized that not living with balance . . . not being obedient to the idea of rhythm and balance and rest in the scriptures is . . . not living [how] God called me to be." Calling provides guidance not just for what should be done but for what one should not do. One can identify this, in part, by how God develops the leaders' gifting. Self-awareness of gifting and passions helps to recognize calling manifested in a vocation.

Multivocational leaders also talked of how something learned in one part of their life could be brought into other parts of their life. They talked about cultivating self-awareness and being intentional in their multivocational lives. One leader talked about "having a space to belong" and the value of working with others to have the gifts necessary to create that space. Another leader explained that, in multivocational ministry, "both roles [inside and outside the church] press into me this deep calling." These leaders' references to calling are all related to the unique manner in which God is weaving together the pieces of their lives.

Unique Fit and Implications for Training

The concept of unique fit should be considered for training multivocational leaders. Unique fit means that each multivocational leader has a combination of life circumstances (ministry, family, individual characteristics, additional employment) specific to what God is doing in their lives and what God is calling them to do in a particular context. This is shaped by both general biblical or theological conceptualizations of calling and by the unique understanding they have developed of their specific circumstances. The multivocational leader engages in a partnership with God to identify how this unique fit works in their specific context. Thus, calling can be both a general approach to living and a specific combination of commitments. Self-awareness of this unique fit contributes to clarity of action, minister health, and passion for what God has asked of the individual. Clarity requires discernment and a listening approach to the work of God as it manifests in individual lives, such as through gifting. If we can agree that calling for multivocational leaders is characterized by the concept of unique fit, then there are several training implications.

The first is simply the willingness to assist ministers in development to embrace the complexity and discern the spiritual significance that holds the different pieces together. We have previously argued, "Theological educators should continue to emphasize calling but also help people understand how differentiated and complex it might be. They also need to be explicit that calling can be multivocational" (Chapman and Watson 2020, 8). Some multivocational leaders have been made to feel that their calling is second-class as compared to full-time ministers or ministers with more traditional church responsibilities. Trainers and other resource people could reflect on their students' personal calling to their unique contexts so that curriculum corresponds to the various needs that are present in students' actual lives.

Second, organizations that train multivocational leaders could develop partnerships of discernment between students and the ecclesial body to which they are responsible. Such relationships could contribute to an understanding of how calling applies to different areas of leaders' lives. Theological instructors and academic institution-based spiritual directors or mentors could foster both appreciation for the biblical understanding of calling and its application to diverse combinations of vocational commitments. It could also reduce the conceptual disconnect that some in ministry encounter between their training and the application of that training to the real world.

Third, the value of the different roles leaders fill and how those roles interact with each other should be taken into account in the exploration of calling to avoid, as much as possible, a disconnect between different work responsibilities. Multivocational leaders need to be supported in the integration between spiritual calling, non-traditional ministry careers (business, trades, medical, and other examples), and daily life. A broader sense of calling that encompasses more than just church roles is necessary.

Finally, this leads to the necessity to train multivocational leaders beyond the limited range of knowledge skills normally associated with pastoral ministry. It may be argued for all ministry practitioners that other life factors such as family responsibilities and personal and spiritual care should be considered, but these take on added importance in the complexity of multivocational ministry. Additional skills with general applications beyond congregational leadership (such as team development or professional ethics) could be considered in addition to any possible instruction that may be specific to a particular career. In this way, multivocational leaders can be equipped to serve God in the lives they actually have.

Calling is a complex and multifaceted aspect of multivocational lives. However, the different understandings, framings, manners of discerning, and applications of calling provided by multivocational leaders challenges us to resist oversimplification. That is, calling is no one thing. It is worked out in the messy business of life and practical ministry. Effective training of multivocational leaders will take into account how the contextual uniqueness of the different elements of specific leaders' lives reflects and contributes to their calling.

Works Cited

Chapman, Mark D. and James W. Watson. 2020. "Canadian Multivocational Ministry Project: Educating Multivocational Leaders."

ureachtoronto.ca/wp-content/uploads/2020/11/Educating-Multivocational-Leaders-White-Paper.pdf.

Hagaman, Ashley K., and Amber Wutich. 2017. "How Many Interviews are Enough to Identify Metathemes in Multisited and Cross-Cultural Research? Another Perspective on Guest, Bunce, and Johnson's (2006) Landmark Study." *Field Methods* 29, no. 1: 23–41. *doi.org/10.1177/1525822x16640447.*

Malcolm, Wanda M., Karen L. Coetzee, and Elizabeth A. Fisher. 2019. "Measuring Ministry-Specific Stress and Satisfaction: The Psychometric Properties of the Positive and Negative Aspects Inventories." *Journal of Psychology and Theology* 47, no. 4: 313–27. *doi.org/10.1177/0091647119837018.*

Root, Andrew. 2019. *The Pastor in a Secular Age.* Grand Rapids, MI: Baker Academic.

Watson, James W., and Narry F. Santos. 2019. "Tentmaking: Creative Mission Opportunities Within a Secularizing Canadian Society." In *Mission and Evangelism in a Secularizing World: Academy, Agency, and Assembly Perspectives from Canada*, edited by Narry F. Santos and Mark Naylor, 131–48. Evangelical Missiological Society Monograph Series 2. Eugene, OR: Pickwick.

Watson, James W., Wanda M. Malcolm, Mark D. Chapman, Elizabeth A. Fischer, Marilyn Draper, Narry F. Santos, Jared Siebert, and Amy Bratton. 2020. "Canadian Multivocational Ministry Project: Research Report." *canadianmultivocationalministry.ca/master-report.*

Wright, Christopher J. H. 2006. *The Mission of God: Unlocking the Bible's Grand Narrative.* Downers Grove, IL: IVP Academic.

Endnotes

1 Some quotations have been edited for grammatical clarity.

CHAPTER 7

Pitching Our Tent with Bivocational Ministry

KRISTEN PLINKE BENTLEY

Within a few months of graduating from seminary, I was called to a pastorate. Both the congregation and I knew it was going to be short-term, and we acknowledged it from the start. We agreed that, while I served with them, they would continue to look for a permanent pastor, and I would look for a church where I could stay longer. Staying longer with them was unsustainable for me. The commute was two hours each way, my husband and I had three young children at home, and I had just agreed to teach an evening course at a college near where we lived. The congregation was three years old and worshiped in a storefront located in a strip mall. For an hour or so each Sunday morning, the storefront housed approximately twenty worshippers and, on Wednesday evenings, a slightly smaller group for adult Bible study and congregational meetings. It was a great fit while it lasted. The congregation was short on financial resources, but they had enough to cover the storefront and a monthly stipend for me, as well as some funds to support those in need and the occasional creative mission effort. With a working spouse whose job provided adequate income and health insurance to support our family, I was able to accept what the congregation could afford.

That year-long experience with the United Church of the Cumberlands in Somerset, Kentucky, provided a glimpse of vitality that did not fit with my expectations. The congregation's statistics would not catch anyone's attention: small membership, small budget, and short-term pastorate. Yet a positive sense of gratitude and discipleship permeated the congregation. Almost every church member came to worship every Sunday (except for a couple "snowbirds"), and after Sunday worship, the whole congregation ate lunch together at a restaurant down the road (we gave them a "heads up" when we were coming) or in the food court of the nearby shopping mall. They worked on church activities together and communicated with each other during the week. As I came to know this group of Christians, I grew to admire their commitment and positive energy. Some weeks I did not even mind the long commute home on Wednesday night; it was 1997, and the Hale-Bopp comet was high in the night sky. When I was called to a ministry position closer to home, it was bittersweet. The church found their next pastor through the same informal fashion they found me. That pastor was able to stay with them for many years, having additional employment and health insurance. When the congregation closed a number of years later, they had given it all they had. Their members dispersed, and they gave away their material goods, sending items such as hymnals and communion ware to ministers and congregations they knew. Now, as I look back nearly twenty-five years later, I remember that ministry as a late twentieth-century version of what the apostle Paul called *koinonia*.

The goal of this chapter is to share several stories of bivocational ministry from research at Lexington Theological Seminary, much of it resonating with my experience with the United Church in the Cumberlands. Expanding the storehouse of strong stories connected to bivocational ministry aids in understanding the diverse experiences within bivocational ministry and congregational ministry at large. In this chapter, we also will step back in time and explore the biblical narrative of the tentmaking ministry of the Apostle Paul and its connections to bivocational ministry of the twenty-first century. These expanded narratives point toward better ways to support and provide resources for those engaged in bivocational ministry, contributing to a better understanding of this model of congregational ministry.

Context of Church in North America

It is increasingly clear that a significant number of churches in North America are led by ministers who hold employment outside the congregations they serve. This has long been the case for many Protestant congregations, especially those in rural geographic areas, as well as for African American, Hispanic/Latinx, immigrant, and refugee communities. It also has been a strategy for planting new churches in a variety of contexts. According to the National Congregations Study, which contacted a representative cross-section of more than 3500 congregations in the United States, roughly one-third of congregations have lead ministers who also hold another job: 37% in the 2006–2007 survey; 34.3% in 2012; and 35% in 2018–2019 (Chaves et al. 2020, 22). The current awareness of the reality of bivocational ministry is also expressed in the vocational expectations of theological school graduates. Responses to the Graduating Student Questionnaire of the Association of Theological Schools show that 30% of graduates from theological schools in the United States and Canada in 2017 expected to hold another paid position in additional to ministerial work after graduation, with higher percentages among African American (57%) and Hispanic/Latinx (41%) graduates (Deasy 2018, 65–66). The vocational expectations of theological students related to bivocational ministry are providing insight to leaders of theological schools as they consider how theological education can best equip and prepare students for bivocational ministry (78).

The number of ministers earning supplemental income outside a congregation is increasing as churches face economic challenges. Because bivocational arrangements supplement what a congregation pays, it contributes to financial stability. This appeals to many congregations, especially those with smaller membership (an average of less than fifty in weekly worship) struggling to adequately compensate their ministers. While the impact of the COVID-19 pandemic is still unfolding, it appears to add to the challenges. When most congregations in the United States ceased in-person worship in mid-March 2020 and the majority (86%) moved their worship online, financial contributions were negatively impacted, since most congregational giving comes through individuals during a worship service (Lake Institute 2020, 3). The Lake Institute's COVID-19 Congregational Study indicates that the pandemic hit smaller congregations particularly hard: 30% reported they had to reduce personnel expenses during the pandemic (more than twice the overall rate of the congregations in the study). This study found that, "with little access to PPP [Paycheck Protection Program] funds and already leaner budgets, clergy in smaller congregations were most likely to feel the direct financial effects of the pandemic" (Lake Institute 2020, 5). In this, the pandemic magnified existing challenges facing smaller congregations, which make up the majority of all congregations (Chaves and Eagle 2015, 5–8). The pandemic exacerbated an already existing resource gap for smaller congregations, impacting their potential for vital ministry and their capacity to compensate ministers. Many of these smaller congregations are led by bivocational pastors.

Research with Bivocational Ministers

The research project at Lexington Theological Seminary focused on Christian Church (Disciples of Christ) ministers serving congregations in Kentucky. We surveyed 110 ministers (44 of whom were bivocational ministers) in 2015 and interviewed 13 solo bivocational ministers and 20 lay leaders in congregations they served (in 2016–2018).[1] In that inquiry, we learned through the experiences of bivocational ministry.

Early in that research, bivocational ministers expressed the nagging feeling that their work was valued "less than" other forms of ministry. Conversations with them helped the research project's advisory team perceive how much bivocational ministry has been peripheral to the understanding of ministry, despite its long and honored history, reaching back to the Apostle Paul and his co-workers. They began to realize more fully how their understanding of ministry had relied on a sense of ministers as the pastor/professional "who can do it all" and as being seminary-educated and ordained, then employed, with full benefits, by congregations as their sole employers. Although many ministers were left out of that description, it has functioned as the primary way of thinking and speaking about ministry within the Christian Church (Disciples of Christ) and other mainline Protestant denominations in North America for some time. Mark Edington (2018, 3–7) described this as the "Standard Model" and explained how much of what we understand related to the church, ministry, and congregational leadership—and the underlying economic arrangements—has been designed around this model of ministry. However, that model of ministry does not fit with the diverse needs of congregational ministry.

Thankfully, there is more to the story of ministry than that one model alone; congregations in various contexts rely on different models to pursue vital ministry and support those who lead them. It is dangerous, warned novelist Chimamanda Ngozi Adichie (2009), to rely on a single story to understand people and places. She stated, "The single story creates stereotypes, and the problem with stereotypes is not that they are untrue, but that they are incomplete." Recognizing many stories of ministry, alongside one that has become dominant and standardized, resists the tendency to submerge distinctive differences, and leads to understanding all forms of ministry more fully.

In our research, we encountered diverse experiences. Several themes emerged from the interviews:

- bivocational ministry contributes to financial stability for the pastor and congregation;
- calls to bivocational ministry are often in response to a congregation's needs and financial limitations;
- individuals frequently become bivocational ministers after they are already employed elsewhere;
- bivocational ministers often pursue theological education and training for pastoral leadership after they are already serving congregations;
- because bivocational ministers are not dependent on congregations for their livelihood, their financial independence realigns the minister-congregation relationship; and
- shared ministry (where lay leadership partners with pastors) is key to successful bivocational ministry.

These themes contribute to a more expansive description of bivocational ministry and the diversity of experiences within it. We learned from pastors who described their experience in various ways. Some celebrated that bivocational ministry brought financial independence that empowered them to teach and preach more prophetically. Some explained how working outside the congregation helped them better understand the "everyday world" in which their congregations' members live. Others expressed their sense of being overwhelmed by challenges facing the congregation and demands on their time (in both workplaces). One stated, "The biggest thing is that I find myself, over the long haul, being mentally exhausted at times, and that mental exhaustion can lead to spiritual exhaustion . . . It all hinges on how tired I am, how long I can continue to go without real rest." The similarities and differences noted in these conversations reflect the importance of learning from those involved in bivocational ministry. Diverse congregational contexts and employment arrangements of pastors lead to different experiences and interpretations of bivocational ministry. To paraphrase an insight about human personality, each bivocational ministry arrangement is, in certain respects, like all others, like some others, and like no other (Kluckholn and Murray 1948, 35; Lartey 2003, 34). There are no "one size fits all" descriptions of bivocational ministry.

The Story of Paul's Ministry

Often, when the topic turns to bivocational ministry, the apostle Paul is cited as evidence of a biblical model present in the earliest times of the church. Paul's centrality is reflected in the use of "tentmaking" as a term for certain styles of bivocational ministry (Ferris 2001, 81; Francis and Francis 1998, xv). According to Acts 18:3, Paul supported himself as a tentmaker or leather worker while he ministered in Corinth, and, in Acts 20:34, Paul is quoted as stating he worked with his own hands to support himself and his companions. Paul confirmed this practice himself when he wrote to the church in Corinth (1 Cor. 9:3–18), and he referred again to a practice of supporting himself and others when ministering at Thessalonica (1 Thess. 2:9) and at Ephesus (1 Cor. 4:12).

Paul's letters provide information about his practice in addition to other ways that teachers, preachers, and missionaries were supported in the earliest times of the church. Four patterns of support emerged at that time, sometimes used in combination: payment from the church to those who preached and taught there, gifts given by the church to those working in the broader mission, lodging and meals provided by church members, and voluntary labor of some evangelists to support themselves. In working to support himself while teaching and preaching, Paul preferred one strategy while other church teachers, preachers, and missionaries adopted other strategies. These strategies also reflected those widely debated by Hellenistic philosophers and teachers at that time, such as charging fees, entering the household of a wealthy patron, begging, and working (Hock 1980, 52–59). One of the reasons given by philosophers who favored working to support themselves was the way it empowered their independence to speak and think freely. The vigorous patronage system present at that time was understood to undermine the freedom of thought and speech for these philosophers.

Paul gave several reasons he and other companions supported themselves through their labor. The reasons included: not being a burden to those to whom they preached (1 Thess. 2:9; 1 Cor. 9:18; 2 Cor. 11:9, 12:13–15); the furthering of the gospel of Christ (1 Cor. 9:12b); his right to relinquish privilege (1 Cor. 9:15); avoiding indebtedness to the church (2 Cor. 12:14b); and serving as an example to the church (1 Cor. 11:1).

His work also provided opportunities to further his evangelistic mission. Although he did not describe it explicitly in scripture, as a tradesperson, Paul would have encountered a variety of people on a regular basis. In Corinth, for example, work such as Paul's took place in shops near the agora, where people of various walks of life gathered and shopped. Archeological work has revealed that, during the time Paul was in Corinth, a series of small shops were located around a central square. Working in one of those shops, with proximity to the agora, ample workspaces, as well as numerous windows and doorways, Paul had access and opportunity to interact with co-workers, clients, and municipal officials, as well as with the crowds of people passing by in the streets (Murphy-O'Connor 1983, 175–78). It is likely Paul followed well-established patterns of Hellenistic philosophers (such as Stoics and Cynics) by using public buildings and workshops of the marketplace for teaching. Paul certainly would have used his workplace as a setting for teaching and preaching to further the gospel, just as he did in local synagogues and in houses throughout his missionary journeys (Hock 1980, 37–42).

While people in the present time look back on Paul's practice with general approval, his practice at the time was controversial, at least in Corinth. His vigorous arguments in 1 Corinthians 9:1–18 and

2 Corinthians 11:5–15 reveal that working to support himself instead of accepting economic support from the church in Corinth was opposed by some in the church. Opponents impugned Paul's apostolic authority because he did not accept their support (as others had); they implied Paul's ministry was "less than" those who accepted pay. However, Paul claimed his hard work as validation of his apostleship (1 Cor. 9:1–14). In response to opponents, he put forth his willingness to lower his social status through manual labor for their benefit as an example of the way God works through weakness (2 Cor. 11:7). Paul reinterpreted the perception present in the surrounding Hellenistic culture—that by working with his hands Paul lowered his social status (and perhaps that of the church in Corinth) in an inappropriate way (Bassler 1991, 70–73).

While Paul continued a strong defense of his practice as furthering the gospel in Corinth, he also asserted the right of ministers to be paid for their work (1 Cor. 9:3–18). Paul was aware his model of self-support through labor was one of many models of economic support necessary in the gospel movement at work in diverse contexts. His own practice was not identical in every context. While refusing financial support from the church in Corinth, he accepted it from the Philippians (Phil. 4:15–18). It is not surprising that, in connection with financial support for ministry, Paul found that "what seemed appropriate to the gospel in one setting was not acceptable in another" (Sumney 2014, 170). His acceptance of support from the Philippians and refusal from the Corinthians reveals the complexity of economic relationships—then and now.

Contemporary Narratives of Bivocational Ministry

Much has changed since Paul's time and place, when various models for financial support for those teaching and preaching in the church were still emerging. In the present time, churches have primarily adopted the strategy of paying ministers who teach, preach, and serve. The model of bivocational ministry is re-emerging as a significant part of the larger conversation about strategies for financial support of ministers who are working in the church or as missionaries. In this re-emergence, bivocational ministry is interpreted in various ways.

In interviews conducted in the research project at Lexington Theological Seminary, three primary narratives emerged as ministers and lay leaders described the way bivocational ministry related to the economic challenges they experienced. They all perceived that "being bivocational" contributed to financial stability, but they interpreted it in different, sometimes overlapping, ways. Some spoke of bivocational ministry primarily as a "sign of the times"—a response to increasing economic challenges that ministers and congregations are facing in the present. Others focused on its missional potential, pointing to its more sustainable use of congregational resources and its natural connection to the wider world; they described it as being on the "cutting edge" of ministry. Others still, such as those in rural contexts, or in African American and Hispanic/Latinx communities, with a long experience with bivocational ministry and economic challenges, said, "It's the way we've always done it." These narratives were not mutually exclusive; in some congregations, they coexisted as the pastors and lay leaders interpreted what was working well as well as what was challenging in their contexts.

The "Sign of the Times" Narrative

Some pastors and lay leaders interpreted the financial stability related to bivocational ministry primarily as response to the financial challenge and congregational decline they experienced—a "sign of the times." They understood bivocational ministry to have some benefits but pursued bivocational ministry largely due to a sense of scarcity in their context. Guided by this interpretation, some congregations called a bivocational minister for the first time because of budgetary concerns, or their current minister had to find supplemental income through other employment because the congregation could not provide sufficient compensation. In such cases, they hoped for financial relief but had not yet realigned their way of ministry or their pastoral expectations. Bivocational ministry had extended them a lifeline, but they remained less hopeful about potential for vital ministry.

Lay leaders of one congregation in particular spoke of bivocational ministry primarily with this "sign of the times" narrative. The historically European American congregation, founded in 1829, owned a well-maintained, brick church building on the Main Street of a small town in central Kentucky. The town's population, now less than 900, had declined over the past decades, with many young families relocating to larger towns nearby. The pastor and congregational leaders of this congregation reported they had a good relationship; they had learned to share the work of ministry well during the minister's tenure of more than ten years. This was the pastor's first experience with bivocational ministry; he had shifted to it after several years of "trying the full-time route." It was a move that made sense to him over time, and he has not regretted it. For him, the most challenging aspect of serving this congregation is the 40-minute commute from a town where he lives and works as a teacher. He is not this congregation's first bivocational minister. However, he is the first one to commute instead of living in the parsonage near the church. Having a pastor not living in the parsonage required lay people to learn to take care of issues related to the building they had previously left to the minister. The change also freed space in the parsonage, which the congregation began renting at that point.

Both the minister and lay leaders were concerned about the congregation's future. They were concerned with the church's small size (30 people in worship on a "good" Sunday) and advanced age of the membership. The church membership had declined gradually over the previous 40 years, reflecting the declining population of their town. While grandchildren came to worship with their grandparents on some weekends, the youngest member of the church was 45 years old. The congregation was careful with its finances, but lay leaders lamented the increasing costs of "keeping the doors open and the lights on" in their aging church building, and they wished they could pay their pastor more. The pastor was satisfied with what the congregation paid but wondered about the challenge of finding the next pastor when the time came. Leaders anticipated the congregation would look for a bivocational minister again, being all they could afford. They had some investment funds and had discussed (before calling this minister) using those funds to support a minister who could work "full-time" and "perhaps help the church grow." However, they decided that was unsustainable. The church's annual budget included support for the minister, a custodian, and both an organist and pianist. They gave 14% of their annual budget to various non-profit missions and gave faithfully to denominational funds. Years earlier, they had needed help with significant repairs to their church building after a natural disaster, and denominational funding had saved the day. They continued to be grateful for that support and wanted to repay the generosity shown to them.

As this congregation thought about the future, they were anxious. They had tried educational programs to strengthen their understanding and practice of evangelism. However, four other Protestant churches were located in their small town, with three of them struggling to make ends meet. During the COVID-19 pandemic, the congregation suspended in-person worship. As an alternative, lay leaders and the minister expended a great deal of energy to record videos for worship at home. The recordings were made available on the church's YouTube channel and posted to the church's Facebook page. They returned to in-person worship in their building in the spring of 2021 and were experiencing declined giving and participation. While grateful for the financial advantages of bivocational ministry, they were not hopeful about how to sustain themselves as a congregation in the future.

The "Cutting Edge" Narrative

Some pastors and lay leaders spoke of bivocational ministry as offering a unique chance for transformation, for financial stability, and for missional advantage. Some were part of new congregations which have intentionally called a bivocational minister as a strategy to "jump start" their new church and help them connect with the surrounding community. However, not all who understand bivocational arrangements this way are new churches; some are established churches that have caught a vision of new life. They see how realigning financial priorities can reinvigorate the mission and ministry of their congregation and connect them more fully with their community.

One bivocational minister who spoke of bivocational ministry as the "cutting edge" of ministry for the future was a female minister leading a church she helped establish in Louisville, Kentucky. She attributed much of the success of the church's accomplishments to the financial and missional advantages of bivocational ministry. This predominantly African American congregation was less than seven years old. They first began meeting in an office building and then relocated when they began nesting in the building owned by an established congregation, which was predominantly European American. While the two congregations worshiped separately on most Sundays, access was shared to all parts of the building, including kitchen and office space. Over time, members and ministers of the two congregations became more acquainted and combined worship and other activities on occasion. When the pastor of the established church retired, the bivocational new church pastor stepped in to help provide pastoral care for that congregation in the interim period.

This minister received very little financial support from the congregation she pastored; her employment outside the church made up the bulk of her income. She was a small business owner and also employed by the metro city government when the church first started. Later she retired from the job with metro city and continued as a small business owner. As the financial stability of the church increased, the congregation began providing her a housing allowance and contributing to her retirement funds. This minister, who actively participates in denominational activities, has found helpful support for the congregation. For instance, during the COVID-19 pandemic, she was able to identify grant funding that enabled the church to purchase needed equipment for recording and broadcasting worship services when they suspended in-person worship services.

Lay leadership was very important in this congregation from its very beginning. Church members trained to serve in significant leadership roles and partnered with the pastor in planning and leading worship as well as leading other dimensions of the church's ministry. The church sponsored a social enterprise where many church members volunteered to develop community partnerships and host community programs to help people in their neighborhood. Their work included providing a food pantry, helping people with utility bills, and assisting with workplace development. A large part of the church's identity and mission is related to this community-based ministry, and much of the church's financial resources are used for its support. It is an investment of finances and energy enabled through the model of bivocational ministry the church employs.

The "We've Always Done It This Way" Narrative

Some pastors and lay leaders explained they have been involved in bivocational ministry for decades, some for as long as they can remember. They spoke of it as "the way we've always done ministry" instead of as a sign of decline or enabling new opportunities. Many of these congregations are located in under-resourced contexts with a history of financial distress, due to lower population density, economic and population decline, or marginalization that has suppressed their capacity to call and compensate ministers. They have practiced bivocational ministry as a strategy of financial support for ministry that reduces the burden upon congregations and some also see it as a way their pastors share the financial burdens. In response to their context, these congregations developed traditional practices of nurturing, supporting, and honoring their pastoral leaders. These traditions include making "love gifts" at different times of the year, honoring pastors with well-established "Pastor Appreciation" programs, and identifying gifts for ministry within their congregation. Sometimes this led to individuals becoming pastors in communities and congregations where they were baptized and "raised in the faith." Some practices emerged from intertwined connections of congregations and their surrounding context—a mutual benefit of pastors' extended, long-term relationships within the community and to their church ministry and employment experiences outside the church.

The "we've always done it this way" narrative was reflected clearly in an historically African American congregation located in western Kentucky. The congregation was founded in 1898. They own a building located on a side street in a town with a population of approximately 10,000 people. They have been led by the same male bivocational minister for most of the previous twenty years. He was called into congregational ministry while employed as a radiation worker and mechanic for a government corporation in the area. He liked to say that God called him into the ministry later in life, as a so-called "second career" minister, because "the church needed a mechanic to fix some things." As all tend to do, he learned how to be a pastor while pastoring; he also engaged in continuing pastoral education offered over a span of time while serving the congregation. This education led him to become a commissioned minister. He took this route of theological education and training rather than going to seminary and becoming ordained; it fit with the congregation's needs and permitted him to serve the church while also retaining his employment.

A similar pattern emerged with the person who became assistant pastor and was being nurtured to become the next lead pastor (when the current one retires). This younger man was being mentored by the pastor and the congregation at large while he was also employed in the local public school system, first as a teacher and later as a principal. The congregation had known him since he was baptized there as a twelve-year-old. These two men worked well together, balancing their work at the church to provide time for each one to adjust their schedules when needed due to other responsibilities related to employment outside the congregation.

During the COVID-19 pandemic, this congregation struggled like others. The decision was made to enable online giving so members could contribute more readily when in-person worship was suspended for a period. The congregation also began broadcasting worship services via Facebook Live, led by a core group of worship leaders and musicians. They continued both practices after resuming in-person worship. Contributions and participation remained steady, and the live streaming of worship services continued after the congregation resumed worship in the church building.

The pastor of this congregation looked back on his experience and explained that the income and benefits provided through his and his associate's bivocational arrangements had enabled this congregation to maintain committed leadership. He believed it had allowed him to continue a long-term pastorate in this congregation through serious challenges and financial distress impacting the community he serves. He recounted periods of time when the congregation could not afford to pay him anything at all. In this context, "being bivocational" contributed to financial stability for both the pastor and the congregation, even though it had not solved all financial woes. Meanwhile, it contributed to the development of sustainable leadership development practices that fit with the bivocational arrangement in that congregation and strengthened the ministry there.

Making the Most of Bivocational Ministry

Some congregations found ways to make the most of having a pastor who also is employed outside the congregation, even alongside financial challenges. These congregations found ways to experience financial stability, shared ministry, and a sense of hope for the future despite uncertainty.

An historically European American congregation in rural Montgomery County, Kentucky, provided one example of thriving bivocational ministry. Founded in 1829, just down the road from where they meet, this church claims a well-known nineteenth-century circuit rider in the Stone Campbell tradition, "Raccoon" John Smith, as its founding minister. Its approximately 100-year-old white clapboard building sits at an intersection and is well cared for by lay leaders and a sexton (the only paid employee of the church other than the minister). Through the years, the pulpit has been filled by circuit riders, seminary students, ministers who were called "full-time," as well as those who were bivocational. This church is not facing financial challenges as many others do. They have a financial reserve due to a generous bequest made decades earlier, designated to pay the pastor. This financial reserve allows them to pay their pastors well enough that pastors often do not seek other employment income. Their pastor was well-educated and had earned both Master of Divinity and Doctor of Ministry degrees. He came to this church after serving many years in a nearby city where he had pastored a congregation without holding any other steady employment.

In this rural congregation, to hear the minister and the lay leaders of the congregation speak about it, bivocational ministry was the best of all possible worlds. They all were aware that having an available financial reserve designated to compensate pastors was helpful to their congregation. The key to making bivocational ministry pleasurable in this congregation, according to the pastor, was the collaborative leadership he has with the congregations. He attributes some of this to having well-defined boundaries and expectations. For him, the shared ministry leadership in the congregation embodied the "priesthood of all believers." In this sharing of ministry, he encountered freedom to be creative and to attend to the central things that ministers need to do, such as preaching, teaching, providing pastoral care, and leading worship. He praised the good stewardship of financial resources in this congregation and the way they lived within their means. Regarding his own experience being bivocational, this pastor said flexibility is helpful. He said that it does not hurt for a pastor to have a "large talent stack" that allows flexibility. For instance, he could fill in at the piano when needed. He also pointed to the flexibility of his work as a potter and musician that permits him to adjust his work schedule when important needs emerge for the congregation, such as funerals. The lay leaders also expressed appreciation for the way their pastor saw their gifts for ministry and helped them "better understand the needs of the community" through his work outside the congregation.

Before the beginning of the COVID-19 pandemic, the congregation discussed making some building improvements, which they decided they did not need to do. The decision was providential; it allowed them to navigate the first year of the COVID-19 pandemic without significant financial challenges. They made other adjustments during the pandemic. When they discontinued worshiping in their church building for a time, they shifted worship to Facebook Live. The pastor offered a conversational-style message on Sundays, accompanied by music, prayer, and communion. They were first offered from his home, then later from the sanctuary, and this was received well. When the congregation returned to their traditional, in-person worship in the church building on Sundays at 11:00 a.m., they changed the time of the Facebook Live worship to 9:00 a.m. on Sunday, retaining its conversational-style message. While the Facebook Live crowd grew smaller than it had been months earlier, the in-person crowd increased slightly. Both pastor and congregation are satisfied with having these two different worship opportunities on Sundays. It seemed to be reaching people and was sustainable for them.

Living with Bivocational Ministry

The interviews with pastors and lay leaders affirmed the value of bivocational ministry. In contrast to seeing it as a model that is "less than" others, they experience it as having unique benefits. It contributes to financial stability for pastors and congregations and provides opportunities for missional advantage. It helps reframe the pastor-congregation relationship in ways that support strong shared ministry and resist the temptation "to think of ministry as only the job of the minister" (Bentley 2019b, 2). It serves as a strategy of financial support for ministry needed by congregations that cannot adequately compensate pastors on their own. Despite many of these congregations serving in communities and contexts at the periphery of a larger and "standard" story of ministry, they engage in vital ministry that impacts the lives of individuals and communities on a daily basis. When stories of success and vitality related to bivocational ministry are highlighted, we resist the tendency to associate it primarily with decline and a scarcity of resources (a "sign of the times" narrative).

The survey of ministers and interviews with pastors and lay leaders involved with bivocational ministry revealed benefits and drawbacks. While they appreciated the financial stability and connections to the community of bivocational arrangements, they also noted that ministers had less time to devote to the congregations, to household members, and to the replenishing of their own energy. The ministers would benefit from support and resources. They also benefit from congregation members who appreciate as fully as possible the challenges ministers face trying to meet expectations at both the church and other places of work.

Bivocational ministry does involve challenges, and, because of these challenges, many may fear its growing presence. Yet its growth also provides opportunities for leadership. As Jessica Young Brown (2019) stated, "if we prepare for a future with more bivocational ministers, we can equip both ministers and congregations to thrive in it." Taking this step requires truly making a commitment to bivocational ministry, "pitching tent" with this model, to use a biblical phrase, and investing in it as a strategy of financial support for ministry. We already know it is a strategy that missionaries have used for centuries, and it helps address needs of congregational ministry in diverse contexts and communities, just as in the earliest days of the church. This investment includes recognizing its significant presence, acknowledging its challenges, and equipping ministers for success. It would lead to strengthened vitality for many of these congregations still lodged in fear of decline.

The signs of vitality are already present, but they are different from those that have been used as benchmarks in the past, such as the number of people in worship or even church membership. Instead, they testify to the unique qualities of diverse bivocational congregational contexts. In relation to vitality in rural congregations, Allen Stanton (2021, 32) stated that, because congregations and communities are "complex and divergent, they require indicators that foster vitality at the local level, respecting both the deeply relational aspects and the necessity of fostering and living out a shared vision." The same can be said of congregations led by bivocational ministers, many of which are rural: their contexts are tremendously complex and diverse, as we have heard from the various narratives. Perceiving and measuring vitality from a position that understands the realities of bivocational ministry helps move us away from narratives dominated by fears of decline and scarcity.

The Hope of Bivocational Ministry

When the Apostle Paul sat with co-workers, whether as a tradesperson or as church leader, he knew he was but one part of a wider mission in the world. His collaborative work involved numerous co-workers coordinated across a wide geographic area. He was not a "lone ranger" in ministry, by any means. He frequently referred to a shared ministry or partnership (*koinonia*) in his letter to the Philippians. The gifts they shared with him and the broader mission in which he was engaged were "part of a much larger pattern of reciprocity that embrace[d] Paul, the gospel, and God" (Bassler 77–78). Bivocational ministers and the congregations they serve in the twenty-first century continue to thrive when participating in such patterns of reciprocity.

Today, bivocational arrangements like Paul's provide financial support to congregational ministry in a myriad of contexts. Congregations led by bivocational ministers are engaged in vital ministry along rural intersections, on Main Street in small towns, nested in established urban congregations, and in the storefronts of strip malls. Being bivocational allows many pastors to serve congregations that otherwise could not afford to support them in the work they have been called to do. The ministry of these pastors and congregations furthers the gospel and provides hope for communities as part of the wider mission of the church in the world. Equipping these pastors for the challenges they experience and supporting bivocational ministry as a viable model of financial support for ministry is a good strategy to strengthen ministry in the twenty-first century.

Works Cited

Adichie, Chimamanda Ngozi. 2009. "The Danger of a Single Story." TED video, 19:16. Oxford, England. *youtube.com/watch?v=D9Ihs241zeg.*

Bassler, Jouette. 1991. *God and Mammon: Asking for Money in the New Testament*. Nashville: Abingdon.

Bentley, Kristen Plinke. 2019a. "Perspectives of Bi-vocational Ministry: Emerging Themes in Bi-vocational Ministry Research at Lexington Theological Seminary." *Lexington Theological Quarterly* 48: 115–51. *lextheo.edu/wp-content/uploads/2021/09/j-4-Perspectives-of-Bi-Vocational-Ministry.pdf.*

———. 2019b. "Stability amidst Turbulent Times: The Benefits of Bi-vocational Ministry." *Colloquy Online*. May. *ats.edu/uploads/*

resources/publications-presentations/colloquy-online/stability-amidst-turbulent-times-the-benefits-of-bi-vocational-ministry.pdf.

Chaves, Mark, and Alison Eagle. 2015. *Religious Congregations in 21st Century America*. November. Durham, NC: Department of Sociology, Duke University. *sites.duke.edu/ncsweb/files/2019/02/NCSIII_report_final.pdf.*

Chaves, Mark, Joseph Roso, Anna Holleman, and Mary Hawkins. 2020. "National Congregations Study: Waves I–IV Summary Tables." Duke University Department of Sociology, Durham, NC. Last modified January 11, 2021. *sites.duke.edu/ncsweb/files/2021/01/NCS-IV_Summary-Tables_For-Posting.pdf.*

Deasy, Jo Ann. 2018. "Shifting Vocational Identity in Theological Education: Insights from the ATS Student Questionnaires." *Theological Education* 52, no. 1: 63–78. *ats.edu/files/galleries/2018-theological-education-v52-n1.pdf.*

Edington, Mark. 2018. *Bivocational: Returning to the Roots of Ministry*. New York: Church Publishing. *bivocational.church.*

Ferris, Robert. 2001. "Of Tents and Taxonomies." *Christian Education Journal* 5, no. 1: 79–82.

Frances, James M. M., and Leslie J. Frances, eds. 1998. *Tentmaking: Perspectives on Self-Supporting Ministry*. Herefordshire: Gracewing, Fowler Wright Books.

Hock, Ronald F. 1980. *The Social Context of Paul's Ministry: Tentmaking and Apostleship*. Minneapolis: Fortress.

Kluckhohn, Clyde, and Henry A. Murray, eds. 1948. *Personality in Nature, Society, and Culture*. New York: Alfred A. Knopf.

Lake Institute on Faith and Giving. 2020. "COVID-19 Congregational Study." Indiana University Lilly Family School of Philanthropy. *scholarworks.iupui.edu/bitstream/handle/1805/23791/lake-covid-report2020-2.pdf.*

Lartey, Emmanuel Y. 2003. *In Living Color: An Intercultural Approach to Pastoral Care and Counseling*. 2nd ed. New York: Jessica Kingsley.

Murphy-O'Connor, Jerome. 1983. *St. Paul's Corinth: Texts and Archeology*. Collegeville, MN: Liturgical.

Stanton, Allen T. 2021. *Reclaiming Rural: Building Thriving Rural Congregations*. Lanham, MD: Rowman & Littlefield.

Sumney, Jerry. 2014. *Paul: Apostle and Fellow Traveler*. Nashville: Abingdon.

Young Brown, Jessica. 2019. "Don't be Afraid of a Future with More Bivocational Ministers." *Faith & Leadership*. November 12. *faithandleadership.com/dont-be-afraid-future-more-bivocational-ministers*.

Endnotes

1 The research project included a 2015 survey and semi-structured interviews in 2016–2018. The survey had a 60% response rate. In total, 110 ordained, commissioned, or licensed ministers serving Christian Church (Disciples of Christ) congregations in Kentucky responded. Of these, forty-four identified themselves as bivocational ministers. In 2016–2018, semi-structured interviews were held with thirteen bivocational solo pastors and twenty lay leaders in congregations they served. The survey was a quantitative study supported with qualitative responses and provided insight regarding ministers' education, ordination status, compensation and income, the positions and types of congregations in which they serve, the congregations' stewardship practices, and their economic challenges. The interviews shed light on the experience of solo pastors and lay leaders within their congregations. Additional information about this research project can be found in Bentley (2019a).

CHAPTER 8

Exploring Distributive Ministry

KWASI KENA

Change. The mere mention of the word seems to spawn coalitions of resistance in the local church. Churches typically do not choose to talk about change until a catalyst sparks a conversation. As I write, the pernicious spread of the Delta variant of COVID-19 has become the predominant external catalyst forcing congregations to change their perceptions of what church is and how it should be conducted. The pandemic has rendered churches' previous practices and structures ineffective. Change, however, is what transition to bivocational ministry requires: something must be altered, and something must be lost, so a new thing can be created. Becoming a bivocational congregation is now a change more churches are willing to consider.

The pandemic created a forced-choice environment in which congregations had to reimagine church. Critical questions, such as "What is church?" and "What is church for?" needed thoughtful responses. Thankfully, many churches learned to pivot and launched innovative ministry practices during the pandemic. Congregations considering how to function in partnership with bivocational pastors have an opportunity to change their current ministry configurations and imagine how non-ordained followers of Christ participate in bivocational congregations.

For these churches, the shift to bivocational ministry includes a shared-ministry framework I call *distributive ministry.* Distributive ministry employs a team approach to leadership in which all persons in the congregation function as ministers. In this radical form of congregational life and ministry, the pastor and congregation flatten the hierarchy that elevates clergy over laity. In distributive ministry as normative practice, the church becomes a bivocational congregation, an egalitarian community in which the ordained and the non-ordained share pastoral responsibilities. Through corporate and collaborative discernment, ministers divide pastoral responsibilities according to their gifts and graces.

Conceptualizing Distributive Ministry

Before beginning an exploration of distributive ministry, it may be helpful to clarify what distributive ministry is not. The current pandemic thrust "the distributed church" into common parlance. The distributed church refers to the forced distribution of the gathered church community. Distributed church attenders congregate via technology. These churches often emphasize equipping and sending congregants to bear witness to Christ wherever they are situated geographically (Briggs 2020). In contrast to distributed churches, which frequently function under a single-pastor model of leadership, distributive ministry features an egalitarian model of multiple ministry leaders.

My distributive ministry model is a radical return to the ancient priesthood of believers doctrine. The increasing online prevalence of the terms "bivocational pastor," "bivocational congregation," and "distributive leadership" indicates the need for thoughtful consideration of new shared-leadership models of ministry, such as distributive ministry. I derive my understanding of distributive ministry from four schools of thought: (1) the priesthood of all believers from both scripture and Martin Luther's articulation of the universal priesthood of all believers, (2) missional ecclesiology as articulated by Lesslie Newbigin and others; (3) distributive leadership theory, and (4) the distributed pastorate model of Jeffrey MacDonald.

Distributive ministry begins with a biblical examination of the priesthood of all believers. A passage from 1 Peter, "like living stones, let yourselves be built into a spiritual house, to be a holy priesthood, to offer spiritual sacrifices acceptable to God through Jesus Christ" (1 Pet. 2:5, NRSV), offers strong affirmation of distributive ministry. The passage enjoins believers to build themselves up as the living stones that constitute God's dwelling—a "house"—which is a common reference to the temple in both testaments (2 Sam. 7:13; 1 Kings 3:2; Matt. 21:13; John 2:16–17; Acts 7:47). The passage also establishes Christians as God's new priesthood charged with offering spiritual sacrifices. I agree with Schreiner's interpretation of holy priesthood. He stated, "The focus here is on the church corporately as God's set-apart priesthood in which the emphasis is likely on believers functioning as priests. . . . All of God's people are now his priests" (Schreiner 2003, 106). The New Testament mentions nothing of reestablishing the type of separate priesthood that existed in Judaism.

Martin Luther's articulation of the universal priesthood provides further validation of distributive ministry as a viable model. During the Reformation, Luther articulated a robust understanding of vocation and emphasized the universal priesthood of all believers. Nessan (2019, 12) noted, "At the time of the Reformation, the universal priesthood was a radical claim about the equal status of all believers before God based on baptism. It was designed to overcome the dependency of the laity on the ministrations of a clerical hierarchy." Baptism was the ministry equalizer for Luther. He believed Christians should live out their baptismal vocation in three arenas: home, state, and church. Nessan expanded Luther's description, adding work as a fourth arena (11).

Revivifying the practice of the universal priesthood remains relevant for the twenty-first century North American church. Nessan declared,

> Luther's affirmation of the universal priesthood largely has remained an unfulfilled promise of the Reformation, insofar as, the churches themselves have perpetuated their own forms of ecclesial *incurvatus in se* and defended a clerical hierarchy instead of focusing their efforts on equipping the baptized for ministry in all arenas of daily life (Eph. 4:11–16). (Nessan 2019, 14)

The priesthood of all believers as articulated in scripture and explicated by Luther support distributive ministry as a normative practice of the *ecclesia*.

Missional church literature, particularly Lesslie Newbigin's provocative articulation of missionary ecclesiology, is my second major influence. Newbigin's comprehensive exposition of ecclesiology highlights the importance of educating congregations about the church's identity. He emphasized equally the church as the gathered community and the scattered community. Newbigin affirmed the formative aspects of communal life together as the gathered community. He emphasized the church's role in helping Christians learn how to be the new humanity resulting from salvation through Jesus Christ. Living into that new reality causes the church to be a distinct community. In *Truth to Tell: The Gospel as Public Truth*, Newbigin noted, "The most important contribution which the Church can make to a new social order is to be itself a new social order. [When a congregation] understands its true character as a holy priesthood for the sake of the world . . . then there is a point of growth for the new social order" (quoted in Goheen 2018, 78–79).

The scattered community refers to congregants' practice of their vocation in the world. Newbigin noted various ways Christians can bear witness to the gospel revealed through Jesus Christ. Goheen (2018, 78) stated Newbigin's points of special emphasis for the church that feature lay participation in ministry: "The distinctive life of the community, the calling of the laity, deeds of mercy and justice, evangelism, and missions to places where the gospel was not known." Newbigin reaffirmed Luther's emphasis on baptismal vocation that commissions all Christians to engage in ministry through their various callings. In "Our Task Today," Newbigin said, "The enormous preponderance of the Church's witness is the witness of the thousands of its members who work in field, home, office, mill, or law court" (quoted in Goheen 2018, 83). Newbigin clearly stated the ministry charge to Christians. In *Unfinished Agenda*, he wrote, "The entire membership of the Church in their secular occupations are called to be signs of his lordship in every area of life" (quoted in Goheen 2018, 83).

Missional church scholars and practitioners like David Bosch, Darrell L. Guder, Alan J. Roxburgh, Allen Hirsch, Ed Stetzer, Reggie McNeal, Elaine Heath, Michael Goheen, and others build upon Newbigin's missionary ecclesiology and echo its common themes: God is a missional God, the church's primary task is to join God in God's mission, the church is a sent people, the church must engage Western culture with the truth of the gospel, and the normality of lay participation in incarnational ministry in the community. Collectively, these themes outline a missional mandate to the church's corporate body to partner with God in God's mission in the world.

The abovementioned missional church writers regularly emphasize the importance of all Christians' participation in ministry rather than reliance on a separate class of ordained clergy as the primary ministry conduits. For example, Roxburgh declared,

> Across the varieties of today's models of ministry, there remains this underlying notion of church leadership functioning as specialized professionals. . . . This view effectively eclipses the gifts for leadership in the non-ordained contingent of God's sent people, those known in Christendom as the laity. (Roxburgh 1988, 195)

Hirsch highlighted the virtues of lay participation in incarnational ministry. He stated, "By living incarnationally . . . mission becomes something that 'fits' seamlessly into the ordinary rhythms of life, friendships, and community, and is thus thoroughly *contextualized*" (2016, 144, original emphasis). Newbigin's missional ecclesiology and current missional church literature highlight the missional mandate compelling all Christians to ministry.

My third major influence came from the articulation of distributive leadership in select higher education and business literature (Brown and Gioia 2002; Gronn 2002; Zepke 2007). Distributive leadership emphasizes a team approach to goal achievement rather than dependence on a single leader. This body of work provides clarity about the aim, the function, and the practice of distributive leadership. Just as the COVID-19 pandemic has forced church operations to change, the literature on distributive leadership routinely notes the impetus of change strategies. When some environmental stimulus destabilizes the organization, community, or constituents, the stimulus acts as the initiator of a change strategy. The challenges of leading more frequently under unstable and unpredictable conditions underscores the need to explore more effective leadership practices during times of uncertainty.

My fourth influence is Jeffrey MacDonald's model of "the distributed pastorate," in which "clergy and laypeople divide up pastoral responsibilities according to the gifts of the Holy Spirit" (2020, 111). Distributing the pastorate—that is, pastoral responsibilities—first involves helping Christians identify their call and their gifts to specific ministry. Once identified, individuals are then prepared to fulfill their ministry responsibilities ethically and effectively.

Reorientation to a Distributive Ministry Model

Congregations that have transitioned into bivocational congregations are positioned for reorientation to a distributive ministry model. The bivocational pastor's focus during reorientation is to nurture the gathered community as they discern their future. At this juncture, the congregation can begin to reimagine *ecclesia* by returning to questions like, "What is church?" and "What is church for?"

Distributive ministry should emerge from the corporate discernment of the gathered Christian community. As the gathered community discerns their future identity, bivocational pastors can encourage congregants to consider adopting a relational paradigm. To move toward this end, bivocational pastors and congregants can explore the priesthood of all believers and the doctrine of vocation together. These central teachings provide the foundation for all believers to respond to the call of God in all their relational spheres of life.

As the congregation becomes "a new humanity" that understands its character as the priesthood of all believers, bivocational pastors can invite members to discern how God wants them to fulfill their Christian vocation. Bivocational pastors can initiate simple conversations to encourage congregants to pray about and discuss specific ways they can live as faithful witnesses to Christ at home, work, the community, and the church.

Lay ministry initiatives can encourage congregants to move from discernment through prayer and conversations to action. For example, Charles Arn offered a user-friendly strategy to invite non-ordained believers into short-term ministry experiences in his book, *Side Door: How to Open Your Church to Reach More People*. Arn referred to these experiences as "side doors." A lay ministry initiative encourages non-ordained believers to create ministry experiences about which they are passionate. People's passions come from myriad sources, such as hobbies, like riding motorcycles, or life challenges, like being a recent widower. The point person forms a ministry team of people with similar passion who collaborate to design and launch four- to six-week ministry experiences. The ministry leaders strive to attract at least 25% of attenders who are non-Christians from the community. "The goal of an effective side door is to provide a place in which participants (both church members and nonmembers) can develop friendships around important things that they share in common" (Arn 2013, 26).

When the ongoing formation of the gathered community creates a critical mass of Christians willing to live as the priesthood of all believers, bivocational pastors can invite the congregation into conversations about creating a distributive ministry model of leadership. Luther's doctrine of vocation informs an understanding of the priesthood of all believers. His doctrine claims that "all Christians hear a call to the gospel and God's Kingdom, and then to a station in life or profession" (Doriani 2016). This declaration indicates a two-tiered aspect of call. First, we are called to be Christians who follow God and promote God's kingdom. Second, we are called to a particular station of work. In this regard, all honest work is sacred. The work of the pastor and the work of the mechanic, the stay-at-home parent, or the business manager are equally worthy. When Christians view all work as calling, they will no longer believe work outside of the church building is "secular" and discounted as ministry.

Bivocational pastors can facilitate these conversations by presenting distributive ministry as a two-tier configuration for consideration. All Christ-followers populate the first tier because, according to Luther's doctrine of baptismal vocation, all believers are commissioned ministers. First-tier ministry consists of participation in the general ministry to which all Christ-followers are called, namely: (1) Christian discipleship, and (2) bearing witness to Christ in all arenas. Congregants, as the priesthood of all believers, respond to the call to live as Christian disciples who bear witness to Christ at home, work, the community, and the church. This is first-tier ministry.

More specialized ministry occurs in second-tier ministry. In this category, the bivocational ministry and congregants corporately discern their gifts and graces and divide pastoral responsibilities among them. The corporate body affirms tier-two ministers. Examples of specialized pastoral ministry include preaching, teaching, counseling, visitation, and so on.

Implementing Distributive Ministry

A church cannot begin practicing distributive ministry without undergoing a culture change. In a distributive ministry model, the congregation of bivocational ministers collectively discerns how to distribute ministry among those with the demonstrated call and appropriate gifts and graces for the ministry responsibility. The bivocational minister functions in a supportive role. This designation represents a fundamental change from pastor as primary dispenser of religious services to supporting cast member (MacDonald 2020, 65). This change in the function of the pastor promotes a more egalitarian perception of ministry leadership.

Those called to specialized ministry undergo training to prepare them to serve knowledgeably and effectively. MacDonald urged democratization of theological education by training laypeople for effective ministry. I concur with him that ministerial training be required for all designated leaders of specialized, second-tier ministry. Such training could occur within the local church, at denominational certification education events, or through seminary classes and continuing education courses. Responsible administration of ministry responsibilities includes creation of a ministry training process and curriculum. I contend that non-seminary trained persons have the capacity to learn the theory and practice of ministry to enable them to serve as credible ministers.

Bivocational congregations can develop specialized training curricula for the ministry areas a bivocational minister leads. Instruction may be available through denominational resources or not-for-profit Christian organizations, like Stephen Ministries (Stephen Ministries St. Louis, n.d.). Bivocational congregations could form partnerships with other churches to develop training courses. In-house, bivocational congregations may discover persons gifted with abilities to provide specialized instruction. Non-clergy have an established track record of creating significant instructional resources for Christian service. Consider Catherine Marshall's study on *The Holy Spirit in The Helper* (2002), Dorothy Sayers's articles on work and vocation, such as "Why Work?" ([1942] 2020), or Amy Sherman's theological and practical presentation on vocational stewardship in *Kingdom Calling* (2011).

A distributive ministry model regards leadership as a team function. A major benefit of this model is sharing pastoral responsibilities among a larger group of people with the gifts and graces to conduct ministry effectively. Pastors are generalists who have stronger abilities in certain areas of ministry. The intent of distributive ministry is to play to the strengths of each believer in the congregation. This model requires faith that God will provide persons with varying ministry gifts that complement those of the bivocational pastor within the local body of believers.

A distributive ministry within a bivocational church culture regards the bivocational pastor and the congregants as egalitarian partners in ministry. To symbolize this egalitarian relationship, I recommend the congregation refer to both clergy and laity as bivocational ministers. The aim of this naming convention is to eradicate the rhetoric that perpetuates the clergy/laity divide—a division that can imply that laity are ill-equipped and spiritually inferior to clergy in matters of ministry.

To ensure clarity of ministry roles and processes, I recommend local churches create a bivocational pastor agreement that specifies the pastoral and administrative responsibilities expected of the pastor by the congregation. Similarly, I recommend local churches create ministry covenants for each non-ordained bivocational minister engaged in specialized second-tier ministry. Additionally, I encourage congregations to create a covenant that outlines how the bivocational congregation will function. This should be a fluid process as the congregation will be learning and refining this definition as they live into this new experience.

There are many ways to employ distributive ministry within the church. By using the team approach to goal achievement, worship teams can be formed consisting of persons responsible for proclamation, music, liturgy, audiovisual technology, and logistics. The worship team can create a quarterly worship schedule with scripture and sermon themes at the center. The advanced notice provided by such a schedule enables the participants to do in-depth preparation for their area of responsibility.

To emphasize collaboration, a Christian education or formation team could work with the worship team to design a comprehensive Christian formation curriculum in which the worship content and Christian formation align. Ample worship, preaching, and music resources are available online. Two examples are *The Text This Week* (*textweek.com*)—a curated website of lectionary, scripture study, worship links, and other related resources—and Hymnary.org (*hymnary.org*)—a comprehensive index of hymns and hymnals.

Similarly, teams responsible for external ministries, such as visitation, emergency response, mission, and other ministry areas can create response strategies to address emerging needs. Each team can monitor ministry effectiveness by incorporating an action-reflection review process. Periodically, teams can review the planning and execution of the ministry endeavor and address any problems. Embedding collaborative and action-reflection review processes into the distributive ministry model promotes ministry excellence and effectiveness.

Denominational Judicatory Concerns

Internal organization of the distributive ministry model is not the only task of the bivocational congregation. In addition to the congregants and the bivocational pastor adopting a distributive ministry model, they will need to negotiate with the denominational hierarchy. Denominational judicatories may regard distributive ministry as heterodoxy. Denominational authorities may raise questions like the following: (1) "Who is responsible for corporate oversight of the congregation?" (2) "Who will administer the sacraments?" (3) "To whom do denominational judicatories relate for reporting and for supervising the congregation's fidelity to denominational polity?"

These questions reflect honest concerns. I encourage bivocational congregations to regard such inquiries as opportunities for creative dialogue about how to be faithful witnesses to the gospel in our quickly changing environment. For example, I believe the distribution of the general oversight of congregational ministries is possible through a highly coordinated communication system among the bivocational ministers. Through technology, ministers can provide immediate feedback to the point persons in the ministry area and to the bivocational pastor. Congregations would need to develop instructional protocols to determine which persons need particular types of information. Likewise, administration of the sacraments can be worked out according to the expectations of the denominational polity. Often, a sanctioned clergy person from a sister church can administer the sacraments in the absence of an ordained clergy. While the bivocational pastor is the likely denominational point of contact, there could be flexibility for allowing the pastor to designate proxies to attend denominational meetings. Ultimate responsibility to the denomination would still reside with the pastor.

The COVID-19 pandemic disrupted the environment sufficiently to form new spaces for churches and denominations to rethink ministry practice. This liminal environment has created a great opportunity for the church community to dialogue about what distributive ministry could contribute. Denominations are also reconsidering their previously immutable positions on congregational practices. For example, in 2003, the administration of online communion by a pastor in the United Methodist Church sparked a heated debate and launched an episcopal study resulting in a moratorium on the practice. Sixteen years later, United Methodist episcopal leaders, confronted with the COVID-19 pandemic, decided to relax the moratorium. One bishop declared "the COVID-19 pandemic a time of '*In Extremis*' (an extremely difficult situation)" (Brooks, n.d.).

There are many other conversations between bivocational congregations, pastors, and denominational leaders to be had. The priesthood of all believers, the doctrine of vocation, and contemporary endorsements of "every member in ministry" provide a solid foundation upon which to discuss the validity of the distributive ministry model in the local church.

Conclusions

This chapter has articulated a clear path for congregational transformation through participation in distributive ministry. Initiating the discussion of distributive ministry presumes the following: (1) a critical mass of congregants self-identifies as the priesthood of all believers, (2) the congregation affirms the practice of bivocational ministry, and (3) the congregation regards the call of non-ordained believers as ministers as valid. These fundamental affirmations provide the environment needed to explore what distributive ministry is and how it affects ministry practice. Implementing distributive ministry in the local church facilitates transformation of the *ecclesia* in several significant ways, with associated challenges.

Distributive ministry promotes a compelling vision for all Christians to take an active part in ministry in all relational areas. It elevates laity from passive recipients of ministry goods and services to active, capable ministers. This approach dispels the clergy-laity caste system that elevates ordained ministers over non-ordained laity. Distributing pastoral responsibilities among congregants qualified by call, ministry gifts, and proper training decentralizes clergy as the primary ministry conduits. Distributive ministry encourages congregations to build ministry teams of people whose strengths and gifts complement the pastor's strengths and gifts. This collaborative, team approach enables ordained and non-ordained ministers to serve more effectively. Not all members will make the adjustment to distributive ministry. Congregations should expect some membership attrition. Though some members will leave, other new members who favor distributive ministry will join the church.

The distributive ministry model creates a congregational ethos that values Christian vocation and equipping congregants for ministry. This ethos requires a robust ministry training process. Innovative leaders can design a flexible ministry education curriculum in which congregants form affiliate groups that focus on the types of skill development required for ministry in specific community settings. From teachers to mechanics to community developers, affiliate group members can then discuss how best to bear witness to Christ at work or in the community.

This ministry model will disturb clergy and laity who prefer the familiarity of the single-pastor model of leadership. Congregants may resist the communication and relationship changes associated with shared ministry. Congregants may assume they will be forced to contact multiple persons with requests formerly directed to the solo pastor. This highlights the need for a highly coordinated communication process that designates one contact person who directs requests to the proper person. Ministry is highly relational, and people develop preferences for who preaches, teaches, or visits them. Initially, new persons assuming ministry responsibilities previously handled by the pastor will need to demonstrate competency both in ministry practice and in interpersonal relationships.

Denominations can benefit from the ministry multiplication produced through distributive ministry. More members actively engaged in meaningful ministry creates more church vitality. This is good news for denominations, as church attendance and congregational rolls in North America continue to decline. Correspondingly, the deployment of bivocational ministers will only increase in the future. Distributive ministry offers denominational judicatories a viable option to address these factors.

Denominational judicatories may regard the commissioning of ministers by the local church as a threat to the established ministry credentialing system currently in place. To minimize confrontation, a collaborative investigation of the potential of distributive ministry will be helpful. The initial aim of the collaborative process is to create allies who engage in spectrum thinking, which considers multiple options, alternatives, and possibilities.

A think tank consisting of innovative thinkers from denominational judicatories, credentialing entities, seminaries, and bivocational ministry practitioners could study the distributive model, note its desired outcomes, and create an educational support system. The aim of the think tank is to design an endorsed ministry education system that prepares bivocational pastors and congregants to develop and implement distributive ministry. Denominational decision-making processes are slow and cumbersome; nevertheless, investing in such collaboration can attract the denomination's imprimatur.

The distributive ministry model commissions believers to serve as ministers in all relational areas, which extends the congregation's reach into private and public spaces. I believe bivocational congregations that use the distributive ministry model are well positioned to offer the gospel to people in an ever-changing environment.

Works Cited

Arn, Charles. 2013. *Side Door: How to Open Your Church to Reach More People*. Indianapolis: Wesleyan Publishing House.

Briggs, J. R. 2020. "Becoming a Distributed Church: Why It's Worth the Shift." *Fresh Expressions US*. March 23. *freshexpressionsus.org/2020/03/23/becoming-a-distributed-church-why-its-worth-the-shift*.

Brooks, Philip J. n.d. "Remembering While Apart: Online Communion and Love Feasts." Accessed October 23, 2021. *resourceumc.org/en/content/remembering-while-apart-online-communion-and-love-feasts*.

Brown, Michael E., and Dennis A. Gioia. 2002. "Making Things Click: Distributive Leadership in an Online Division of an Offline

Organization." *Leadership Quarterly* 13, no. 4: 397–419. *doi.org/10.1016/S1048-9843(02)00123-6.*

Doriani, Dan. 2016. "The Power and the Dangers in Luther's Concept of Work." *Covenant Theological Seminary. covenantseminary.edu/theology/the-power-and-the-dangers-in-luthers-concept-of-work.*

Goheen, Michael W. 2018. *The Church and Its Vocation: Lesslie Newbigin's Missionary Ecclesiology.* Grand Rapids, MI: Baker Academic.

Gronn, Peter. 2002. "Distributed Leadership as a Unit of Analysis." *Leadership Quarterly* 13, no. 4: 423–51. *doi.org/10.1016/S1048-9843(02)00120-0.*

Hirsch, Alan. 2016. *The Forgotten Ways: Reactivating Apostolic Movements.* 2nd ed. Grand Rapids, MI: Brazos.

MacDonald, G. Jeffrey. 2020. *Part-Time Is Plenty: Thriving Without Full-Time Clergy.* Louisville: Westminster John Knox.

Marshall, Catherine. 2001. *The Helper.* Ada, MI: Chosen.

Nessan, Craig L. 2019. "Universal Priesthood of All Believers: Unfulfilled Promise of the Reformation." *Currents in Theology and Mission* 46, no. 1: 8–15. *currentsjournal.org/index.php/currents/article/view/155.*

Roxburgh, Alan J. 1998. "Missional Leadership: Equipping God's People for Mission." In *Missional Church: A Vision for the Sending of the Church in North America,* edited by Darrell L. Guder, 183–220. Grand Rapids, MI: Eerdmans.

Sayers, Dorothy. (1942) 2020. "Why Work?" In *Letters to the Diminished Church.* Center for Faith & Learning Scholar Program. *villanova.edu/content/dam/villanova/mission/faith/Why%20Work%20by%20Dorothy%20Sayers.pdf.*

Schreiner, Thomas R. 2003. "1, 2 Peter, Jude." *The New American Commentary* 37. Nashville: Broadman & Holman.

Sherman, Amy L. 2011. *Kingdom Calling: Vocational Stewardship for the Common Good.* Downers Grove, IL: InterVarsity.

Stephen Ministries St. Louis. n.d. “What is Stephen Ministry?” *stephenministries.org/aboutus/default.cfm/721.*

Zepke, Nick. 2007. “Leadership, Power and Activity Systems in a Higher Education Context: Will Distributive Leadership Serve in an Accountability Driven World?” *International Journal of Leadership in Education: Theory and Practice* 10, no. 3: 301–14. *doi.org/10.1080/13603120601181514.*

CHAPTER 9

Incarnating Christ through Bivocational Ministry

STEVEN C. VAN OSTRAN

It has been my experience that, despite the best efforts of denominational types like myself, bivocational ministers see themselves and are looked upon by others as second-class ministers—ministers who are not on the same level with those who serve full time. Not all hold this view, to be sure, but most bivocational ministers and most other ministers, church members, and people in the community do—or at least that is how it feels according to the bivocational pastors I know. It has also been my experience that some of the finest, most godly, and long-tenured pastors I have ever had the privilege to serve alongside were and are bivocational.

So why the disconnect?

I suspect a large part of the reason for this is that, in this "Show me the money!!" environment and culture, we naturally presume that the brightest and the best will be called to full-time positions, be paid well, and not have or even want to do anything but live out the call to pastor God's people. We presume that, when God calls someone to serve in ministry, that call is to full-time ministry. But that simply is not the case.

In fact, while estimates vary, a survey by Faith Communities Today reported that just 62 percent of congregations had a full-time, paid senior or sole pastor in 2015 (Roozen 2015, 8). This percentage was down from the 2010 survey. Accurate data from specific denominations are often unavailable. One Southern Baptist Convention commentator speculated that between 40 and 60 percent, and maybe as much as 80 percent, of their churches were served by bivocational pastors (Gray 2016). My experience as a denominational leader in the American Baptist Churches—where the small, single-cell, solo-pastor congregation is the norm—suggests similar numbers.

Yet, these dedicated, talented, hard-working, and tireless men and women of God are too often looked down upon by their full-time colleagues. They endure questions from friends and family about when they will become "real" pastors. Too often, they are passed over for opportunities to speak to and address their colleagues and constituents at conventions and associational meetings. I say this not to malign full-time pastors—I was a full-time local church pastor for eighteen years and continue to serve in full-time Christian ministry to this day.

Even pastors who are classified as full-time are likely to be involved in some sort of "side-hustle," either for economic reasons or simply because of other advantages that employment outside the church offers. In my own experience, I served as solo or senior pastor to four different congregations. In only one did I not have some sort of outside employment. In the first two ministries, my decision to work outside the pastorate was economic. In my most recent local church pastorate, I served as an adjunct professor at the local university—not because we needed the money but because of the opportunities it gave me to connect with the students, faculty, and staff of the university. Serving on the university staff, even if some would not classify it as being truly bivocational, afforded me and my congregation some critical advantages for ministry in our community that we otherwise would not have had.

In this chapter, I present bivocational ministry as a means of incarnating Christ to the community, drawing on my pastoral experience, my experience as an executive minister in the American Baptist Churches, and the experiences of many bivocational pastors I know personally. First, I offer the "incarnational church," based on 1 Corinthians 12 and Luke 10, as a model of holistic mission. Then, I present four benefits of bivocational ministry that might lead churches and pastors to engage in bivocational ministry even when a full-time ministry is possible. The incarnational benefits of bivocational ministry include breaking down the sacred-secular divide, creating community and relationships outside the local congregation, uncovering new opportunities for ministry and mission outside the walls of the church, and reducing the dependencies of the pastor that hinder authentic leadership and prophetic action, both in the church and in the community. I conclude by encouraging the church to reframe its understanding of bivocational ministry as a positive way of incarnating Christ.

The Incarnational Church Model

The incarnational church model is based upon Paul's declaration to the Corinth church that "you are the body of Christ, and each one of you is a part of it" (1 Cor. 12:27, NIV). This text is often interpreted to speak to the universal Church, not the local church, and to be figurative and aspirational rather than literal. However, Paul was writing to a local church and, even had he known that the letter would become an encyclical circulated to other churches, his target audience was still local congregations, not the Church universal. Paul was saying, in effect, "You, the church at Corinth, are supposed to be the Body of Christ for Corinth." By extension, the text challenges every local church to be the Body of Christ to its community. This model then offers the church a huge challenge and gives it direction in how to operate. Even if one views this challenge as aspirational rather than fully attainable, it tells us that the core mission of the church is to be Christ to its community!

But how do we do that? One might begin to analyze the Gospels and try to discern and lift out Christ's actions while here on earth to understand how we are to fulfill our mission of being Christ's Body. Alternatively, we might simply look at Jesus's charge to the disciples as He sent them out on mission in Luke 10. Many believe that this passage depicts Jesus's soft opening of the church, like a restaurant has a soft opening before the grand opening to familiarize staff with the menu and how the restaurant will be run. In this passage, Jesus summarized the mission of the disciples in four simple tasks: being physically present, dwelling with and entering into relationship with the people, doing acts of mercy, and proclaiming the gospel. These tasks summarize not only the mission of the disciples but also the church and Jesus's own ministry here on earth. God's love for humanity offers the opportunity to enter into relationship with God through Jesus.

These four actions are the hallmark of the New Testament church—the incarnational church model, to which reformers through the ages have sought to return. One example of this is Martin Luther's decision to translate the Bible into German (the "September Bible") in 1522. By doing so, Luther was doing all but "acts of mercy" for the commoners of Germany of his time.

Common areas of emphasis for the church—being missional, doing social justice, and even the classic revivalism—often truncate the incarnational model by focusing on a single task without the holistic mission of being present and engaging in relationships before moving to the more measurable goals of hands-on mission work and winning souls. Churches whose leaders engage in bivocational ministry, whether intentionally or out of economic necessity, often find themselves engaged more fully in the community because the pastor is engaged more fully in the community. This engagement leads to more effective missional activities and broader opportunities to proclaim the gospel. Four benefits evolve from being bivocational and, while not directly related to the four tasks of being incarnational, enhance the pastor and church's ability to be incarnational.

Breaking Down the Sacred-Secular Divide

Bivocational ministry can break down the divide felt between sacred and secular. This divide happens in part because of a kind of hyper-holiness. In scripture, the Temple is designated a sacred and holy place. Jesus, in driving out the money changers from the Temple, seems to affirm this view—that the place of worship is holy and set apart. But God's acts of rending the veil in the Holy of Holies and the in-dwelling of the Holy Spirit seem to eliminate this separation. Instead of a certain place or certain person being holy, Jesus's action on the cross made everything holy. God can and does dwell within us, and it is God's presence that makes a person or place holy, not the place itself.

Still, this attitude that some places and people are holier than others continues in US culture. Indeed, the actions of many congregations, the architecture of their buildings, and the honor that churches confer to their pastors and leaders proclaim this difference. By creating physical separation between the altar and the people, by limiting access to the altar, and by the costuming and vestments of clergy, we have created an attitude that all clergy and all church buildings are to be treated as sacred. Some churches even extend this separation to the point of having separate bathrooms for the pastors. While the intention for this may simply be for the convenience of the pastor, the implicit message is separation. And, to be honest, many of us who are in ministry like this special treatment. We, like Moses, work to preserve the illusion of our holiness even after the glory has long faded away (2 Cor. 3:13)!

But this special treatment—this separation—creates problems in communicating the message that Christ died for us all and that we are all sinners saved by grace. To combat this false message, one of the members of my doctoral cohort—a former Jesuit who was serving a Lutheran congregation—began sitting in the congregation to visibly make the statement that he was coming from the same place as the rest of the congregation when he went to the pulpit to offer a Word from the Lord. This was a dramatic step for him, coming from his Roman Catholic tradition.

Pastors choosing to work bivocationally take the message of being among the congregation one step further. By working alongside laity in the community to earn their living, they are sending the message that they too are dependent upon God's grace and their own hard work for their livelihood. Yes, we know full-time pastors work hard, as well, but congregants may perceive their tithes and offerings as fully providing for the pastor, creating a feeling of separation and division.

By working alongside their congregants, either literally or symbolically, this division is attenuated. As a student pastor, I worked as a farm hand for members of my congregation. There were many times when my sense of "holiness" was brought into check, either by a ripped seam in my jeans or by some expression of frustration due to an animal or my own clumsiness. While all pastors face the same day-to-day challenges and temptations as their parishioners, the congregation sees this a bit more clearly in those working bivocationally.

In addition to the holiness divide between pastor and parishioner, there is also the "Marie Antoinette divide." Marie Antoinette, of course, was infamous for reportedly having replied to the complaints of the commoners having no bread by saying, "Let them eat cake." Whether true or not, it speaks to the real perception that many people hold—that those who are privileged do not really understand what the common person faces day to day. Clergy are often perceived as being among the privileged. Further, there is the belief that they (the privileged) are unable or unwilling to do some of the practical things necessary for day-to-day living and are dependent upon others to meet those needs. A practical example of this is the pastoral spouse who called a plumber to change a toilet seat rather than doing it themselves, expecting the plumber to bill the church. This action communicated to the congregation that the pastoral couple should not be expected to do this common task or even to know how to do it and that their privilege and their holiness meant they were above common skills and abilities.

The bivocational pastor who works in the community, even in another professional position, generally communicates that they are not above learning and doing common everyday tasks. When a pastor is willing to serve school lunches or drive a delivery truck, they are saying they are on a par with the other members of the congregation, not above them. They show they are willing to do even menial labor to provide for themselves rather than create a dependency upon the congregation.

Further, when a pastor serves bivocationally, they must count on lay leaders of the congregation to do more of the work of the church, thus further breaking down the sacred-secular divide. A bivocational pastor, for example, may depend on a lay leader to plan the worship service, make hospital visits where they will give communion, or work with vendors and volunteers to take care of the building. The bivocational pastor is forced "to equip the saints for the work of ministry" (Eph. 4:12a) more often than the full-time pastor.

Creating Community and Relationships

Perhaps one of the greatest advantages of bivocational ministry is in building community and relationships outside the walls of the church. One of the great challenges of the US church is its dependence upon full-time staff, whether that be the pastor, a pastoral team, or ministry leaders, to bring people into the church. This dependency is problematic in several ways, including limiting disciple-making efforts to "professionals." Furthermore, outside of family, most fully compensated ministers limit their primary relationships to other church folks, whether in their own or in other congregations. Full-time pastors must be very intentional about building community and relationships outside of their own congregation. And when they are intentional about this, they often face jealousy from members of their congregation, who may accuse them of dereliction in their service to the membership of the church.

Bivocational ministers, however, naturally build these connections, and their being bivocational often strips away the congregation's idea that they own the pastor's time. Indeed, this idea was communicated to me by a bivocational pastor whose full-time predecessor had come under fire because he was "spending too much time on the golf course," where he was trying to build relationships with young professionals in the community (personal communication, January 7, 2021). While the predecessor may indeed have had some responsibility for not clearly communicating his intentions in playing golf versus being in the office of the church, that church's expectations of pastoral office hours were necessarily changed when they called a bivocational pastor. In this case, the pastor was already working in the school system and had community and relationships established when he came to the church. In fact, those very relationships, built in the community, allowed him to connect with the church when they needed a pastor.

This attitude of owning the pastor's time is common. Another colleague, employed full-time by a small congregation located just outside a metropolitan area, shared the following story. The small town in which the congregation was located had become a bedroom community for the nearby metropolis. My colleague was asked to coach the wrestling team for the local high school. The church was out in the country, and the nearby families all sent their kids to this local high school. In his desire to make this effort a congregational outreach, the pastor made plans for many of the practices to be held at the church building, in their large community room. When the pastor approached the church leadership, however, they were unable to see the community connections that might have been made. They expressed concern about how this program would affect the pastor's availability to them and asked that he not do this. Obviously, when the boss (or in this case the leadership of the congregation) asks you not to do something, the wise employee bends to the desires of the employer. Ironically, this congregation, who were largely baby boomers, struggled to keep youth in the congregation. Perhaps they were legitimately worried about the pastor's use of time, but, if so, this was not communicated. In contrast, they had no problem with the pastor's involvement with and time commitment to the Christian Motorcycle Association.

Discovering Unique Ministry Opportunities

A third way in which bivocational ministry helps the church incarnate Christ is through discovering unique ministry opportunities in the community. Due in large part to breaking down the sacred-secular barrier and the pastor's broader community and relationships, bivocational pastors find unique connections for ministry.

One of my "side-hustles" during one pastorate was working as day labor for a heating and air contractor who was a member of the congregation. Through his work, he discovered a number of elderly clients and widows who not only needed to have work done on their HVAC (heating, ventilation, and air conditioning) systems but also had small tasks around the house that they either did not have the ability to do or were no longer capable of doing. This contractor could have simply taken on these jobs and charged these folks for the work. Instead, he asked me to help. The two of us, along with his teen-age son, took one day a month to do odd jobs for these people—many of them members of my congregation. Some were simply members of the community in need. Sometimes the people would be able to pay for the parts, sometimes not. My friend saw it as a way he could "look after widows and orphans" (James 1:27; see also Acts 6:1–4).

Another pastor, whose ministry career has been largely bivocational, told me about the time he was working in banking, and a relative of one of his customers committed suicide. The customer reached out to him to care for the family because "you're the only pastor I know!" (personal communication, January 4, 2021).

One of my denominational colleagues, who served many years bivocationally, was able to minister to groups of people to whom he would not otherwise be able to minister through his work as an adjunct professor at the local community college. As an African American pastor serving in the South, this professorship enabled him to minister across racial lines, generational gaps, and cultures (Harrison 2021).

Another congregation entered bivocational ministry by calling a full-time, practicing attorney and college president as their pastor. This shift to bivocational ministry allowed them to increase their giving to missionaries to 29% of their budget (personal communication, January 20, 2021). They also increased volunteer leadership support significantly and saw their attendance grow under the leadership of this capable individual.

These examples illustrate the many ways in which a bivocational pastor may open unexpected pathways for the church to encounter ministry opportunities to love others as Christ has loved us.

Reducing Pastoral Dependencies

Bivocational pastors who earn their livelihood outside the church have a freedom of the pulpit not enjoyed by fully compensated pastors. For example, I am aware of many full-time pastors holding egalitarian views on gender yet reluctant to challenge the complementarian practices of their congregation by elevating capable women into positions of leadership, for fear of creating too much turmoil in the congregation. Their reluctance is based on more than simply maintaining order. Job security also plays a part in these actions and lack of action. Bivocational ministry arrangements can reduce pastoral dependencies and increase prophetic potential.

An example of how financial dependency can affect the work of the pastor is recorded in *Rocket Boys* (Hickam 1998). Hickam tells the story of the pastor of the company church in Coalwood—a coal town in West Virginia—who was brow-beaten by the coal mine's ownership into condemning the actions of Hickam and the other young rocket engineers. The pastor initially came out in support of the boys and the opportunity this would provide them to break out of Coalwood through education. The pastor's change of mind came about solely because of the pastor's dependency on the mine for his salary, home, and way of life. This incident—a classic example of how the economic dependency of a pastor can limit their prophetic ministry—was left out of the popular movie adaptation, *October Sky*.

Hickam's pastor was not alone in this experience. During my full-time ministry, economic dependency and pragmatic wisdom also caused me to edit my prophetic stances on various issues. When serving a rural church whose members' cash crop was tobacco, I did not preach about the evils of tobacco. Further, when serving a congregation whose membership included managers of the Shell Oil Refinery, a major employer in our community, I did not pass along the denomination's call to embargo Shell and other Dutch-owned companies to protest apartheid in South Africa.

In contrast, bivocational pastors who earn their livelihood outside the church have a freedom of the pulpit not enjoyed by full-time pastors. I am aware of another situation where a bivocational pastor confessed it was financial independence that allowed him to move the congregation out of some long-held theological and liturgical beliefs and practices. He led the church to soften their views about the sacredness of the sanctuary and building, leading them to open it up to tenants. This action gave them greater viability and prompted them to consider selling the building and buying another that served their needs better. He also challenged them to move away from a staid, rigid form of worship to a more inviting and culturally relevant style of worship. He was able to accomplish this in a very short amount of time because he was unafraid of the consequences of his actions and could be prophetic from the pulpit—not only in these very pragmatic areas but also in the arena of social justice.

Prophetic ministry is but one of the areas in which financial independence gives freedom. Another is pastoral tenure. One colleague, specifically called to serve as a bivocational minister, served for seventeen years at one small-town congregation. This congregation had experienced regular turnover of their pastors every three to five years as a result of the stepping-stone practice that is a part of our Baptist tradition. Pastors would serve this congregation in their first pastorate and then move on to a larger congregation after gaining experience. My bivocational colleague was able to interrupt this tradition and help the congregation make several critical moves that set them up for future success because of his practice of a personal trade (personal communication, January 6, 2021).

Another pastor came to a church with a similar pattern. He was allowed to work bivocationally as an adjunct at the local junior college, interrupting the stepping-stone tradition. Because he was not financially dependent upon the church, he was able to continue in ministry in the small, isolated community. This pastor will soon retire from the church after thirty-plus years in the community.

Shifting Our Understanding

While the economic benefits of bivocational ministry have long been evident, I believe that the incarnational benefits will be of greater importance to the church in the coming years. For that reason, the church, through its various leadership and training structures, needs to do a better job of preparing and supporting bivocational ministries and pastors. One reason this has not happened is the current bias against being bivocational—a bias shared by church executives, pastors, seminaries, denominational leaders, and even the people in the pews. This does not have to be.

Recognizing that bivocational ministry has been the most common form of pastoral ministry throughout generations and that bivocational ministry is still the most broadly practiced model in most areas of the world should indicate to us that bivocational ministry is formative rather than regressive. The current negative or regressive view of bivocational ministry comes from an established church perspective, which sees bivocationality as a sign of failure. It is the same feeling experienced by a large program church declining to the point of being a single-pastor congregation: the memory of "what was" prevents celebrating "what is" or even dreaming about "what could be." A new, growing church will celebrate having a special service of 100 people while the old, established church laments the same size of service.

If the church can reframe its understanding of bivocational ministry as formative—that its very nature is advantageous to incarnational ministry and helping the church be Christ to its community—great strides will have been taken. Whether or not we make this shift in understanding the value of bivocational ministers, their service will be required for the sustainability of the church. Surely, then, we should be doing all we can to support and sustain this vital work, instead of discouraging it by asking the pastor engaged in bivocational ministry, "When are you going to become a real minister?"

As we enter a new age of the church—as God prepares to do a new thing—I suspect that bivocational ministry will once again become the norm. Historically this has been the case and still is the case in most parts of the world, especially in areas where the church is thriving. And the church is thriving in these areas not because of the economic benefits, but because of the incarnational benefits bivocational ministers offer to the local church and to the Kingdom of

God. Bivocational ministry simply enhances the incarnational model of church depicted in the New Testament. The incarnational model for ministry is what previous reformations have striven to re-create and what I believe will be the aim of the coming reformation as well.

Works Cited

Gray, Rudy. 2016. "Is Bivocational Ministry the New Normal?" Courier. November 2. *baptistcourier.com/2016/11/bivocational-ministry-new-normal.*

Harrison, James. 2021. Participant in "Rethinking Bi-vocational Ministry," workshop presentation at ABC-USA Biennial Mission Summit—An Online Experience. American Baptist Churches USA. June 26.

Hickam, Homer H., Jr. 1998. *Rocket Boys: A Memoir.* The Coalwood Series 1. New York: Delta.

Roozen, David A. 2015. *American Congregations 2015: Thriving and Surviving.* Faith Communities Today. *faithcommunitiestoday.org/wp-content/uploads/2019/01/American-Congregations-2015.pdf.*

CHAPTER 10

Bivocational Ministry as a Path of Unexpected Spiritual Growth

BEN CONNELLY

Everyone loves unexpected outcomes; from the surprise ending to movies like *The Sixth Sense* and *The Usual Suspects*, to the heart-racing twists of spy novels, to the breath-taking excitement of sudden turns in a theme park roller coaster, people are often thrilled when things turn out differently than they expected. Bivocational ministry—like so many other aspects of life—often leads to an outcome unexpected by those who pursue it.

Throughout the holy scriptures, we see that God is in the business of unexpected outcomes: "so those who are last now will be first then, and those who are first will be last," our Lord Jesus tells his first disciples (Matt. 20:16, NLT). The Apostle Paul echoes the Messiah's words: "God chose things the world considers foolish in order to shame those who think they are wise. And he chose things that are powerless to shame those who are powerful" (1 Cor. 1:27). And, of course, the Gospel account portrays the greatest unexpected outcome of history. There is one expected outcome of death: the dead person stays dead. But in earth's greatest surprise ending, "the Spirit of God . . . raised Jesus from the dead" (Rom. 8:11). The story does not end there. To finish the verse, that same "Spirit of God, who raised Jesus from the dead, *lives in you*" (emphasis added). Christianity affirms that God created each human in the divine image and for God's glory. God uses every circumstance in one's life to form us, God's children, increasingly into this image. God guides both our lives and our ministries.

In this chapter, I share the results of a survey administered to bivocational ministers regarding their motives and outcomes related to ministry and spiritual growth. I begin by discussing a hypothesis based on personal experience and observation: bivocational ministry is often an unexpected path of spiritual growth for the bivocational minister. The results of the survey validate and reinforce this hypothesis. Individuals pursue (or, perhaps, find themselves in) bivocational ministry for many reasons, including finances, missional motives, and personal convictions. And, my research shows, bivocational ministry often leads to unexpected personal spiritual growth within the bivocational minister. The pattern proved surprisingly common; nearly every minister surveyed entered bivocational ministry for one or multiple reasons, hardly any of which related to their personal spiritual growth, and nearly every minister surveyed shared personal spiritual growth as an outcome of this unique form of ministry.

A Hypothesis Based on Personal Experience and Observation

I have served in bivocational ministry for over 20 years. Early in my ministry, I worked part-time in churches while in school. Later, I taught at a local university while planting a church. Most recently, I have worked with parachurch ministries while pastoring. My initial impulses for pursuing bivocational ministry were primarily pragmatic (for example, pastoring while pursuing a degree or, later, trying to save the church plant money). But, as with many things in life, there were unexpected outcomes.

I had not considered the missional implications of teaching at a university while planting a church. While many North American churches excel at teaching disciples, the making of new disciples is more commonly forgotten or neglected. My own conviction came from the Lord Jesus's final charge to his followers at his ascension: "go and make disciples of all the nations, baptizing them in the name of the Father and the Son and the Holy Spirit. Teach these new disciples to obey all the commands I have given you. And be sure of this: I am with you always, even to the end of the age" (Matt. 28:19–20). Indwelled with the Spirit of God, the rest of the New Testament contains, among other elements, the story of Jesus's followers displaying and declaring the gospel, both individually and collectively. Based on similar reasons and convictions, many ministers I know choose to be bivocational so that they can be proactively and regularly sent into the world as the Father first sent the Son into the world (John 17:18). In my case, God used my teaching to grow his kingdom on campus. Over the years, God has drawn me closer, grown my own faith, and changed my view of the church in deep and unexpected ways, specifically because of being bivocational.

Having trained other ministry leaders and church planters across the world through my work with the Equipping Group, I am aware that my story is not unique; ministers choose to be bivocational for certain reasons (often logistical, as in my case) but commonly experience unexpected outcomes from their bivocational lives. Over time, I observed that these unexpected outcomes were more personal and spiritual than the initial motives; bivocational ministry is often an unexpected path of spiritual growth for the bivocational minister. In early 2021, I set out to test this hypothesis and learn from my bivocational peers.

Survey Participants

From March 1 to April 12, 2021, I surveyed bivocational ministers (also called covocational, tentmaking, and so on) specifically around the motivations and spiritual formation involved with this unique form of ministry. This online survey, open to any practitioner of bivocational ministry, was administered via Google Forms by Saturate, a non-denominational resource and training organization for which I served as director of training, largely focused on North American church leaders. Participants were found by posting invitations in various online groups dedicated to supporting the practice and philosophy of bivocational ministry. In addition, a link to the survey was posted in four Facebook groups: Covocational Church Planting, Saturate the World, Soma Leaders, and Acts 29 Family.

The "Bivo/Covo Ministry Survey" produced over 500 pages of data from 80 respondents, giving insights into trends across various organizations.[1] The survey focused on motivations, factors, and tangible and personal outcomes of ministry. Geographically, participants were mainly located in North America: 82.5% in the United States, 7.5% in Canada, 5% in Australia, 2.5% in the Netherlands, and 2.5% in Northern Ireland. The survey allowed anonymity, although 83% of respondents chose to divulge their identity. Information about age, ethnicity, and gender was not solicited, but, based on names given, nearly all participants were male. Other information offered voluntarily in responses indicates that, of the 20 pastors quoted in this chapter, 18 are male, 17 are White, one is Native American, and two are anonymous.

Respondents spanned several Protestant denominations and networks. More identified themselves by affiliation with church planting networks than denominations, though 20% of participants indicated some form of dual-alignment—thus the following percentages add up to more than 100%. Of participants, 30% were Southern Baptist and 10% affiliated with other Baptist organizations, such as the Canadian National Baptist Convention; 23% were part of Acts 29 church planting network (*Acts29.com*); 15% were involved with the Soma Family of Churches (*wearesoma.com*); 10% were affiliated with Wesleyan traditions, such as the United Methodist Church and Free Methodist; 13% were affiliated with other networks and denominations, such as Vineyard, Assemblies of God, or localized networks; and 8% indicated unaffiliated churches ("none").

Eighty-seven percent of respondents identified themselves as "Senior/lead pastor or minister (or team leader, regardless of title)"; the rest filled other pastoral or support staff roles within local church ministry teams. Forty-two percent had been in full-time ministry before becoming bivocational. In addition to serving in local churches, respondents worked across the vocational spectrum, as postal carriers, educators, city, state, and federal employees, healthcare workers, retail workers, drivers, psychologists, maintenance workers, consultants, students, realtors, handymen, beverage and hospitality industry workers, as well as serving in non-church ministries, such as chaplaincy or parachurch ministry. Among those surveyed, 40% reported that their non-church job provided 100% of their income, 42% said it provided half or more, and 18% said it provided less than half of their income. As one might expect, none of these bivocational respondents said, "My ministry role supports 100% of my income."

Motives for Bivocational Ministry

Multiple factors contribute to consideration of bivocational ministry. Seventy-five percent of participants in this survey "intentionally pursued bivocational ministry"; the rest were bivocational due to factors beyond their control. One Australian Baptist captured a common theme of many respondents: "I didn't originally pursue [it], but now wouldn't have it any other way."[2] Participants were asked to evaluate the following motivations for their own bivocational ministry: missional living, biblical/theological convictions around money, biblical/theological convictions around ministry, your personal ministry philosophy/methodology, your church's ministry philosophy/methodology, your personal spiritual formation, your personal financial needs/abilities, and your church's financial needs/abilities. The survey asked respondents to rate each motivation on a five-point Likert scale: "not at all a factor," "not very much a factor," "somewhat a factor," "very much a factor," or "the primary factor." Participants were also given the opportunity to add further explanation as an optional follow-up.

Financial Motives for Bivocational Ministry

The most commonly expected motive for bivocational ministry is financial. Historically, bivocational ministry has been viewed by many North American churches as a consolation prize. This viewpoint assumes that ministers are only bivocational because either the church's finances could not support a full-time minister or the minister's household necessitated greater income than their church could provide. Survey respondents indicated that finances—both personal and congregational—were indeed a common motive for their pursuit of bivocational ministry. On one hand, 73% of respondents cited "personal financial needs/abilities" as somewhat, very much, or the primary factor in their consideration, with 20% claiming it as "the primary factor" for their being bivocational. On the other hand, 68% of respondents cited "your church's financial needs/abilities" as at least "somewhat a factor," with 23% claiming it as their "primary factor." When asked for further explanation of their answers, one participant candidly summarized a theme common to many responses: "our church cannot financially support full time staff, and our family has not been able to raise funds for full time support."

While many full-time ministers view bivocational ministry through a negative lens, it is worth noting that most ministers who added further explanation in this survey did not view a lack of finances as a negative reality: many saw it as neutral—simply a fact of life—while others viewed bivocational ministry as a positive way to provide for their household needs without putting undue strain on the church. As one minister said, "I found freedom and wisdom in Paul's example of being supported, working, and being able to support his own team." Other ministers saw bivocation as a proactive way to free up funding to support other ministers or to give more financial support to their church's mission and ministry. To this end, one lead pastor offered a representative perspective: "My education/skills afford me the ability to work outside the church. My associate pastor and other church planters do not have as many options, so I've opted to free up the church finances to fund them." Sometimes mission and finances were intertwined, as one participant explained:

> the people I know and love in my own sphere of influence are skeptical of organized religion, particularly because of its association with money. So when we planted, we wanted to do everything we could to remove the things that might cause people to question our motives and allow them to see that we're loving/serving them with no strings attached.

In summary, while situations and views varied, finances were a primary, real, and prevalent motivation for bivocational ministry among the survey respondents. But, perhaps contrary to common views, finances were not always seen as negative among those who minister bivocationally, and finances were not the only motivation for this unique ministry pursuit.

Missional Motives for Bivocational Ministry

The minister's and local church's role in God's mission emerged as a significant motive for many ministers being bivocational—even more than finances, according to the survey. Fully 90% of respondents cited "missional living" as at least "somewhat a factor" in their consideration of bivocational ministry, with 33% claiming "missional living" as "the primary factor" for bivocationality. This was the highest reported "primary factor" of the eight categories on the survey. The ability to participate in God's mission personally, equip churches for collective mission, see churches multiply, send and plant new churches, and see their ministry outside the church as complementing (rather than competing with) their ministry inside the church body—these are all factors that participants affirmed in multiple-choice and open-response survey questions.

When asked to explain their missional motivation, respondents were unified in their views. One said frankly, "full-time vocational ministry was not getting me in the path of people." Another echoed, "By working outside the church organization, I'm able to stay connected to the wider culture while also serving as a model for people who want to follow Jesus while still working (i.e. bivo/covo is a great way to destroy the clergy/lay divide)." A bivocational minister in the Netherlands served as a reminder that this is true outside North America as well, in a more post-Christendom culture: "Working in [a] high tech industry gives me credibility in the mission field." As indicated by these and similar responses, some ministers intentionally pursue bivocational ministry so that they can personally live out God's mission, even while concurrently serving as a minister in their local church.

Related to their desire for personal missional living was a focus on the church's collective missional impulse. One survey participant chose to be bivocational so that his church could be involved in "church planting with a reproducible model." Another saw his bivocational role as an opportunity to equip his church's members to view their workplaces, neighborhoods, and cities as a mission field:

> We want to be and raise up leaders who spend a majority of their time in everyday spaces where they live, work and hang out and less time spent in a church office or building. A simpler, multiplying structure with covocational leaders allows for this in ways traditional ministry does not.

Two questions about the compatibility of work and ministry employed a five-point spectrum, from "Not well at all" to "Very well." When asked, "How well do(es) your other job(s) complement your bivocational ministry role's FOCUS/MISSION?" 95% indicated a three or higher. In a separate question, "How well do(es) your other job(s) complement your bivocational ministry role's SCHEDULE?" 95% also indicated a three or higher.

Convictional Motives for Bivocational Ministry

A third motive for pursuing bivocational ministry pertains to convictions about money and ministry. Many layers to this term were explored and inquired into throughout the survey, some of which also relate to finances and mission. For example, just over half of participants agreed that "Biblical/theological convictions around money" were at least "somewhat a factor" in their "decision to pursue bivocational ministry," while 55% named their "church's ministry philosophy/methodology" to be at least "somewhat a factor" in their decision. Very few indicated either of these reasons as "the primary factor" in their decision to be bivocational (3% and 13%, respectively). Meanwhile, nearly three-quarters of participants said their "biblical/theological convictions around ministry" were at least "somewhat a factor" in that decision, with 20% responding that it was "the primary factor" in that decision. And 88% of participants indicated that their own "personal ministry philosophy/methodology" was at least "somewhat a factor" in their decision to be bivocational, with 25% responding that it was "the primary factor" in being bivocational.

Two survey respondents captured a common theme behind these statistics. One declared, "Being covocational really had nothing to do with church finances or personal finances, but a conviction on how to most effectively reach our culture for Jesus with principles of how Jesus made disciples." A second minister explained a shift in his personal ministry convictions, from initially pursuing full-time ministry toward becoming bivocational:

> Despite having a desire to become a full-time pastor—not to mention having the social pressure to do so by other pastors within my denomination—I continued to work full-time [at another job] as the church did not have the budget to hire a full-time pastor. After a few

> years of being bivocational I came to the personal and theological conviction that being bivocational was a GOOD thing that should be pursued rather than dreaded . . . I'm currently a few years into a new church plant and I have no desire to become a full-time pastor working for a church organization.

Many ministers indicated that their bivocational experience led to a shift in personal views of church finances, ministry roles, and vocation. Several of these shifts are echoed in another bivocational minister's convictional motives: "My calling, personal conviction and our church's ministry philosophy dictates here. We want to be and raise up leaders who spend a majority of their time in everyday spaces where they live, work and hang out and less time spent in a church office or building." Yet another wrote, "I wanted our church to be generous. It was the only way. . . . our staff of five is all bivocational, and we only support and send bivocational leaders and missionaries."

Whether one agrees with all the convictions listed above is beside the point. For many ministers in the cross-section of this survey, the point is simply that various convictions, around a variety of factors of mission and ministry—whether personal or informed by their church—proved a common motive for many ministers to become bivocational.

An Unexpected Path of Spiritual Formation

For all the common motives that led various ministers to pursue bivocational ministry, one motive was uniformly low. When responding to a survey question regarding one's "personal spiritual formation" as a motive for pursuing bivocational ministry, only 10% of participants referenced it as "the primary factor"; 62% said that it was only somewhat, "not very much," or "not at all" a factor. And yet, when asked more specifically about their experience in bivocational ministry, participants consistently indicated that their bivocational experience influenced their personal spiritual formation. Respondents were asked to rate the degree to which "bivocational ministry enhanced or hindered the following: your view of God; your view of God's care & provision; your view of the church; your view of church leadership; your view of Christian community; your view of God's mission; your personal identity in Christ; your personal spiritual thriving; and your personal sanctification." Respondents were also asked to rate the degree to which "bivocational ministry has enhanced or hindered your view of" nine different areas: "dependence on God; dependence on others; personal humility; realizing personal limits; accepting personal limits; embracing others' giftings; ministry as a team; activating the 'priesthood of all believers'; and seeing Jesus as 'head of the church.'" Both questions utilized the following Likert scale: greatly hindered my view; somewhat hindered my view; neither hindered nor enhanced my view; somewhat enhanced my view; greatly enhanced my view. Specific themes emerged, each of which plays a part in bivocational ministers' personal spiritual growth. Through bivocational ministry, respondents reported growth in humility and dependence, a deepened need for a team, and growth in sanctification. The survey also revealed a few hindrances to spiritual growth.

General Spiritual Growth

Over 75% of respondents indicated that bivocational ministry had somewhat or greatly enhanced their view of God, "God's care and provision," "Christian community," and their "personal spiritual thriving." Additionally, over 80% of participants said that bivocational ministry had at least somewhat enhanced their views of the church, Christian leadership, their "personal identity in Christ," and their "own sanctification." Furthermore, 90% responded that bivocational ministry had either somewhat or greatly enhanced their views of "God's mission" and "Jesus as 'the head of the church'." Correspondingly, bivocational ministry had somewhat or greatly hindered the views of these areas in no more than 10% of participants, with "your view of church leadership" as the highest (10%). Responses to these questions indicated a consistent pattern: while "personal spiritual formation" was seldom a motivator in participants' pursuit of bivocational ministry, it was a common outcome.

One survey participant explained specifically how bivocational ministry had formed him spiritually:

> Being bivo/covo allows me an additional context through which to view myself outside of ministry. This helps me recognize and battle my idolatry of ministry and ministry success. It also challenges me

> to be a faithful witness of Christ where others do not care about my ministry leadership role. Here I find a unique type of accountability.

Another credited his bivocational pursuit for helping him focus his ministry—and reveal temptations to pull away from what matters most:

> The simplicity of discipleship being loved by God, church as family, and hospitality-based mission has removed a lot of the veil on my own character (and those with us). It keeps a laser focus on whether we really trust God, listen to his voice, and are dependent on his grace. So many other organizational opportunities and hurdles were distractions to the simplicity of life with God and his family.

Yet another respondent said, perhaps a little tongue-in-cheek, "I have seen God provide over and over and am 'forced' to give Him credit. With a larger budget I might think I played a bigger part than I did." Each of these quotes represents the general spiritual formation that occurred because of participants' pursuit of bivocational ministry.

Growth in Humility and Dependence

Humility and dependence on God and on others are specific forms of spiritual growth commonly produced in those who pursue bivocational ministry. Of the bivocational ministers surveyed, 80% responded that their humility was greatly or somewhat enhanced by being bivocational; only 5% said their humility had been "somewhat hindered." Since increased humility, in part, leads to increased dependence on God and others, it is worth noting that over 75% of participants said that bivocational ministry has greatly or somewhat enhanced their dependence on others, while a full 90% indicated that bivocational ministry has greatly or somewhat enhanced their dependence on God. No participant said their dependence on God was hindered by bivocational ministry. One participant explained his answer, saying that bivocational ministry "makes me realize that I have limited capability and that I am not my church's savior. He [Jesus] is!" Another confessed, "This really comes back to the struggle I have with viewing myself in a healthy way when I'm in ministry full-time. Working another job allows me another context to simply be with Jesus, follow Jesus and live on mission with Jesus."

Deepened Need for a Team

Further explanations by many participants showed their growth in personal humility and dependence accompanied another area of spiritual growth: accepting personal limits and thus trusting and equipping a team to pursue mission and ministry together. As difficult as these things may be, participants viewed both as signs of God's work in their lives. Considering their own capacity for humility and dependence, 88% of survey participants noted that bivocational ministry has greatly or somewhat enhanced their view of "realizing personal limits," and that 80% said that bivocational ministry has greatly or somewhat enhanced their view of "accepting personal limits."[3] Nevertheless, some of the highest percentages of the survey came from questions regarding ministry with others: 85% of participants indicated that bivocational ministry had somewhat or greatly enhanced their view of "embracing others' giftings"; 90% said bivocational ministry has somewhat or greatly enhanced their view of "activating 'the priesthood of all believers'," and 95% of participants said bivocational ministry has somewhat or greatly enhanced their view of "ministry as a team."[4]

Perhaps as a natural overflow of ministers' personal growth in dependence and humility, respondents reported that bivocational ministry nearly always deepened their need for a team to minister with them. Three respondents summarized their view of teamwork. One said, "having a full-time job outside of the church has made me understand the importance of 'equipping the saints for the work of ministry.' With a bivo ministry philosophy, everyone gets to play . . ." Another wrote,

> The ONLY way bivocational works for a lead pastor is if he is able to raise up other leaders and trust God to use them. It has forced me to avoid having the 'CEO pastor' mindset and embrace having a strong leadership team. It's helped to highlight the importance of the congregation's role in ministry.

Still another said, "I am cognizant of the fact that there is absolutely no way we can reach our city and mobilize laborers to the nations with Jesus without being part of a multi-functional team." And the vital nature of a team is perhaps perfectly captured by this respondent: "Empowering others to use their gifts is a must. Delegation and discipleship are your friends." Humility, dependence, sharing work, and activating others' giftings were all common elements of spiritual growth revealed in the survey.

Growth in Sanctification

While humility and trusting a team are signs of spiritual growth, many participants also saw bivocational ministry as a venue by which they became more holy. Multiple answers in the survey pointed to this theme of sanctification. Survey participants were asked, "What are specific ways that your personal sanctification has been enhanced by your involvement in bivocational ministry?" Respondents explained many ways that they had seen themselves becoming more holy and credited bivocational ministry as a means of that growth.

Many said bivocational ministry helped grow their awareness of God in everyday life outside of the church, with implications for their own daily lives. One said,

> I have become more aware of the hand of the Creator around me—in the workplace, my neighborhood, etc. The importance of walking out the faith in daily life has become more and more real as I have to push into Jesus in order to deal with the stress of life. There is no separation of "holy" and "unholy", "sacred" and "secular." It is just life and him around me.

Another echoed,

> It has introduced me to incarnational living, which strengthens my dependence on Jesus and leads me to pursue his likeness. Being with people who are either marginal followers of Jesus or not at all on a consistent basis makes me more conscious of his presence with me and his work through me.

Others listed many areas of life that have been refined because of their involvement in bivocational ministry. One participant said, "My personal growth in Christ likeness is directly linked to my ability to merge worship as a lifestyle, life together in community, and mission and service for the sake of Jesus and good of the world," while another answered with a list of areas of growth: "Work ethic. Marriage. Parenting. Friendships. Money. Purpose. Identity. All these things have been refined by the fire of bivocational ministry in a way that is clarifying because none of them can be overshadowed by 'success'."

Still others said they found that bivocational ministry enlarged their view of God and Jesus, while concurrently giving a more accurate view of themselves and their abilities. Many shared the implications of that view for ministry. "It's helped me to realize that the sacrifices I've made in being bivocational are nothing compared to what Jesus has done for me. It's shown me that I am not sufficient, but he is," said one. Another referenced one of Jesus's miracles, saying, "I feel like I don't even have five loaves and two fish. But with the few resources I have, I realize more and more that God can multiply them." As a bivocational minister myself, I certainly concur. I cannot be 100% of what my church needs! Only Jesus can be that.

Hindrances

The survey also revealed a few hindrances to spiritual growth. In addition to asking about ways personal sanctification has been enhanced by bivocational ministry, the survey also asked, "What are specific ways that your personal sanctification has been hindered by your involvement in bivocational ministry?" Only 15% of participants shared a response to this question, and every one of them mentioned time and energy. Capturing the heart of these responses, one participant said, "Time is definitely an issue as it is easy to get overbooked. I have to be careful not to plan too many things within a week or to dream too big as my family and my soul cannot handle it. Slow and steady are words that have grown on me as well as patience and humility." Another explained how time and energy relate to his inner life: "Time management, performance pressures, and responsibilities becoming too much have at times hindered sanctification simply because I have gone through seasons in which I didn't handle [these] well and might have been 'performing' but without joy [and] without trust, burning myself out." Another response simply stated, "I am often envious of full time ministers and the flexibility of their schedules." However, 85% of participants in the survey did not share any areas in which bivocational ministry hindered their personal sanctification. Rather, the overwhelming majority indicated that, because of their bivocational ministry, their own dependence and humility grew, their own need for a team deepened, and their own personal sanctification increased.

Reflections on Spiritual Growth

An overwhelming majority of survey respondents greatly valued the areas of personal spiritual growth they experienced because of their involvement in bivocational ministry, notwithstanding the pressures of time and energy required. But most did not expect such outcomes as they first pursued bivocational ministry. It is common, even expected in most Christian traditions, that ministers are used by God to enliven biblical truths in the hearts and minds of their congregations. Ministry is generally thought to enhance the growth of others. But, as this survey revealed, God often uses bivocational ministry to enliven biblical truths in the hearts and minds of bivocational ministers themselves, regardless of their motive for pursuing this unique calling.

While most entered bivocational ministry for financial, missional, and convictional reasons, many survey participants found themselves drawn closer to God through bivocational ministry, promoting the minister's own spiritual growth. One bivocational minister summarized this theme beautifully:

> Bivocational ministry increases my sensitivity to the mission of God and what the Spirit is doing to pursue people far from Jesus. This has a forming effect on me spiritually because it heightens my desire to draw near to God and walk with him as I find myself in need of his guidance as I pursue gospel opportunities. In addition, it forms me emotionally because it puts me in situations to slow down, listen carefully to and empathize with people.

Another explained the freedom in Christ he feels by being bivocational:

> I feel far less pressure than when I was a senior pastor, I'm having way more fun, ministry is still challenging, but more natural. My position/title as pastor was at times a hindrance to normal relationships with some people. It's relieving to be accepted as just another person.

Still another minister saw bivocational ministry as a test of his calling: "Bivocational ministry, above all, has deepened my commitment to pastoral ministry. It's made me consider whether or not being a pastor was what I was really being called to do simply because of how easy it would be to quit." Bivocational ministry also helps ministers live for God in everyday life: "My Christlikeness isn't restricted to a sacred space but is formed in very secular places as I choose to respond to the spirit," and "it's taught me to integrate faith into all of life, as we ask our people to do." But the overarching reminder for the heart of every bivocational minister is that "the work of God doesn't rise and fall, nor is it dependent on me."

These responses resonate with my own experience in twenty years of being bivocational. I have long known that I am gifted in a few areas of ministry—and very "un-gifted" in many others. Bivocational ministry has thus helped produce humility in me, which has in turn led to my need for a diversely gifted team to minister alongside. With everyone thriving in their gifting and helping to shape a local church in their gifts and from multiple perspectives, the church's ministry is more holistic and stronger. Together, our team points our congregation to Jesus, rather than shaping them into the image of "me." (As it should for any self-reflective minister—the alternative makes me shudder!)

Conclusion

My own experience in bivocational ministry and working with other bivocational ministers in various contexts led me to anticipate the major findings of this research: that the outcomes of bivocational ministry are more personal and spiritual than the initial motives for pursuing them and that bivocational ministry is often an unexpected path of spiritual growth for the bivocational minister. I was not surprised to learn that this dynamic was common among bivocational ministers. The surprising element of the survey was how common the pattern was: nearly every minister surveyed entered bivocational ministry for one or multiple reasons, hardly any of those reasons related to their personal spiritual growth, and nearly every minister shared personal spiritual growth as an outcome of this unique form of ministry.

There are many benefits to bivocational ministry and many motives for pursuing such a path. Some of these relate to finance, mission and ministry philosophy, and theological conviction. But in God's grace, God often has more in store for bivocational ministers than they know when they start that journey. There is often an outcome that matters far more to the life of the minister than even the best surprise ending to a movie or the thrill of a roller coaster. The Apostle Paul, in his letter to the Church at Rome, made the bold claim, "everything comes from him and exists by his power and is intended for his glory" (Rom 11:36a). "Everything" necessarily includes bivocational ministry. Bivocational ministry exists for the same reason "everything" exists: "for [God's] glory . . . forever! Amen" (Rom. 11:36). In addition to other ways bivocational ministry glorifies God, it is a pathway to unexpected spiritual growth in the lives of those who pursue it. It is that spiritual growth, produced by this form of ministry, that leads me to close this chapter with the words of two survey respondents: "I went bi-vo mostly out of necessity, but would never go back to anything different," and "I recommend it to every pastor."

Endnotes

1 The survey instrument is available online: *benconnelly.com/bivoandbeyond-chapter-survey.*

2 All quotations from survey participants are used with permission.

3 Concurrently, 10% of respondents said bivocational ministry has "neither hindered nor enhanced" their view of "realizing personal limits," while 18% said it has "neither hindered nor enhanced" their view of "accepting personal limits." At the same time, 3% of participants said bivocational ministry has "somewhat hindered" both their realizing and also their accepting personal limits.

4 Only 5% to 15% of respondents expressed that bivocational ministry has "neither hindered nor enhanced" their need for others' giftings or teamwork, and none stated that their view of others' giftings or teamwork has been hindered by bivocational ministry.

CHAPTER 11

The Bivocational Congregation

ANTHONY PAPPAS, ED PEASE, AND NORM FARAMELLI

Editor's note: What is the shape of tomorrow's church? The authors of this chapter answered this question in 2009 by describing an array of bivocational congregations. They presented five case studies illustrating a variety of ways that churches faced mounting pressures to adapt to declining membership in North America. Their prescient analysis remains timely and relevant and is still valuable for teaching and learning. The names and locations of the congregations have been de-identified in this adaptation of the text.[1] The authors pose several questions for discussion at the end of this chapter. Additionally, Ed Pease provides a new epilogue on how to prepare a congregation for bivocational ministry.

Any garden-variety atheist, agnostic, or even religiously indifferent materialist knows that if—and we do mean *if*—the church is to survive well into the future in the northern hemisphere, it will not be through a linear extension of today's church. (The only ones who do not seem to realize this are pastors, seminarians, and some denominational people!) Every index of the church as it has been indicates a decline, and many indicate a precipitous decline. So, what might tomorrow's different church look like? What should we call it? And what are its qualities?

We believe the bivocational congregation offers a viable model for tomorrow's church. We begin with the initial premise that a bivocational congregation is a local church that operates upon (and may even self-consciously understand) two callings: the first is the calling of function and the second is the calling of mission. We believe the bivocational congregation is more likely to survive into tomorrow to do God's will and be God's people because it is essentially organized around spiritual realities in tune with God's redemptive work. These include:

- healthy team functioning
- a high commitment to place and to being a ministering presence in that place
- a willingness to die to self, if need be, in the cause of serving others
- an acceptance of this expression of the church as a full expression of the church, not a second-rate, temporary, expedient form of the church
- a willingness to experiment and trust that a higher power has something wonderful in store for tomorrow

The following five cases help to illustrate these qualities of bivocational congregations as they exist in very different churches.

Case 1: The Always-Been Bivocational Congregation

Fellowship is a small Baptist church in southern New England that recently celebrated its 175th anniversary. The two to three dozen people that gather on Sunday mornings know each other well, and each of them has a role to play that helps keep the church going. A shopkeeper is their pastor, a schoolteacher their treasurer, and a retired woman their clerk.

This congregation needs someone to fill the pastoral role—a very strictly defined role of preaching and pastoral care. Otherwise, the people expect to work together to accomplish whatever needs doing. "The pastor preaches and guides us, but he doesn't really have to do much else," they told us. "We know what needs to get done and we each pitch in and do it. If something out of the ordinary arises, we huddle up and figure out how to handle it."

The members' relationships with one another have morphed over the years so that they exhibit a high degree of complementarity. They function as a team. People know what motivates their fellow members and for the most part they stay out of each other's way. Realizing that energy is limited, they do not waste much time on turf battles. New members are incorporated slowly into this dynamic organism. Giftedness and interest are discerned over time and offered and used for the common good. Occasionally something may happen that galvanizes the congregation around a new opportunity or threat, but usually business as usual prevails. The members are "not anxious about tomorrow." They are comfortable living out the mutually determined roles that are so familiar to them as to hardly need conscious definition. This semi-aware team functioning may not respond well to a rapidly changing environment, but, since it has a nearly two-centuries-long life, that fact is seldom brought to mind. This bivocational congregation functions as a simple organism. Each part has a role to play. The pastor is important but not crucial. In fact, this type of congregation can keep on going for long periods of time without a pastor, if need be.

Recently we had conversations with two people from different congregations. Each of their churches has a full-time pastor and each is considering closing! Why? Fatigue. "We're just too tired to do everything," one explained. In contrast, Fellowship, despite not having a full-time pastor, has members who have developed focus and complementarity. They know what needs to be done (and what does not) and who is going to do it (and who is not). Yes, their ministry is basic and not extensive. But they own it, they do it, and they will keep on doing it indefinitely. And maybe that is enough.

Case 2: The Rooted-Here Bivocational Church

Savior Church is in a blue-collar section of urban Boston that the majority of the residents have made their permanent home. Most can tell you where their best friends in elementary school lived—and often where they live now—and whose mother always sets an extra place for you for dinner.

Savior Church combines two different denominational heritages in addition to at least two other neighborhood churches and their members who have been subsumed into it over the preceding half-century. Its ecumenical spirit is even greater now, as Roman Catholics, shut out of their old sanctuary just around the corner, are finding their way into Savior. Their bishop intended for them to move into a Roman Catholic parish nearby, but that parish just does not seem like home to them. Instead, they have found a home at Savior, which has existed for over a century to minister to the people of its neighborhood.

Savior is an example of what happens when a congregation is truly bivocational. When, after a successful 20-year part-time ministry, Savior's pastor left for a university position, the congregation began a search process for a new pastor. Their goal was clear: they desired a clergy companion for a bivocational ministry. There were no illusions about getting a replica of their outgoing pastor nor about switching to a full-time pastor. They sought someone who could serve as pastor and who was as committed to bivocational ministry in this place as they were. That meant having local roots and being committed to doing outreach to the local community.

This bivocational congregation has a ministry not only to its own members but also to its community. They understand the need for a presence in the local setting—a presence from which outreach programs can flow. Since their pastor's departure, Savior received a denominational award for exemplary work in operating a successful food pantry. The commitment of Savior to the community was also seen when, upon the closing of the local Roman Catholic parish church, Savior immediately extended an invitation to continue the work of its branch of the Society of St. Vincent de Paul—an outreach program. Today, the St. Vincent group operates from Savior's facilities. Although they could have relocated to another Roman Catholic parish, they, like the members of Savior, understood the need to stay in the neighborhood where they had been serving.

Members of Savior told us that, even if they had the funds available for a full-time pastor, they would use those funds in other ways, especially for community outreach. The congregation understands the need for roots in its community, and it also understands that the concept of bivocational ministry is not just a clergy thing—that it needs to be embedded in the minds and hearts of all the members.

This bivocational congregation was missional long before the term came into vogue. They know that their internal life and health depend on their external service. Churches in their neighborhood that didn't understand this have long since closed. Savior lives incarnational ministry right there in their neighborhood, and, consequently it, too, lives.

Case 3: The Transitional Bivocational Congregation

In Massachusetts, on a residential street near a large university, is Founder's Church, which emerged from the closing of three churches in the 1960s. Today, Founder's Church is in the midst of what it calls its Five-Year Holy Experiment, which involves two congregations working together in the same building. One is a small congregation of English descent and the other is a new, large, and growing congregation primarily of Korean heritage. The English congregation of Founder's Church is bivocational, with a call to live its own life as a congregation, yet also with a call to house and nourish the Korean congregation.

Founder's Church Council, made up of five members from each congregation, meets monthly. Church committees also comprise members from each congregation. The treasurer of the church was appointed from the Korean congregation—a move supported by the English congregation. The budget for the church is supported by both congregations, with some help from the regional judicatory. Lay leaders in the English congregation monitor telephone messages and follow up as needed—for both congregations. They also lead a weekly Bible study session open to all. One Sunday a month both congregations worship together.

The church has a paid staff, including two paid clergy. One is a Korean-speaking man who works with the Korean congregation full-time. The other is a woman who works with the English congregation

20 hours per week. The two pastors see themselves as sharing worship and preaching responsibilities.

The two congregations also share a custodian, and one church member is a choir director who supervises a full music program and leads a choir largely composed of Koreans, many of them students. The choir performs primarily for the Korean congregation but also for the English congregation on special occasions.

The English congregation is concerned about its continuing decline in numbers, but its overall attitude is one of joyful celebration for the blessings of the present and the unknown but promising future of this vibrant parish venture. Where will they end up? God only knows, but this transitional bivocational congregation is enjoying the ride!

Founder's Church is ready to die to self—the worship style they are accustomed to, their identification with "our" pastor and building, indeed their whole self, if need be—to see that ministry to their community continues. Unlike so many other congregations that ensure their death by holding on tightly to life as they have known it, Founder's Church will live on—possibly in resurrected form and speaking Korean! They understand that letting go of "what has been" is the only way to see what will be.

Case 4: An Experimental Bivocational Congregation

Five small, centuries-old congregations sit sprinkled around the Connecticut River valley. A few decades ago, each struggled to make ends meet, to maintain its high-maintenance building, to keep its Sunday school staffed, and to manage with a part-time rector. Then along came a rector who introduced to them to a concept he called "clustering," an arrangement in which certain functions are collectively managed by a board comprising members from the different churches in the cluster. He had heard of such arrangements in Nevada and had developed one in northern Vermont. He was convinced of the efficacy of clustering. He had charts and reports to show that clustered congregations were better off and did more mission than isolated, atomized, suffering-in-silence parishes. One by one, the five congregations agreed to cluster.

Under the cluster arrangement, each parish maintains its own building and vestry. Each votes its own budget and raises its own funds. Each may have its own ministry in its own community. And each sends representatives to the cluster board. There, such synergies as common missions, Christian education, music, and social activities may be developed. But the critical task of the cluster board is to develop and execute a plan for a staff of professional leaders. Typically, this is done by assessing the needs and desires of the constituent parishes and, within the various parish contributions to the cluster budget, call and deploy an array of leaders. Clergy coverage for the worship of each parish is arranged on a rotating basis. Other staff members contribute from their skills and calling as the cluster board determines best. What this means in practice is that any one parish has access to a wider array of skills than it could afford on its own. But it also means that their pastor is a functionary, rotating in and out of their pulpit every eight weeks or so, according to a set schedule. So, parishioners do not develop the same kind of dependence on their pastor that they might otherwise.

Although potentials are always variously attained, clusters offer the potential for parishioners to develop the kind of ownership and commitment that occurs in what we are calling the bivocational congregation. Clusters call forth the lay leadership of the congregation. Clusters clearly say: "The responsibility is yours. The rector will assist you in achieving your call, but he or she is not going to do for you what is yours to do. You are the permanent part of this equation."

That is both freeing and challenging. Clusters are hard to sustain over time. In fact, this one is currently in the process of breaking up—but after 27 years! Cluster boards must keep working constructively together while being pulled in various local directions. Another layer of organization is added, and some may mourn the lack of a priest they can call their own. But clusters also allow congregations to mature in vibrancy and self-direction if they are willing to accept a new role for pastoral leadership. This is not always easy. As one weary vestry member notes, "The cluster fosters independence. [The clergy] were able to keep their distance and let the lay people do the work. We found and are still finding it hard to balance doing the deeds of Christ and learning the Mind of Christ and sharing the love of Christ and still have a family and a job." Even so, she concludes, "the premise of the cluster model is a very good one."

Clusters are one experimental form that aligns with this emerging concept of the bivocational congregation. Undoubtedly others will become visible now that we know what we are looking for.

Clustering invites lay ownership of the ministry. Yet there are dangers inherent in this model, which tantalizes the laity with the ability of more professional resources, inviting more extensive ministries, and—due to the additional time and energy necessary to manage such ministries—eventually resulting in more fatigue. Clearly this model will not work everywhere, nor forever. But for churches willing to define their ministry and focus, it offers hope.

Case 5: The We-Backed-Into-It-and-We-Want-Out-of-It Bivocational Congregation

Unless the concept of bivocational ministry is firmly rooted in the minds and hearts of the congregation, it can fall apart when the pastor leaves. St. Luke's is such a church.

St. Luke's was originally organized in 1893 as a mission. It provided worship, fellowship, and settlement help to the town's small population of English-speaking immigrants, most of whom had moved from the British Isles and the Canadian Maritime Provinces to work in the town's mills. In 2002, after serving for 119 years as a mission, the congregation finally attained the status of parish. However, despite growth in the town and, to a lesser extent, in the size of the congregation, in recent decades St. Luke's has not been able to afford a full-time priest. As a result, it has been served by a succession of bivocational pastors.

Today the congregation continues its original mission of worship, fellowship, and help, and it has turned outward to provide the same opportunities to people in the area who are not members of the congregation.

Strong lay leadership has emerged to maintain and expand the ministry of the congregation. The Sunday school, youth ministry, routine pastoral care, and outreach efforts are organized by members of the congregation. One person has organized a weekly women's spirituality group. It has grown over time to include a number of people living in the community who would not consider themselves members of the congregation. The pastor orders the worship services, presides over the parish vestry, gives encouragement and counsel to the lay volunteers, and makes emergency calls on parishioners.

After their last "permanent" part-time pastor of seven years retired, the congregation struggled to find a successor. In the course of searching for three years, the vestry decided to use the congregation's small endowment to seek a full-time pastor. They hope to be able to support this person at full time for three years, during which time the congregation may grow sufficiently to be self-supporting. If not, they will have exhausted their financial reserves, failed at growing, and possibly become terminally discouraged. Though the laity have taken on significant and fruitful responsibilities in mission and in the life of their church, this church seems to have been simply a congregation with a bivocational pastor rather than a bivocational congregation.

This example, replicated so very often, is not a particularly hopeful one, barring a miracle. The desires deeply rooted in the hearts of the parishioners for their own full-time pastor, to be a "legitimate" church, and to have someone to define and do ministry represent a model of doing church that is unlikely to lead us very far into the future. Spending broke in that quest will not be as productive as learning the lessons God desires to teach us in order to move into a new future.

Embodiments of Change

Each of the first four of these examples lifts up qualities of faithful congregations that may presage the characteristics of the church in the future. Fellowship illustrates the power of focus and complementarity of functions. Savior is an example of presence, rootedness, and the primacy of mission. Founder's Church embodies the willingness to take risks and even die to self, if need be. The cluster model demonstrates a willingness to experiment and take responsibility for one's congregation. And St. Luke's teaches us of the danger of giving in to the constant temptation to slip back into old patterns.

Does a congregation need to have a bivocational pastor to exhibit the positive qualities of a bivocational congregation? We think that, though it may help, it is not necessary. What makes a congregation bivocational and more likely to thrive into the future is the dual calling of the congregation to fresh understandings of mission and function—mission that is rooted locally, focused, and so primary that the church is willing to risk self in the cause, and functioning that is responsible, complementary, experimental, and not pastor-dependent but lay-owned. Such a church, we believe, will warm God's heart and serve its neighbors for years to come.

Questions for Reflection

- Which case comes closest to describing the character of your congregation?
- Under what circumstances would your congregation consider becoming a "bivocational congregation" as distinct from offering a bivocational-level clergy salary package?
- Would your congregation ever consider engaging a bivocational pastor to work in a bivocational setting?
- How might your congregation develop the qualities identified in this chapter?

Epilogue

BY ED PEASE

How can the congregation prepare for bivocational ministry? My conviction that congregations benefit enormously by increasing their understanding and commitment to bivocational ministry has grown over the years because of my experiences of working in them. Reflecting on those experiences, I have learned a few lessons about preparing the congregation for bivocational ministry. My definition of bivocational ministry is a sharing among pastor and participants in the congregation of ministries that traditionally were done only by the pastor. Whether a congregation is about to make a fresh start on a new phase of its life or could benefit from a refreshing change of pace in one or more areas of ministry, I believe that two steps will be useful: forming a leadership team and initiating a project.

The first step is to form a leadership team for bivocational ministry. If the team is not identical to the parish council or vestry, it should report to them. The team would include volunteers from the congregation, the pastor, other paid members of the staff, and, of course, God, who is present and should have a voice in the deliberations. That is why, when the team meets together by Zoom or in person, the first order of business really must be a time of Bible study and prayer.

The team should then engage in ongoing discussion to understand the emotional and spiritual condition of the congregation. Many congregations have been badly damaged by the decline in membership that has been taking place since the mid-1960s (see Wright, chapter 3 in this volume). Remaining congregants may be exhausted from still trying to do the things they used to do in the days when the congregation was growing. One of the differences between then and now is that there are far fewer people to do the work and provide financial support. In the decades immediately after World War II, congregations would call one or more pastors to do all the pastoral care while the people of the congregation made sure that the buildings were in repair, that there was enough food made for every spaghetti dinner, and that there were enough dollars coming in to cover all the costs. Decline can be traumatic, and members may be numb from the experience.

The next task for the team is to survey the current needs of the congregation, seeing to it that as many as possible are being met, particularly those that require immediate attention. The congregation should be informed via newsletter or email of every action of the team, preserving the privacy of individuals as appropriate. In starting a bivocational ministry team, it should always be made clear that the ongoing needs of the parish are, and will continue to be, met. Maintaining trust in the running of the parish is most important.

When everything is running as smoothly as possible, the leadership team can then turn its attention to discerning a project in bivocational ministry. A study of the texts of the temptations of Jesus after fasting in the wilderness can be helpful for discerning a project in vocational ministry (Matt. 4:1–11; Luke 4:1–13). What does God want the church to be like? A Baptist minister in Bellingham, Massachusetts, frequently told our ecumenical clergy Bible study group, "Remember, God has a bigger stake in this than we do." The team could use these texts in its Bible study time for meetings while the congregation could hear sermons on the same texts. If the congregation has experienced a significant level of trauma, an additional approach might be appropriate.

In the past ten years or more, scholars have increasingly developed a theological understanding of trauma. *Spirit and Trauma*, by Shelly Rambo of the Boston University School of Theology, is a great example of these writings (2010). The book is about what happened in Jesus's tomb between Good Friday and Easter Day. How was Jesus resurrected? In a moving description of the events of the Resurrection, Rambo described the love poured out on the cross from Jesus and toward Jesus. In the tomb, Jesus was brought back to life through the Holy Spirit. Jesus descended into hell. On Easter morning, Jesus rose from the dead, but that was only the beginning. The women who stayed at the grave became the first witnesses and provided the first sign that there was more to the Resurrection. They did not recognize Jesus at first because he did not look like they expected. When they did recognize him, their tales of witness went out among people and continued to spread so that, on Pentecost—the fiftieth day from Easter—the church itself burst into existence. Pentecost—the birthday of the church—is part of the Resurrection.

Those who have remained active in the church throughout this current decline are like the women at the tomb. They are the first witnesses that the church that existed in the 1950s and 60s is now rising from death. This resurrected church will come in a form that no one has fully imagined—and many may not recognize, with a strength that no one has anticipated. This resurrection includes the clergy and the people of the church—the body of Christ. Bivocational ministries are among the most important events of the unfolding resurrection. Bivocational ministry builds on the Reformation concept of the priesthood of all believers—that all who are followers of Jesus are called to ministry, including but not limited to the ordained. Biblical studies among the team members and preaching of the Crucifixion and Resurrection, the Resurrection appearances of Jesus, the Ascension, and the Day of Pentecost are important at the beginning of a new bivocational ministry.

The second step involves starting a project in bivocational ministry. When the team members are ready to begin an activity, they should ask for volunteers to help in the chosen area. One of the most successful introductions to bivocational ministry I have seen took place when a consultant was engaged to gather and train volunteers from the congregation for the ministry of pastoral care in partnership with the clergy. The pastor alone could not do all the work of pastoral care in the parish. Volunteers generously made themselves available. Working with the consultant, the volunteers devised a method of communicating with the parish office and with the pastor. One person assumed the role of dispatcher. The pastoral care visitors called on people in their homes, in nursing homes, and hospitals. Volunteers asked the pastor to step into situations of the greatest need for care. In addition, they consulted privately with the pastor about the visits that they had been making. The volunteers and the pastor met together occasionally to talk about how the ministry of pastoral care was going among them. Over time, the volunteer pastoral visitors became acceptable to the other parishioners.

It is important that the people doing the bivocational ministry of pastoral care be visible to the congregation. It is easier for people to understand what bivocational ministry is when seeing the people involved in this work. The first chosen activity of bivocational ministry may not be the one described above—assisting in pastoral care. Whatever project is chosen will go a long way in the preparation of a congregation for more bivocational ministry.

A congregation usually does not go from zero to full speed ahead in bivocational ministry overnight. It is important for the pastor and the leaders to begin with one activity and then go on from there. It might take a year or more for one bivocational ministry project to be in place before any other projects are undertaken. Sometimes the original plan may not work, and a new one will have to be substituted. The pastor and leadership team should hear from people how they see things are going and be guided by listening to advice from as many as possible. Over time, an understanding of the possibilities of bivocational ministry will develop in the congregation, and a rich sense of God's activity in the life of the congregation will grow.

Works Cited

Pappas, Anthony G., Ed Pease, and Norm Faramelli. 2009. "The Bivocational Congregation: Tomorrow's Church?" *Congregations* 35: 11–15.

Rambo, Shelly. 2010. *Spirit and Trauma: A Theology of Remaining.* Louisville, KY: Westminster John Knox.

Notes

1 Adapted and reprinted with permission from Alban at Duke Divinity School. Pappas, Pease, and Faramelli (2009).

CHAPTER 12

Bivocational Ministry and the Mentoring Relationship

HERBERT FAIN

The writer acknowledges the invaluable contribution of Kimberly Fain, JD, PhD, Texas Southern University.

The Apostle Paul provides a model for the bivocational, mentor-mentee relationship. Working as a tentmaker, Paul mentored Timothy and Titus in the faith and in ministry. Shadowing Paul, both had the opportunity to observe their mentor, imitate his zeal for ministry, and assume delegated tasks. By observing, imitating, and assuming authority, Paul's mentees were prepared to assume leadership upon his death. Following the Apostle's spiritual model, this chapter presents shadowing as a type of mentoring methodology in which bivocational pastors permit protégés to accompany them in ministry.

Shadowing is a strategy for a mentee to imitate their mentor's service to the church. To communicate the meaning of mentoring, this chapter adapts Walter Brueggemann's (2018, 7) definition: "mentoring is a relationship between someone of an older generation with more experience providing guidance and counsel for someone in a younger generation." Although the concept of mentoring is modern, "The practice of mentoring, however, is quite old." Jack Wellman (2020) argued for its contemporary relevance: "Every older Christian man and woman should be mentoring someone because they have so much to offer a younger believer in the faith, chiefly, their experience." Nevertheless, it is important to mention that mentoring is not age-dependent. A mentor does not need to be older to provide guidance. Instead, the mentor should possess faith and more experience than their mentee. When a mentor shares their expertise, a mentee experiences how Christians should behave in both public and private spaces. Mentoring is a significant part of growing the faith—a practice in which every Christian should participate.

Mentoring offers an opportunity for a bivocational minister to share their faith and experience with another person. For the purposes of this chapter, "the term bivocational describes the work life of a pastor (paid or unpaid) who also holds another job (paid or unpaid)" (Stephens, chapter 1 of this volume). Some ministers may have multiple jobs. Thus, the term *multivocational* may be more appropriately suited. This author will use the term *bivocational* to encompass both. Yet bivocational ministers face challenges in terms of time management, perhaps wondering how to balance mentoring with the leadership demands of their church work and another job. Is it any wonder that, although mentoring is "more important than ever," it is "a dying art in the church" (Wellman 2020)? Despite money or time constraints, bivocational ministers should take advantage of the opportunity to train the next generation of leaders. Bivocational ministers have an opportunity to spread the word of God and grow the church by engaging in a mentor-mentee relationship.

This chapter contributes to leadership studies by showing how Paul's spiritual model offers a methodology for shadowing that is mutually beneficial, providing leadership opportunities for both the mentor and mentee. The shadowing methodology of mentoring is rooted in the Hebrew apprenticeship process, illustrated in the New Testament and adapted in a contemporary way by many popular leadership authors. This chapter begins with a discussion of the methodology of shadowing as a specific form of apprenticeship, requiring modeling and imitation. This is followed by a discussion of Paul and his protégés, Timothy and Titus, drawing primarily on David L. Bartlett's article, "Mentoring in the New Testament," and

Andreas Köstenberger's article, "Paul the Mentor." The discussion of shadowing continues with Kenley D. Hall's "The Critical Role of Mentoring for Pastoral Formation." Then, Paul's model is brought into conversation with contemporary writers on mentoring, including John C. Maxwell and Harley Atkinson. Finally, mentoring is presented as a call-to-action for the purpose of church growth and development. The chapter concludes with a special call to bivocational pastors to engage in the spiritually enriching practice of mentoring the next generation of leaders.

The Method of Shadowing

Paul's mentoring relationship with Timothy and Titus demonstrates how the shadowing methodology works. To express the meaning of the term shadowing, based on Paul's "relationship to his coworkers," Bartlett (2018, 25) stated that there are "clues to what Christian mentoring might look like in our own time." The mentor begins by explaining the rationale behind an assignment and completing the task while the mentee observes. As the mentor-mentee relationship progresses, each person assumes some duties of the other. During this exchange, the mentor offers guidance, constructive feedback, and praise. After the mentor observes that the mentee is proficient, the mentee is ready to work alone. The shadowing methodology is mutually beneficial for both the mentor and the mentee, with the potential to grow the church.

There are three elements of shadowing exhibited by Paul and his mentees. First, "mutuality and partnership" form the basis of "Paul's relationships" (Bartlett 2018, 25). Thus, mentoring provides a mutual benefit to both the mentor and mentee. Each party feels they have gained valuable insight and experience from the mentoring relationship. Second, "the mentee derives much of his authority from his relationship to Paul." In other words, when the mentee exhibits leadership, they derive their authority from Paul's spiritual model. As a result of Paul's ethical leadership style, the mentee learns how to lead others in a caring and Christian manner. Third, "Mentees imitate the mentor, in both their integrity and their zeal for the gospel and for the churches." Through his enthusiasm for the word of God and zeal for church service, Paul provided a model for his mentees to imitate.

Spiritual leaders, such as Paul, are the foundation for effective mentoring and Christian leadership in contemporary practice.

Even a more formal mentoring relationship, such as apprenticeship, can utilize shadowing methodology to teach mentees. In the *Introduction to Educating Clergy: Teaching Practices and Pastoral Imagination*, William M. Sullivan (2006, 1) wrote that clergy play a significant role in "public as well as private life in America." Sullivan stated that clergy "help individuals and communities interpret and respond to the events of their individual and family lives." Specifically, Sullivan discussed how an apprenticeship is a formal way to mentor. Apprenticeships involve students in activities to further their effort to join the clergy. Sullivan wrote, "Simulations, case studies, field placements, and clinical pastoral education are common in today's seminaries" (7). However, even though a mentee may engage in these activities, it does not mean that the mentor modeled effective behavior. A mentor should have a strategy for offering guidance and counsel. For example, while students are in seminary, they should have access to "the spiritual resources of their religious traditions" and should consistently engage "in the spiritual practices of those traditions" (Foster et al. 2006, 273). However, if modeling is absent from the mentor's instruction of the mentee, the apprenticeship does not include shadowing. In shadowing, the mentee must observe and emulate the mentor's behavior in various settings.

Mentees gain expertise from interacting with the mentor and learning from church activities. Mentees gain valuable lessons from observing pastoral care, sitting in meetings, participating as team members, and completing modest tasks. Impactful mentors communicate the purpose and significance of each task. When pastors give and receive feedback, there is a beneficial exchange of reflection and introspection between both mentor and mentee, contributing to spiritual growth. Thus, mentorship through shadowing can be a mutually rewarding endeavor.

Paul and His Protégés, Timothy and Titus

Paul was a productive bivocational minister who found value in mentoring. The founder of churches and the author of many New Testament books, Paul found time to cultivate these collegial relationships. Although Paul spread "the gospel everywhere he went and planted numerous churches, perhaps his most important contribution was mentoring men such as Timothy and Titus" (Köstenberger 2018, 11). Paul knew how to identify mentees who were spiritually skilled to spread the word of God. For example, he perceived Timothy as "the right person for the job" (Hoehl 2011, 35). Applying Paul's mentoring strategy, contemporary church leaders can "develop followers who are committed, motivated, and personally satisfied by their work." As an effective church leader, Paul knew how to inspire his mentees via service to communities.

Mentees such as Timothy learn how to tend to church followers and confront leadership issues by shadowing their mentor. Through a mentoring relationship, Paul "equip[ped] him for ministerial tasks, empower[ed] him for success, employ[ed] him in a challenging environment to develop effectiveness, and communicate[d] to Timothy the value of their friendship" (Hoehl 2011, 35). After observing and working with Timothy, Paul felt comfortable delegating tasks, motivating, and providing invaluable feedback to him. Paul then assigned Timothy to the community of Christians residing in Ephesus. While working in Ephesus, Timothy addressed issues that plagued the church, such as "removing sinning elders" (Köstenberger 2018, 11). For purposes of leading a church, it is important to have elder members who follow the teachings of Jesus Christ. If elders are conducting themselves in a wayward manner, this is not a positive message for young people in the church. Thus, Paul knew that for the church to succeed, it is important to have elders in leadership who exhibit a Christian lifestyle.

When a mentor engages with his mentee, they should make all expectations clear. Mentees should know the objectives of the assignment and have a complete understanding of their role. In Paul's first letter to Timothy, there is a respectful urgency to his tone (Köstenberger 2018, 11). Paul's language demonstrated his concern in a tactful manner. Since Timothy was aware of his mission, Paul made it clear that his assignment "was to 'command certain people not to teach false doctrines.'" When Paul stated his reasonable expectations for Timothy, Paul demonstrated effective leadership. Paul considered Timothy to be "his 'true son in the faith'" and referred to Timothy in this way because "Timothy genuinely reproduced Paul's own spiritual characteristics, as a biological son would reflect his father's natural characteristics" (12). In other words, Timothy imitated Paul's positive characteristics in the manner that a natural-born son would do. Thus, both Paul and Timothy benefitted from this healthy mentoring relationship because it mirrored a healthy father-son relationship. Since Timothy followed his mentor's guidance with ethical integrity, Paul trusted him to communicate with the church members.

After shadowing their mentor, the mentee is ready to assume control in their mentor's absence. Paul's second and final letter to Timothy made clear his intentions. "Paul's ministry was about to end; after his passing, his legacy would devolve to Timothy and other apostolic delegates such as Titus" (Köstenberger 2018, 13). Since Paul had taught his mentees Timothy and Titus well, he had a positive sense that his legacy would continue. When an effective leader's legacy continues, the church grows and benefits the community it inhabits. As a result, the community is filled with authentic believers equipped to follow the teachings of Christ and grow in the word of God.

Like Timothy, Titus had an important service assignment. Paul assigned Titus to appoint "elders in every city" in Crete (Titus 1:5, NKJV; Köstenberger 2018, 13). At the time, this was a challenging assignment because people worshiped false gods. Knowing these obstacles to church growth, Paul's letter provided encouragement to his mentee. According to Köstenberger (14), "evangelizing the entire island was an ambitious undertaking"; there were false teachers that opposed the authentic teachings of Christ and widespread immoral behavior among the Cretans. False teaching encourages wayward behavior in a culture. If leadership wants their church to grow, it is important to teach the gospel truth to the community. Leading a community in the right direction provides endless possibilities for Christian growth.

When a mentee feels respected and empowered with choices, the importance of shadowing becomes apparent. Although Paul was Titus's mentor, he used language denoting the mutually respectful nature of their relationship. He did the same with Timothy. Mentor leadership requires ethical treatment of the mentee. Thus, when Paul asked Titus to go to Corinth, he made it clear that his mentee was not forced to comply. While it was apparent that Paul was the "senior partner in this relationship," he used terms like "partner" and "co-worker" to emphasize their joint service work (Bartlett 2018, 25). Observation is also an important element of shadowing. Mentees should observe their mentor in meetings. For instance, when Paul met "with the leaders of the Jerusalem church concerning the gospel he preached, he took Titus with him" (Köstenberger 2018, 13). By allowing the mentee to see how to interact and speak with church leadership, the mentee learns how to solve problems when they are not in the presence of their mentors.

Furthermore, Paul and Titus's relationship demonstrates two other elements of shadowing: authority and trust. Even though a minister may be busy, sharing authority with a competent mentee is a way to teach them how to serve a community. Paul's willingness to delegate authority to his mentee, Titus, demonstrates Paul's strength as a leader. Delegating authority to a skilled mentee expresses trust. The willingness to delegate authority also teaches the mentee how to lead. By working with congregations, Titus assumed some of Paul's authority (Bartlett 2018, 25). When Titus spread the word of God and assisted Paul with his duties in Crete and Corinth, he took on some of Paul's authority.

Imitation demonstrates that the mentee sees value in the lessons they are learning from their mentor. When Titus imitated Paul, he did not just go through the motions. Instead, he exhibited the same enthusiasm and spirit that his mentor displayed (Bartlett 2018, 25). Undoubtedly, shadowing Paul benefited Timothy and Titus because they received decades of training. When a mentee is trained over a long period of time, they learn to recover from mistakes and how to make improvements. If a mentee is not given time to learn from their mistakes, they may not be ready to lead. After Paul's faithful training of Timothy and Titus, they knew they "were poised to take the baton their mentor was about to pass to them" (Köstenberger 2018, 14). As Paul reached the end of his life, he could confidently know that "his influence was to continue through the work of his trusted associates whom he had strategically trained over decades of faithful ministry." Like Paul, if a mentor fulfills their spiritual duty to teach mentees, the mentor may feel comfortable knowing that the Lord will bestow them a "crown of righteousness" when the day comes (2 Tim. 4:7–8).

Pastoral Formation through Shadowing

Pastoral formation is rooted in the same principles as shadowing. As an alternative term for shadowing, Kenley D. Hall (2017, 44) offered "pastoral formation," when a mentor prepares young ministers to manage the expectations of ministry. Pastoral formation encourages mentors to shape mentees based on their church culture, not the surrounding secular culture. If a mentor fails to guide a mentee, the new minister "will be shaped by the surrounding ethos and culture." In other words, the belief system of the secular world could negatively impact the new minister—unless they have the guidance of an older minister. In essence, the community benefits from leadership that is reflective of Christian values established by the church.

Understandably, there is an added layer of intimacy when a mentee can experience how ministers live via observation. As previously discussed, Paul and Timothy provide a model of what pastoral formation looks like. Paul invited Timothy to observe him, giving him the opportunity to witness the way Paul engaged in ministry and to "observe how Paul lived" (Hall 2017, 47). According to Hall, observing "how Paul lived" is a "deeper level" of pastoral formation engagement. An effective mentor must invest time, energy, and heart to provide the opportunity for a new minister to observe how to balance both their work life and personal life (48–49). When time, energy, and heart are the basis of pastoral formation, there is a more valuable return on the mentor's spiritual investment. Pastoral formation through shadowing prepares the mentee for the realities of pastoral life, since "the crucial role of mentoring is pertinent to vocational formation in general" (52). Whether a mentor uses the term *pastoral formation* or *shadowing*, both terms have the same meaning and process.

Shadowing in Contemporary Contexts

For shadowing to work in a contemporary context, both the mentor and mentee have duties to fulfill. Impactful mentors delegate tasks and communicate the purpose and significance of each task. Skillful mentees observe the mentor and participate as team members. After completing various tasks or projects, the mentor and mentee should engage in debriefing sessions to evaluate the results. By engaging in a feedback session, the mentor and mentee can determine what was taught and learned. This process is mutually beneficial to both the mentor and the mentee. The mentee builds confidence in their ability to assume increased responsibilities as their leadership skills develop further. As a result, the mentee is in a better position to grow a church because they know how to engage and solve problems with both leadership and followers.

Applying mentoring language to the ancient Hebrew practice of apprenticeship illustrates how to adapt shadowing methodology to a contemporary mentor-mentee relationship. In *Mentoring 101: What Every Leader Needs to Know,* John C. Maxwell (2008, 17) observed that the ancient Hebrews had a tradition of apprenticeship. The purpose of this practice was "built on relationships and common experience." The Hebrew apprenticeship process illustrates how shadowing methodology works. The mentee learns by emulating the behavior of their mentor. The mentor should learn, understand, and perfect the craft. While the mentee observes, the mentor should explain the rationale behind the task. As part of the process of the mentor and mentee swapping roles, the mentee receives consent to assume increased responsibilities, while the mentor remains to provide counsel, constructive feedback, and praise. Once the mentee is proficient, the mentor may allow the mentee to work solo. After the apprentice has worked alongside a mentor, "they master their craft and are able to pass it along to others."

For the mentor-mentee relationship to receive the mutual benefit of growth, the mentor should be a master at their craft. Therefore, when the mentee observes the mentor, they are learning a precise way for completing various tasks. Before the mentor and mentee exchange roles, the mentor should feel comfortable that the mentee is proficient. Thus, prior to assuming authority, the mentee does not have to acquire expertise on the level of the mentor. The mentor should trust that their presence will guide the mentee. As Maxwell (2008, 17) said, the mentor remains "to offer advice, correction, and encouragement." The mentor should not hover and micromanage the mentee. Instead, the mentor's constructive feedback should provide helpful guidance and inspiration. Furthermore, this shadowing methodology builds confidence and independence in the mentee and frees the mentor to accomplish higher tasks. Maxwell asserted that, as soon as the apprentice reaches "that higher level, the teacher is free to move on to higher things." Thus, the mutual benefit of sharing, teaching, learning, and growing is accomplished by the shadowing methodology.

In formal theological education, the opportunity for mentoring is most prominent through field education. By providing guidance on the behavior of effective field education mentors, Harley Atkinson enabled mentors and mentees to visualize how their relationship should manifest itself. After all, the purpose of field education is to provide an understanding of real-life experiences and Christian leadership. Atkinson (2008, 140–1) emphasized the importance of trusted and respected mentors sharing expertise, exhibiting zeal for the ministry, expressing a ministry vision, challenging students to heighten their performance, and protecting students (mentees) from negative outside critique.

The following assertions, summarized from Atkinson (2008), promote understanding of the role of good mentors. First, good mentors refrain from feeling competitive or envious of their mentee. Instead, good mentors enthusiastically share their knowledge, expertise, and skills to inspire the mentee, thus elevating the mentee's performance for a future leadership role. Second, good mentors possess the trust and respect of their peers. If peers lack confidence in a mentor's skills, the mentee may learn habits that stunt learning. Conversely, when peers demonstrate trust and respect for the mentor, the mentee witnesses this and feels confident that they are learning the best way to manage and solve problems. Third, to lead a mentee, a good mentor should exhibit exuberant service and commitment to the ministry. When mentees feel doubtful about their skills or ability to lead, a mentor's positive attitude will provide inspiration for the mentee. Fourth, when a mentor has a vision for the ministry, their goals for growing the church are evident to followers. Furthermore, when the mentor shares their vision, the mentee learns how to identify issues and create a vision for their future leadership in the church.

Fifth, mentees will improve their performance as they gain knowledge and skills and feel inspired by their mentor's leadership vision for the church. In other words, the mentor provides a roadmap for their mentee to adapt to their own purposes as they advance in their leadership journey. Lastly, the importance of protecting mentees from negative interference and criticism is imperative. As previously stated, it is important for constructive feedback to come from the trusted mentor. Why? Because the mentor has trained the mentee, knows the mentee's strengths and weaknesses, and possesses the leadership skills to guide and inspire the mentee. Sometimes outside interference conflicts with the directives of the mentor, and negative criticism may derive from envy. Both interference and criticism from others may erode a mentee's confidence or move them away from the vision provided by the mentor. Thus, it is best to steer unwanted interference and negative intrusion away from the mentee.

A Call to Bivocational Leaders

In a healthy society and a healthy church, senior leaders prepare junior leaders by mentoring them. When mentees shadow mentors, they are shaped and developed by the experiences they encounter. In *The Power of Mentoring: Shaping People Who Will Shape the World*, Martin Sanders (2004, 13) discussed the importance of passing the torch to future leadership. Mentoring "is at the very core of how the next generation of leaders is developed." Sanders noted that "the future health of the church depends upon these mentoring relationships." Without teaching the younger generation how to assume church leadership, the church could suffer from incompetent influences. How do mentors ensure the future well-being of the church? Sanders suggested, "One of the key realities of life and faith is that each generation is required to hand over the reins to the next generation of leaders" (13–14). Sanders reminded his readers that passing the torch from one generation to the next is rooted in Biblical principles: "Moses passed the torch to Joshua" and "Paul passed the torch to Timothy" (14). Since mentoring is a church tradition, bivocational leadership should, without hesitancy, consider this type of service to be a continuation of church growth and development.

As part of this growth and development, the mutually beneficial mentoring process manifests in leaders that will impact the world. Sanders (2004, 16) asserted, "The practice has a long and rich tradition of producing both functional and even world-class masters out of young, emerging apprentices." Since mentoring produces functional and world-class leaders, mentors and mentees should not be surprised if the mentee supersedes the learning of the mentor. Due to the shadowing methodology, a mentee has the potential to learn quickly and surpass their mentor because they have observed good leadership practices. If a mentee is simply instructed on Christian leadership practices, they may not learn as effectively. If the goal of mentoring "is to help the mentoree reach his or her fullest potential," the mentor should refrain from competing or feeling envious of the mentee's increased skills and expertise. After all, the goal of the mentor-mentee relationship is to elevate a person into leadership. As a result, "the mentoring process is not as much about the mentor as it is about the current and future development of the mentoree." Even as mentors benefit by fulfilling God's purpose, experiencing joy, and passing on the torch, mentees benefit by gaining expertise from shadowing that will prepare them for leadership that will grow church and impact the world.

Shadowing methodology teaches mentors and mentees how to have an effective spiritual relationship. Since mentoring is a call-to-action, mentors benefit from guidance on how shadowing works. When mentors understand the significance of modeling leadership, their mentees experience the spiritual benefits of shadowing and feel more prepared to lead. Mentoring is mutually beneficial because the mentee receives the torch from the mentor to continue growing the church. For instance, in the article "Next [Wo]-Man Up: Examining Prophetic Leadership Transition in Moses and Martin Luther King, Jr.," Phillip Allen Jr. (2020) argued that having mentors is important for a healthy leadership transition. Mentoring churches often transition mentees into mentors. For example, a youth pastor may use what they learned from their mentor to counsel a mentee (Stokes and Marler 2015, 82). The mentor-mentee relationship is imperative for growth, spreading the Christian word of God throughout the world. As the church grows, more and more people learn how to live and reach the Kingdom of God.

Bivocational ministers can mentor successfully, despite apparent obstacles such as money and time. There are various ways that a minister may engage with their service. Depending on the resources of a church, a minister may not receive payment for this service. There are also some ministers who contribute to the church by working on a volunteer basis. Furthermore, a minister may receive payment and consider his volunteer work to be vocational in nature. Since a bivocational ministry may consist of a combination of paid and non-paid activities, bivocational status is not determined by payment from ministerial or non-ministerial activities. In addition to monetary concerns, bivocational ministers may struggle with time management and setting priorities. Some individuals may feel they have no extra time to devote to another activity such as mentoring. "At every Bivocational conference" that he has led, Dennis Bickers (2004, 127) reported, attendees "want to know how to find the time to lead the church, work their second jobs, spend time with their families, and have some time for themselves." Bickers suggested that time management helps set priorities. For every bivocational minister, spreading the word of God should be prioritized.

Mentoring deepens life's purpose for the mentor and fulfills the mentor by giving them joy. In *Mentor for Life: Finding Purpose Through Intentional Discipleship,* Natasha Sistrunk Robinson discussed how mentors benefit from the calling of mentoring. Robinson (2016, 27) stated that "mentoring has brought more than a driving purpose to" her life; "It also has ushered in inexpressible joy as" she participates "in the kingdom of God on this earth." This joy reaches beyond the mentor. Robinson explained how trust between mentor and mentee is essential: "Mentoring relationships are intentional, and they are built on the trust and understanding that exists between those who are mentoring and those who are being mentored" (28). Without trust, communication between the mentor and the mentee could falter because the church's mission is not truly understood. Trust and understanding within a mentor-mentee relationship assist in vision building. Beyond trust and understanding between the mentor and mentee, the church also benefits from this relationship. When the mentor engages in this holy and service-related relationship, the mission of God spreads bountifully.

When a bivocational minister accepts the call to mentor, this action not only enhances the well-being of the mentor and mentee but also benefits the community, culture, and world by spreading the Christian message of salvation. Robinson (2016, 28) wrote, "By presenting the kingdom vision and mission of mentoring, I am inviting you to participate in God's mission and purpose to flourish in our lives, in our communities, in our culture, and in the world in which we live." How does it feel to experience heaven on earth? According to Robinson, "By answering the call to discipleship, we have an opportunity to partake in a part of the kingdom of heaven now—because we can experience great joy in living our lives with God's kingdom mission in view." Meaning, when a bivocational minister mentors, they are answering the call to discipleship. Shadowing will assist bivocational ministers with fulfilling this call to discipleship. This call-to-action results in experiencing earthly joy, knowing that the heavenly kingdom is our final resting place.

Conclusion

Bivocational pastors have a spiritual duty to train and prepare the next generation of professionals for church leadership. By engaging in an effective mentor-mentee relationship, both parties mutually benefit from teaching and learning from one another. Apprenticeships are a formal way to mentor in both church spaces and field education. Since apprenticeships are rooted in Biblical principles; they help people understand the mentor-mentee relationship. While not all apprenticeships include shadowing, this author believes that all mentor-mentee relationships should include shadowing.

The shadowing methodology is a specific type of mentor-mentee relationship that depends on both modeling and imitating effective leadership. Shadowing specifically addresses how to engage in an effective mentor-mentee relationship, with implications for leadership studies and field education. Shadowing offers practical guidance for making the mentor-mentee relationship more effective, contributing to the goal of spreading the Word of God and growing the church. Lastly, shadowing helps former mentees become current mentors. Thus, the torch of Christian leadership is passed from one generation to the next.

Works Cited

Allen, Phillip, Jr. 2020. "Next [Wo]-Man Up: Examining Prophetic Leadership Transition in Moses and Martin Luther King, Jr." *Journal of Religious Leadership* 19, no. 2: 28–51. *arl-jrl.org/next-wo-man-up-examining-prophetic-leadership-transition-in-moses-and-martin-luther-king-jr.*

Atkinson, Harley. 2008. "The Mentor Supervisory Meeting: The Heart of Field Education." In *Preparing for Ministry: A Practical Guide to Theological Education*, edited by George M. Hillman Jr., 139–55. Grand Rapids, MI: Kregel.

Bartlett, David L. 2018. "Mentoring in the New Testament." In *Mentoring: Biblical, Theological, and Practical Perspectives*, edited by Dean K. Thompson and D. Cameron Murchison, 23–36. Grand Rapids, MI: Eerdmans.

Bickers, Dennis. 2004. *The Bivocational Pastor: Two Jobs, One Ministry*. Kansas City: Beacon Hill.

Brueggemann, Walter. 2018. "Mentoring in the Old Testament." In *Mentoring: Biblical, Theological, and Practical Perspectives*, edited by Dean K. Thompson and D. Cameron Murchison, 7–22. Grand Rapids, MI: Eerdmans.

Foster, Charles R., Lisa E. Dahill, Lawrence A. Golemon, and Barbara Wang Tolentino. 2006. *Educating Clergy: Teaching Practices and Pastoral Imagination*. San Francisco: Jossey-Bass.

Hall, Kenley D. 2017. "The Critical Role of Mentoring for Pastoral Formation." *Journal of Applied Christian Leadership* 11, no. 1: 42–53. *digitalcommons.andrews.edu/jacl/vol11/iss1/3.*

Hoehl, Stacy E. 2011. "The Mentor Relationship: An Exploration of Paul as Loving Mentor to Timothy and the Application of This Relationship to Contemporary Leadership Challenges." *Journal of Biblical Perspectives in Leadership* 3, no. 2: 32–47. *regent.edu/journal/journal-of-biblical-perspectives-in-leadership/paul-and-timothy.*

Köstenberger, Andreas J. 2018. "Paul the Mentor." *Biblical Illustrator* (Spring): 10–14. *cbs.mbts.edu/wp-content/uploads/2018/02/0318_paul_the_mentor.pdf.*

Maxwell, John C. 2008. *Mentoring 101: What Every Leader Needs To Know*. New York: HarperCollins.

Robinson, Natasha Sistrunk. 2016. *Mentor for Life: Finding Purpose through Intentional Discipleship*. Grand Rapids, MI: Zondervan.

Sanders, Martin. 2004. *The Power of Mentoring: Shaping People Who Will Shape the World*. Chicago: Wing Spread.

Stokes, Charles E., and Penny Long Marler. 2015. "Congregations As 'Multivocal' Mentoring Environments: Comparative Research Among Three Protestant Denominations." *Journal of Religious Leadership* 14, no. 1: 67–104. *arl-jrl.org/wp-content/uploads/2016/02/Stokes-Congregations-as-Multivocal-Mentoring-Environments-2015.pdf.*

Sullivan, William. 2006. "Introduction." In *Educating Clergy: Teaching Practices and Pastoral Imagination*, edited by Charles R. Foster, Lisa E. Dahill, Lawrence A. Golemon, and Barbara Wang Tolentino, 1–16. San Francisco: Jossey-Bass.

Wellman, Jack. 2020. "Why Every Christian Needs a Mentor." *What Christians Want to Know*. November 19. *whatchristianswanttoknow.com/why-every-christian-needs-a-mentor/print.*

Learning

CHAPTER 13

Empowering the Full Body of Christ

KATHLEEN OWENS

As the Apostle Paul traveled across the Mediterranean region in the first century, he sought to help the communities he encountered understand how Jesus had changed the world as they knew it. Jesus's teaching offered a new way of understanding our relationships with one another. The community that Jesus encouraged was based in collaboration, common purpose, and mutual service to one another. Like all great preachers, Paul knew that teaching Jesus's vision of the church community required a good illustration. Hence, Paul presented the image of the church as the Body of Christ, equipped with a variety of gifts for the good of all. This image, which Paul presents in variations through several of his epistles—most clearly in 1 Corinthians, Romans, and Ephesians—continues to guide the church.

The church finds itself in another time of great transition today. The rise of the internet age and the global commerce and connection it enables is changing our political and economic reality. Combined with the experience of the COVID-19 pandemic, the need for new models of local church leadership is unavoidable. While many traditions have long operated with part-time clergy—the gifts of that experience are explored elsewhere in this book—for my own primarily White Presbyterian tradition, like many in the US mainline, the move from a full-time to a part-time pastor is frequently seen as a sign of decline for the congregation. It is often accompanied by a sense of loss and shame in the minds of congregants who have previously supported full-time clergy. These are congregations that have long prided themselves on their well-educated, professional clergy. Their emphasis on the education of clergy also leads to a sense of inadequacy for many members, who feel they do not have the training or knowledge to step into leadership roles. This sense of inadequacy is magnified in the current political climate of disinformation and heightened polarization. I see this dynamic particularly in my own context in the United States, though I know we are not alone in facing this challenge.

When leaders feel they do not have sufficient education, training, or support structures, the experience can be detrimental not only to the leader but also to the congregation. Phyllis Tickle, in her 2008 book, *The Great Emergence*, saw this challenge coming long before some of the most polarizing experiences of the last decade.

The computer, opening up—as it does—the whole of humankind's bank of collective information, enables the priesthood of all believers in ways the Reformation could never have envisioned. It also, however, opens up all that information to anybody, without traditional restraints of vetting or jurying; without the controls of informed, credentialed access; and without the accompaniment or grace of mentoring. It even opens up with equal *élan* the world's bank of disinformation. To the extent that faith can be formed or dissuaded by the contents of the mind as well as those of the heart, then such license has huge implications for the Great Emergence and for what it will decide to do about factuality in a wiki world (Tickle 2008, 107).

In any work that is done to discern the gifts of, educate, or support new leaders within the Body of Christ, we cannot ignore the challenges of establishing authority and fact in the internet age. Providing broader access to our educational resources, spending time in communal discernment, and working to form greater structures for ongoing support and nurture of all our members may be exactly what is needed to maintain our unity as the Body of Christ while celebrating our diversity. Just as the image of the Body of Christ supported previous transformations in the church, this image can guide our understanding of the transformation in leadership needed for the current time.

In just the fifteen years since I graduated from seminary, the changing nature of the church is apparent. The COVID-19 pandemic only escalated the transformation that was already underway. I write as a clergyperson who has served twice as a part-time pastor in a congregation previously served by a full-time pastor. In addition to my pastorates in southern Wisconsin, I also served in leadership roles for my regional Presbytery, covering urban and rural settings, and for the state-wide Wisconsin Council of Churches. As I reflect on the congregations and neighbors I served, I see the need to rethink how we structure our local congregational leadership and how we support those leaders.

In this chapter, I explore how Paul's image of the Body of Christ has informed the church through other times of great transition and the opportunity this image offers for empowering the multitude of gifts in our church membership today. I address the ways in which Paul's image of the Body of Christ has guided the church through great technological and societal shifts, not unlike what we are experiencing now, and how we can build on these experiences to meet the challenges of our time. The image of the church as a multi-gifted, interconnected body is a helpful reminder of the need to educate and support the leadership gifts of the full Body of Christ. A transition from full-time to part-time, or bivocational, pastorates offers an opportunity to utilize the educational resources we already have to empower and equip members with specific gifts for ministry. This exploration then leads to a discussion of new models for empowering the full Body of Christ through discernment of gifts, education and training, and ongoing support of those trained.

Unity and Charism in the Body of Christ

Paul's image of Christian community as the Body of Christ, unified through our diverse gifts, has provided structure for Christian community since the first century. Despite the many interpretations and varieties of ways to understand this metaphor, the image of being united through our varieties of gifts continues to speak to the experience of Christian community. From the first century communities in Corinth, Rome, and Ephesus to current-day international unions and local congregations, we continue to profess that Christ alone is head of the church, that we are connected to one another through our common baptism, and that all who profess faith in Jesus Christ as our Lord and Savior have a calling to serve as his disciples.

In the Body, Christ alone is the head, and all members have gifts to offer. Paul emphasized that every person, every gift, has value, declaring that no part of the body can say to another "I have no need of you" (1 Cor. 12:21, NRSV). He emphasized the dependency of all the various parts of the body on one another:

> For as in one body we have many members, and not all the members have the same function, so we, who are many, are one body in Christ, and individually we are members one of another. We have gifts that differ according to the grace given to us: prophecy, in proportion to faith; ministry, in ministering; the teacher, in teaching; the exhorter, in exhortation; the giver, in generosity; the leader, in diligence; the compassionate, in cheerfulness. (Rom. 12:4–8)

In writing to the Ephesians, Paul also described the ways in which we are called to bear with one another in humility, gentleness, and love as part of the one Body of Christ, united in our baptism (Eph. 4:2–4).

This image of the church as the Body of Christ has informed the church through previous transformations. In the Reformation era, the image of the variety of gifts and the interdependent Body of Christ gave rise to the concept of the priesthood of all believers. Martin Luther spoke to this concept in his treatise, "The Babylonian Captivity of the Church":

> If they were forced to grant that as many of us as have been baptised are all priests without distinction, as indeed we are, and that to them was committed the ministry only, yet with our consent, they would presently learn that they have no right to rule over us except in so far as we freely concede it. For thus it is written in 1 Peter 2:9, "Ye are a chosen generation, a royal priesthood, and a priestly kingdom." (Luther [1520] 2002, para. 7.9)

Luther's emphasis on baptism as the unifying force that brings the Body of Christ together without any right of one to rule over another echoes Paul's call for all the baptized to "lead a life worthy of the calling to which you have been called" (Eph. 4:1). Paul's image of the Body of Christ opened the door wide for Luther's interpretation of 1 Peter 2, viewing the priesthood as a function of all believers.

For the modern era, we see this understanding of the image of the Body of Christ reflected in the ministry section of the 1982 Lima Text adopted by the World Council of Churches: "Baptism, Eucharist, and Ministry." This statement declares, "All members are called to discover, with the help of the community, the gifts that they have received and to use them for the building up of the Church and for the service of the world to which the Church is sent" (World Council of Churches 1982, Ministry II.5). The statement goes on to speak to ordained ministry and does not lose sight of the importance of the variety of gifts, or charisms, found in all members. This is clear in the statement on charisms:

> The ordained ministry, which is itself a charism, must not become a hindrance for the variety of these charisms. On the contrary, it will help the community to discover the gifts bestowed on it by the Holy Spirit and will equip members of the body to serve in a variety of ways. (World Council of Churches 1982, Ministry III.D.32)

Again, there is an expectation that all members of the church—the full community of the baptized—have gifts to share for the good of the whole community.

The Body of Christ and Technology

It is one thing to recognize that every member of this interconnected body has a gift to share; it is far harder to put this statement into practice. How we live into this image, discern the gifts of our members, equip them for the work they are called to do, and support them in that work are unique to our particular times. We must find the ways to respond with humility, gentleness, patience, and love for one another that will best suit our current situation and technology.

In the Reformation, the priesthood of all believers was directly tied to an emphasis on scripture's authority (*sola scriptura*). Reformers were aided by the invention of the printing press, enabling them to equip and empower the people to approach and read scripture directly. As it became possible to print Bibles for use in common households, the importance of increasing the literacy of the people also arose. This technological advance supported and encouraged what was happening in the church and enabled local communities and wider networks to equip and empower their members to develop their gifts in service to the larger mission of the church.

In a similar way, the technological advance of the internet is fueling the current emphasis on developing the gifts of all those who are part of the Body of Christ. We have opportunities to equip, educate, and empower the full Body of Christ that were not available to us before. Once again, the ways in which we communicate and share information are undergoing a rapid change. A new age in the life of the church has accelerated with the COVID-19 pandemic and the sudden shift in development of online worship and new ways of connecting with one another virtually, outdoors, or at greater distance. As a pastor working with a congregation through the first months of the pandemic in 2020, I was impressed with the number of people who had once struggled with email who were quickly able to adapt, using Facebook and YouTube for worship and Zoom for meetings and study groups. There is still a technological gap among our membership, but the comfort levels of the technologically timid have increased dramatically since the start of the COVID-19 pandemic.

This technological development opens doors for more accessible education programs for congregational leaders. As access to and comfort with the internet are increasing, there are more ways to educate and support those in leadership where they currently reside and serve. Online tools create opportunities to provide education to those who cannot travel onsite for theological training. However, the same technological advances also present challenges that can drive us apart.

We should celebrate the reality of the simultaneous diversity and unity in the Body of Christ. We should also celebrate the ways in which the internet and its associated technological advances allow for greater connection. At the same time, we must be aware of the rising wave of disinformation. The rise in polarization and disinformation is a significant concern for the full Body of Christ in our time. When basic facts and authority are routinely questioned, leaders need to seek greater understanding and resourcing to support their work (see Ebertz, chapter 18 in this volume). Anyone who steps forward into leadership roles in congregations today will likely encounter some level of pushback or resistance.

Opportunity for New Growth and Engagement

Today, we have a unique opportunity to engage the gifts of church members in a way that equips and empowers a broader base of leadership in congregations. We can build on the image of the Body of Christ, learn from the ways this image has empowered congregations through history, including other times of great disruption, and meet both the challenge and the opportunity of the current time. Even the smallest congregations and communities have a wide range of skill sets and interests among their members. The role of Christian educators and church leaders across denominations is to identify those gifts and then equip and support those who are called to lead from their various roles.

As a bivocational pastor and leader in the regional Presbytery, I routinely encounter congregational leaders who want to engage in a greater leadership role within the church, according to their gifts and passions. Church members often express interest in taking on greater roles in pastoral care, worship leadership, and the vision and direction work of the congregation but feel they do not have the necessary skills or training. Their own sense of inadequacy, lack of training, or theological understanding stops them from pursuing the work. I know gifted teachers who feel they lack the Biblical knowledge to ever offer a sermon. I know compassionate friends, quick to listen to the concerns of others at any potluck or coffee hour, who are mystified by the idea of visiting a hospital room to offer a prayer and word of comfort. I know committed worship committee leaders who feel they are only qualified to arrange flowers and coordinate volunteers. I know food pantry organizers who are stymied by the idea of engaging in greater advocacy around hunger issues.

At this time, much of the discernment, equipping, and training of church members for specific gifts within the Body of Christ is left to the local pastor, or perhaps a mid-level judicatory. However, it is very difficult as an already-stretched-thin part-time pastor to add the work of training others to lead in specific areas. In the larger body of the church, we have those who are better equipped to provide the needed theological education. Our challenge is to bridge the gap between those with interest at the local level and those with the skills and expertise for training and education.

Traditions that take pride in educated clergy also have the ability to educate and equip the full Body of Christ for a wide range of the gifts and particular skills needed in ministry. The resources we have long relied on for clergy education and support can be adapted and used for the education and equipping of the Body of Christ. The work of discerning gifts and equipping and training leaders is still best accomplished by those with experience in educating church leaders. Seminaries and theological educators already have the expertise required to meet the challenges of our time. The work that is needed is adapting this expertise for use in what Jeffrey MacDonald (2020, 111) called a "distributed pastorate" model.

New Models for Equipping the Body of Christ

The model of theological education needed in our current time differs from what was helpful in the age when the majority of White, mainline churches could support full-time clergy. However, it is not entirely new. MacDonald's image of the "distributed pastorate" is in line with Paul's early emphasis on the variety of gifts present in the Body of Christ. MacDonald argued in his book, *Part-Time Is Plenty*, that we need to use our educational resources to move toward a "distributed pastorate, whereby clergy and laypeople divide up pastoral responsibilities according to the gifts of the Holy Spirit" (2020, 111). We still need people trained for Christian education, liturgy, pastoral care, vision and strategic planning work, mission outreach, ethical reflection, and other areas of ministry. What is changing in our new context is the need for all these skills to be found primarily in one person.

I see an ongoing need for clergy with a full Master of Divinity educational background. Yet, there is a simultaneous need to break out sections of this traditional degree for certification programs or other training opportunities for those with specific gifts. While some individuals within the Body of Christ will be called to full-time ordained ministries, we must also accommodate those who are called to serve with specific gifts for particular ministries. According to Paul, both are equally valued:

> But God has so arranged the body, giving the greater honor to the inferior member, that there may be no dissension within the body, but the members may have the same care for one another. If one

member suffers, all suffer together with it; if one member is honored, all rejoice together with it. (1 Cor. 12:24b–26)

It requires work to establish a community of love and respect, where we serve one another and rise and fall together. As we look to build a "distributed pastorate" reflecting the variety of gifts in the full Body of Christ, I see three areas of focus: discernment of gifts, education and training, and ongoing support of those who are trained (see MacDonald 2020, 111–32, for a related discussion).

Discernment of Gifts

As those who have the gifts and experience of theological education work to provide the training and certification needed for particular ministries, we need a transformation in our discernment process. In many denominations, this work is traditionally done at a middle judicatory level. In my tradition, the Presbyterian Church (U.S.A.), Presbytery committees on preparation for ministry oversee discernment work for those seeking full-time ministry. Just as education of members with specific gifts or skills is best done by those who already have the gift and knowledge of providing theological education, it makes sense that discernment work around the gifts present in any congregation is best supported by those who are already doing this work. Denominational leaders and others already working to identify those with gifts for ministry can adapt to include working with local congregations to discern the gifts of their members.

Discerning and encouraging the gifts of the full Body of Christ takes a willingness to spend time listening for the call of the Holy Spirit, naming where skills and gifts are already present, and identifying areas where training and development are needed. To identify those in need of further education and training, we need church leaders who are able to listen for the Holy Spirit's presence and guide those considering taking on greater leadership roles.

The work of discernment needs to be done primarily at the local level. While middle judicatory leaders and others can help with the discernment of gifts, the initial recognition and encouragement will most often come from a local pastor. Transforming the local congregation into a place for discernment places a larger burden on local pastors, including those who serve bivocationally. Local pastors must be alert to the varieties of gifts that their members have to offer. This will require that seminaries include some training in discernment and recognition of gifts for every local pastor—particularly those intending to serve in bivocational ministry.

Education and Training

Identifying church members with specific gifts for leadership is the first step to empowering the full Body of Christ. However, there is a large gap between identifying a gift and empowering someone to use that gift. Education and training are necessary to address the sense of inadequacy and lack of knowledge that many gifted church members feel when called upon to take on a larger leadership role. Education and training are also helpful to meet the challenges of disinformation and polarization that frame our current time.

Models exist for equipping and empowering church members to use specific gifts. Nearly every denomination and many seminaries already have some form of lay pastor training program. There are also existing non-denominational programs with clearly defined training and certification around a particular gift, such as the Stephen Ministry program with training in pastoral care (Stephen Ministries St. Louis, n.d.). Another form of training is found in various models of weekend or week-long training sessions for congregational leaders around a specific issue, like how to lead children's education, discern the mission needs in your neighborhood, or run an effective stewardship campaign. These existing models for education around specific gifts are scattered and usually disconnected from one another and would benefit from greater collaboration and connection on both regional and denominational levels.

Adapting coursework from the Master of Divinity degree to specific certifications in pastoral care, mission engagement and ethics, or non-profit administration presents another opportunity. Seminaries know how to train and equip students for full-time pastorates. As we discern specific gifts among the Body of Christ, how might current seminary coursework be developed into certification programs for specific gifts in ministry? Meeting the needs of the present does not necessarily involve a complete redevelopment of what has served our churches well in the past. With thoughtful consideration, it is possible to build on existing programs and expand access to education and training for those seeking to develop a particular gift.

The opportunity to expand education programs and increase accessibility is due in part to the increase in comfort and familiarity with online education brought about by the COVID-19 pandemic. As broadband access expands into rural areas, the opportunity for online programs will only increase. While programs similar to the existing weekend or one-week training opportunities will continue to be helpful, the best point of access for specialized educational programs will be online. Internet technology allows those with expertise and experience to share with those who have discerned gifts for ministry and provides greater connection with those seeking to step into new leadership roles in their local congregations.

Discerning the gifts of leadership in the Body of Christ and providing the education and training to support leaders in specific ministries are essential to the transformation of the church of the twenty-first century. However, we cannot take these steps forward without also ensuring support and ongoing care for those in leadership.

Ongoing Support

With the image of the Body of Christ, Paul emphasized the ways in which we are connected to one another. Connection as interdependence is particularly prominent in 1 Corinthians 12 as Paul discusses the ways in which ears, eyes, hands, feet, and head all rely on one another. One part cannot say, "I have no need of you" (1 Cor. 12:21). So it is with the work of supporting the gifts present in our local congregations. We must work not only as the Body of Christ at the local level but also in our larger connections of denominations and the universal church. Empowering the gifts of members at the local level requires ongoing support and connection with one another.

We know that our full-time clergy do not function well when they are isolated. There is a need for support circles, continuing education, and other connection points for clergy. How do we provide similar support for members taking on larger roles of ministry within their congregations? Ongoing training sessions and regular study groups could be helpful. A quarterly Zoom check-in with a continuing education component for those already trained in a specific skill could help to keep the sense of connection and the support needed in place. The form of the ongoing support may differ depending on the skill or gift itself. There are many creative ways to keep members of the Body of

Christ connected to one another. What is important is that those who are trained and equipped for specific ministries be supported and nurtured through a commitment by the Body of Christ as they serve.

Ongoing support for those who are serving in leadership also helps to meet the challenge of the disinformation and polarization that has arisen in our technological age. Those serving in leadership at the local level benefit from a group of colleagues and access to those with more information or expertise when faced with difficult situations. No matter how congenial the congregation may be, or how long a leader has counted themselves a member of their community, there will be times when a congregational leader needs outside support or at least a listening ear. Collegial groups of those with similar training and roles in their congregations can help as problems arise. Ongoing educational opportunities and further training resources can support leaders as they continue to grow and come to understand situations differently.

Conclusion

Transforming into churches that discern, equip, and support requires a massive shift in our church culture. A focus on discerning the gifts of members, equipping and empowering members to share those gifts in the community, and offering ongoing support and accountability—this is a lot to ask of members and current leaders. Even as we look to theological educators and denominational leaders for leadership in education and discernment, the role of pastors in local congregations continues to be paramount. A primary role of bivocational pastors is the work of discernment of gifts and the ongoing support of the congregational leaders working alongside them. Bivocational pastors can help congregations identify the gifts of their members, find education and training programs needed to develop those gifts, and make sure that those who are trained for pastoral care, education, mission coordination, worship leadership, and other areas of ministry are connected with persons who can offer support and ongoing training. However, it cannot fall to our bivocational pastors to be the primary resource for any of these areas. As the Body of Christ, we need to maintain the connections that encourage and support each and every member as an essential part of the larger community.

Any form of education program or training established to equip and empower the gifts of our membership must address the reality of our current polarization, equipping leaders to respond in ways that celebrate both the unity and diversity of the Body of Christ. The challenge is significant—that should not be denied. However, we have witnessed ways in which the faithful have responded time and again throughout the history of the church by coming back to the image that Paul kept coming back to in his letters to the various early church communities of the first century. We are part of the great Body of Christ, with Christ alone at the head, our guide and our focus. Greater collaboration, connection, and leadership will give us a church that truly reflects the Body of Christ, a priesthood of all believers. We are in a new time and place, with ways to connect and new gifts to celebrate. As we come through the COVID-19 pandemic and embrace the realities of our technological age, there is an opportunity before us to grow into a church that continues to express Christ's transforming resurrection as we live into being Christ's body.

Works Cited

Luther, Martin. [1520] 2002. "A Prelude by Martin Luther on the Babylonian Captivity of the Church." Translated by Albert T. W. Steinhaeuser. English text edited and modernized by Robert E. Smith. Project Wittenberg Online Electronic Study Edition. *projectwittenberg.org/etext/luther/babylonian/babylonian.htm#.*

MacDonald, G. Jeffrey. 2020. *Part-Time Is Plenty: Thriving Without Full-Time Clergy*. Louisville: Westminster John Knox.

Stephen Ministries St. Louis. n.d. "What is Stephen Ministry?" Accessed January 9, 2022. *stephenministries.org/aboutus/default.cfm/721.*

Tickle, Phyllis. 2008. *The Great Emergence: How Christianity Is Changing and Why*. Grand Rapids, MI: Baker.

World Council of Churches. 1982. "Baptism, Eucharist and Ministry." In *Faith and Order Paper No. 111*. Geneva: World Council of Churches. *oikoumene.org/resources/documents/baptism-eucharist-and-ministry-faith-and-order-paper-no-111-the-lima-text.*

CHAPTER 14

Preparing to Educate for a Thriving Bivocational Ministry

DARRYL W. STEPHENS

How can institutions of higher learning in theological education respond to an increasing need for bivocational ministry preparation, training, and support?[1] Lancaster Theological Seminary (LTS) established specific action steps to learn to do so in its Strategic Plan 2020–2022. One of these action steps was to explore options "to equip current and future bivocational religious leaders with ministerial leadership skills." Toward this end, the seminary applied for and received a matching grant from the In Trust Center for Theological Schools to fund a year-long effort, "Educating for a Thriving Bivocational Ministry." A significant part of this project involved surveying core constituencies of the seminary and hosting a student focus group to learn how the seminary currently supports and equips students for bivocational ministry. Lancaster Theological Seminary is a school of the United Church of Christ and one of approximately 250 member schools of the Association of Theological

Schools in the United States and Canada (ATS). This chapter presents these findings as a seminary case study in preparing to educate for a thriving bivocational ministry.

Bivocational ministry is not consistently defined in academic literature or popular usage. Thus, one of the first tasks in the seminary's effort consisted of a review of literature and an attempt to define terms. A tentative definition provided initial direction for this grant project. Bivocational ministry was defined as a combination of religious and secular employment (paid or unpaid) by someone called to representative ministry. The research team for the Canadian Multivocational Ministry Project worked from a similar definition, interviewing people who had "more than one job or serious volunteer commitment in addition to a congregational leadership role" (Watson et al. 2020, 5). This researcher prefers the term "bivocational" because it unambiguously connotes pastoral ministry (Stephens, chapter 1 in this volume).

In recent years, White Protestants in North America have increasingly expressed interest in bivocational pastors as leading a "new" way of doing ministry in local congregations. Researchers and writers are quick to point out, though, that bivocational pastors have long been the norm in other parts of the world and for many non-White and immigrant communities within North America (Bentley 2018, 148; Christian Reformed Church in North America 2020, 13; Deasy 2018, 66; MacDonald 2020, 8–9). In 2006, Carroll (2006, 81) reported "18% of mainline Protestants, 29% of conservative Protestants, and 41% of clergy in historic Black denominations [were] bivocational." While popular perception depicts an increase, the actual percentage of bivocational pastors in the US seems to be holding steady. In an article titled, "Are Bivocational Clergy Becoming the New Normal?" researchers observed no increase between 1996–2017, though statistics varied by gender, marital status, and geographic region (Perry and Schleifer 2019). According to the "National Congregations Study," the percentage of congregations served by a "head clergyperson" who "also holds another job" was 37% in 2006–2007, 34% in 2012, and 35% in 2018–2019 (Chaves et al. 2021, 22). Whether their numbers are increasing or holding steady, it is fair to say that bivocational ministry has attracted more attention in mainline churches in recent years.

Increased attention has prompted greater awareness of the distinct challenges and stressors on bivocational pastors and congregations. Finances are, of course, a stressor for pastors juggling part-time employments, but this is neither the only nor the most significant source of stress. Consistently, part-time or bivocational pastors report being less valued and supported within denominational structures and congregations (Carroll 2006, 175; MacDonald 2020, 23–28; Miller-McLemore 2008, 166–67). The need to overcome external bias and stigma is accompanied by the individual's need to balance multiple vocations (Miller-McLemore 2008, 169–71) or "multiplicity" within a singular sense of vocation (Lindner 2016). The Canadian Multivocational Ministry Project focused on clergy health and job satisfaction, exploring the ways that multivocational pastors combined various employments to sustain their vocational identities and ministries (Watson et al. 2020, 16–18). A significant aspect of thriving was intentionality—discerning a "unique fit" for ministry, employment, and the individual's gifts (Watson et al. 2020, 18). Samushonga's (2019, 77) observation in the United Kingdom is applicable in North America, as well: "there is an emerging concept of intentional bivocationalism." For congregations accustomed to the "standard model" of professional ministry, adjusting to bivocational ministry requires more than a lower salary and reduced hours. Intentional bivocational ministry is a paradigm shift toward shared, congregational ministry (Bentley 2018, 147; Bickers 2007, 6; Edington 2018, 8; MacDonald 2020, 65; Pappas et al., chapter 11 in this volume; Stephens, chapter 1 of this volume; Watson et al. 2020, 19). Thus, intentional bivocational ministry also requires changes in perception and expectations, including adjustments to congregational leadership style (MacDonald 2020, 65–69; Watson et al. 2020, 19).

The emergence of intentional bivocationalism challenges ATS member schools to become more intentional in their efforts to prepare students for bivocational ministry. In 2011, Daniel O. Aleshire, then executive director of ATS, observed that "the percentage of part-time pastors has emerged as a growth industry in mainline Protestantism across the past two decades" (76). However, most bivocational pastors seek training outside of accredited master's degree programs and many are credentialed through pathways other than ordination. The usual channels for intentional preparation for bivocational ministry are found beyond ATS member schools (Aleshire 2010, 511; González 2020; Scharen and Miller 2016, 8). Similar challenges exist in the United Kingdom (Samushonga 2020). Researchers in the Canadian Multivocational Ministry Project concluded, "the increasingly diverse and constantly changing nature of ministry calls for more regular curricular review and a constant evaluation of delivery formats" (Chapman and Watson 2020, 12). ATS member schools are feeling some pressure to adapt. Current Executive Director of ATS, Frank Yamada (2020, 32), observed that this generation of theological students is increasingly part-time and "already engaged in a local ministry context while working on a degree." Theological schools are addressing these changes in structured as well as improvisational ways as they learn to meet the needs of bivocational students and pastors.

Lancaster Seminary is not alone in turning its attention to bivocational ministry. Aleshire (2021, 108–9) cited positive examples of ATS programs that cater primarily to bivocational students; one program required students to be employed at least half-time in ministry while completing their degree. Other schools have investigated balancing dual roles (Grand Rapids Seminary 2018), financial stability of bivocational pastors and congregations (Bentley 2018), and joys and challenges of bivocational ministry (Earlham School of Religion, n.d.).

ATS seminaries seeking to meet the needs of bivocational students and prepare students for bivocational ministry are, for the most part, faced with two main avenues for change: adapt existing programs or create new ones. Some schools are adapting the curriculum and delivery of master's degree programs. Other schools are creating and nurturing "alternative educational models" falling outside the scope of ATS-accredited degree programs (Aleshire 2008, 137; see also González 2015, 139; MacDonald 2020, 111–21). Lancaster Seminary has done both. In 2015, this seminary lowered the number of credits required and developed a four-year "weekend" (Friday evening and Saturday morning) track for the Master of Divinity degree. While this track is technically not a part-time program, the intention was to cater to students who work and go to school. In 2019, this seminary launched a part-time, non-degree program for lifelong learners preparing for ordination without going to seminary. However, neither program is explicitly promoted as bivocational.

To improve its support for bivocational students and better prepare them for bivocational ministry, Lancaster Seminary surveyed current students, staff, faculty, and trustees and conducted a series of six focus group meetings with students. This research focused implicitly on this seminary's degree programs. Survey questions pertained to perception and relevance of bivocational ministry, distinct stressors of bivocational ministry, opinions about current degree programs at the seminary, and opinions about institutional changes designed to better support and prepare seminarians for bivocational ministry. This chapter presents the findings of these surveys, augmented with data from a series of student focus group meetings. The chapter concludes with a discussion of challenges and opportunities facing this seminary in its strategic effort to educate for a thriving bivocational ministry, with implications for theological education in general.

Methodology Overview and Demographics

Between November 19 and December 3, 2020, the project director (this author) administered four surveys, each to a different constituency of Lancaster Seminary (Stephens 2021, Supplementary S1).[2] The project received prior approval for human subject research, and informed consent was obtained from all subjects involved in the study. Surveys of current students and faculty (adjunct faculty as well as fully funded faculty) were conducted through the seminary's learning management system, Moodle. Surveys of staff and trustees were conducted through Google Forms. The entire population invited to participate consisted of 186 persons: faculty (38), staff (29), students (98), and trustees (21). A significant proportion participated: faculty (32%), staff (45%), students (22%), and trustees (38%). In aggregate, N = 55, consisting of faculty (12), staff (13), students (22), and trustees (8).

Demographic information was collected on all respondents except trustees, to maintain greater anonymity among this smaller group. Of those surveyed, 18% of student respondents identified as "BIPOC or Latinx," compared to 43% BIPOC or Latinx among the entire student body (Lancaster Theological Seminary 2020). Of all constituents surveyed, 21% identified as "BIPOC or Latinx," 70% of whom answered affirmatively when asked if they were "affiliated with a US mainline, historically White denomination (UCC, UMC, ECUSA, PCUSA, etc.)." Among all respondents, 79% were affiliated with a White, mainline denomination; inferred is that about 15% of respondents were White persons in a nondenominational, multiethnic, multiracial, or no church setting. Students were also asked their preferred pronouns: they/them/theirs (0); she/her/hers (7); he/him/his (11); four did not answer. At the time of the survey, 51% of the entire student body was female (Lancaster Theological Seminary 2020). Most student respondents were in master's degree programs (19); three were in the Doctor of Ministry program.

Vocationally, staff and faculty respondents were asked if they were "ordained, licensed, or in some form of authorized ministry in [their] faith community": over half said yes, with faculty (9 yes; 3 no) outnumbering staff (5 yes; 8 no) in their affirmative responses. Just over one-third of staff and faculty respondents answered affirmatively to the prompt, "I consider myself a bivocational minister (or have significant previous experience as a bivocational minister)": again faculty (7 yes; 5 no) outnumbered staff (2 yes; 11 no) in their affirmative responses. Among staff and faculty, all who were bivocational were in some form of authorized ministry and 64% of those in authorized ministry were currently or previously bivocational ministers.

The sample of students surveyed skewed more active in ministry and other employments than expected, based on recent ATS Graduating Student Questionnaires for Lancaster Seminary. Two-thirds of student respondents "currently hold a paid position outside of ministry" (Q23 for students), and 55% "currently hold a paid ministry position" (Q22 for students). While 55% of student respondents described their current ministry as bivocational (Q24 for students), not all students holding a paid ministry position considered themselves bivocational. Nearly 60% of current student respondents "expect to be bivocational in ministry after graduation" (Q25 for students)—twice the rate reported over the previous seven years (ATS n.d.; Deasy 2018, 66), though consistent with more recent data (Deasy, chapter 15 in this volume).[3]

Almost all the students participating in focus group meetings were engaged in some form of paid employment, ministerial or otherwise, while attending seminary. Each monthly focus group meeting lasted one hour and was conducted via Zoom. Thirteen students participated in at least one of the six focus group meetings over a span of six months. Meetings were held November 10 and December 15, 2020, and January 18, February 9, March 9, and April 13, 2021. Ten students attended at least three meetings. The group included significant gender and racial diversity: preferred pronouns included 5 she/her, 7 he/him, and 1 they/them; racial representation included 7 Black and 6 White students; and one student identified as Latino. Ages ranged from twenties to sixties.

Survey instruments are available at Stephens (2021, Supplementary S1). The first 17 questions were identical on all four surveys and utilized the same Likert scale: strongly disagree, disagree, neutral, agree, strongly agree. Responses are reported below in the form of color-coded charts (figure 1). Additional questions were asked separately of each constituency.

Strongly disagree Disagree Neutral Agree Strongly agree

Figure 1: Likert Scale, color-coded response legend.

The following analysis presents the findings of these surveys (Stephens 2021, Supplementary S2), arranged in four sections: perception and relevance of bivocational ministry, distinct stressors of bivocational ministry, opinions about current educational programs at the seminary, and opinions about institutional changes.

Perceptions

All groups surveyed perceived bivocational ministry as relevant to the future of the church, even if they expressed ambivalence about this future. Across constituencies, two in three persons agreed that "bivocational ministry is the future of pastoral ministry" (Q1) (figure 2). Staff and students exhibited the greatest intergroup and intragroup disparities. Among students, over 75% agreed; among staff, just over 50% agreed. Approximately 5% of staff and students strongly disagreed. Interestingly, the one student who expressed strong disagreement with Q1 also indicated that bivocational ministry is a first choice for their ministry career (Q19 for students), discussed below.

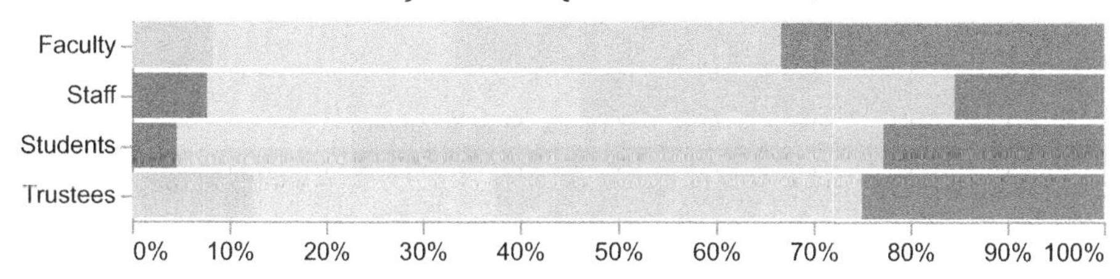

Figure 2: "Bivocational ministry is the future of pastoral ministry" (Q1). 4% strongly disagree; 4% disagree; 25% neutral; 44% agree; 24% strongly agree.

Respondents seemed less than enthusiastic about this perceived future. Among faculty and trustees, only one person agreed that "bivocational ministry is preferable to fully-funded ministry" (Q2); over 85% disagreed and, among faculty, 25% strongly disagreed. Overwhelmingly, faculty and trustees expressed preference for the model of fully funded ministry. Students and staff expressed greater ambivalence. Among students, nearly 60% did not disagree, and over 30% agreed. The gap between student preference for bivocational ministry and that of faculty and trustees was over 40%.

Separately, students were asked if they were intentional about pursuing bivocational ministry (Q19 for students). Student responses were nearly evenly distributed across the entire spectrum of choices (figure 3). The disparity in student responses to Q1 and Q19 is remarkable. There is a significant cadre of students (approximately 45%) who see bivocational ministry as the future yet do not prioritize being part of this future. Nevertheless, nearly 60% of student respondents indicated that they "expect to be bivocational in ministry after graduation" (Q25 for students).

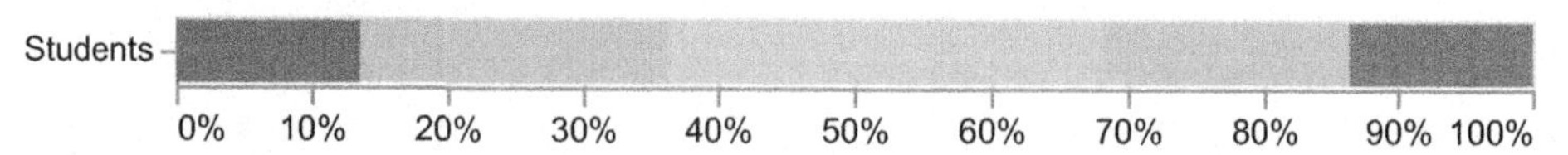

Figure 3: "I consider bivocational ministry a first choice for my ministry career" (Q19 for students). 14% strongly disagree; 23% disagree; 32% neutral; 18% agree; 14% strongly agree.

All groups perceived bivocational ministry to be an intentional career path with vocational integrity (figure 4). Approximately 75% of faculty and staff agreed that "bivocational ministry is an intentional career path for ministry" (Q6); two in three trustees and a majority of students also agreed. There was no disagreement among staff and trustees; however, one in four students disagreed.

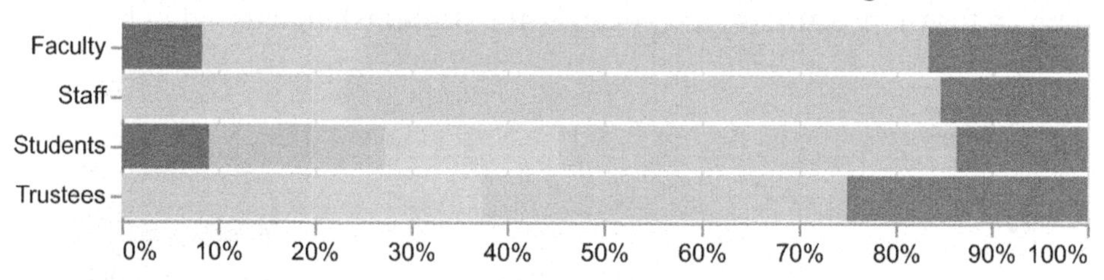

Figure 4: "Bivocational ministry is an intentional career path for ministry" (Q6). 5% strongly disagree; 7% disagree; 22% neutral; 49% agree; 16% strongly agree.

Regarding vocational integrity, 87% of respondents disagreed that "bivocational ministry is a lesser commitment to one's call compared to fully-funded ministry" (Q5); approximately 50% strongly disagreed (figure 5). Interestingly, the three students who agreed or strongly agreed with this statement (Q5) also agreed or strongly agreed that bivocational ministry is the future of pastoral ministry (Q1).

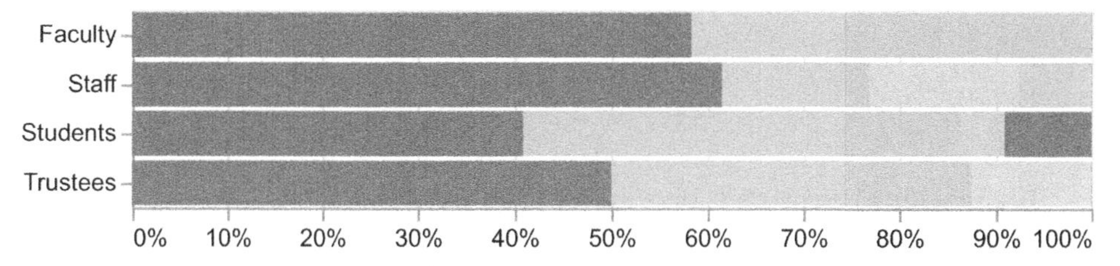

Figure 5: "Bivocational ministry is a lesser commitment to one's call compared to fully-funded ministry." (Q5). 51% strongly disagree; 36% disagree; 5% neutral; 4% agree; 4% strongly agree.

Across constituencies, bivocational ministry seemed to be valued as a distinct and legitimate form of ministry appropriate to all demographics. Over 60% agreed that "bivocational ministry is a way to model for laity the ministry of all Christians" (Q7); only about 15% disagreed. Regarding skills and preparation, 80% disagreed and nearly 60% strongly disagreed that "bivocational ministry is a path for persons with insufficient skills to enter fully-funded ministry" (Q8). Staff and students showed greater ambivalence than other groups: about 30% of staff were neutral, and 14% of students agreed. Furthermore, only 10% of respondents agreed that "bivocational ministry is a short-term necessity when searching for a full-time church position" (Q3).

None of the groups surveyed considered bivocational ministry to be narrowly relevant based on race, ethnicity, denomination, or the pastor's experience or life circumstance. Overwhelmingly, all constituencies disagreed that bivocational ministry is: "mainly for second-career pastors" (Q10); "mainly for young, single pastors" (Q11); "mainly for certain faith traditions" (Q12); and "mainly for certain racial or ethnic communities" (Q13). Of the 55 total respondents, only one person agreed with any of these statements; 75% of staff, 95% of students, 98% of faculty, and 100% of trustees disagreed or strongly disagreed with these statements.

Congregational size seemed to have slightly more, though still limited, relevance than any of the preceding factors. In response to the prompt, "Bivocational ministry is only relevant to small congregations that cannot afford a full-time pastor" (Q9), about 40% of staff and trustees were neutral, two faculty persons agreed, and one student strongly agreed. Given another opportunity, this researcher would rephrase the question to say "mainly" rather than "only."

Stressors

Bivocational ministry was perceived by most to be more stressful than fully funded ministry (figure 6). Of all the groups surveyed, students were the least likely to think so, though student opinions were evenly divided. Most faculty, staff, and trustees said yes. Students expressed less agreement than any other group with the statement, "Bivocational ministry is more stressful than fully-funded ministry" (Q4). About 35% of students agreed, compared to 50% of the faculty, 60% of staff, and over 75% of trustees. Notably, about one in three students disagreed, mirroring the number who expressed preference for bivocational over fully funded ministry. (However, there was no correlation between individual student agreement on Q2 and response to Q4.)

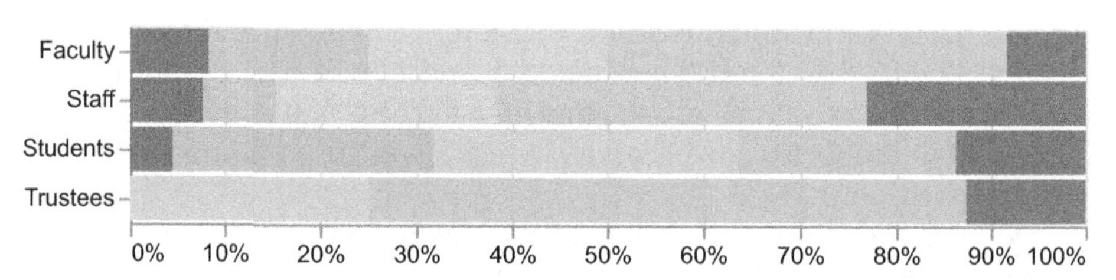

Figure 6: "Bivocational ministry is more stressful than fully-funded ministry" (Q4). 5% strongly disagree; 16% disagree; 27% neutral; 36% agree; 15% strongly agree.

Staff and faculty had no difficulty naming examples of the sources of this stress. In an open-response question, they were prompted to identify "three distinctive stressors faced by bivocational students" (Q18 for faculty; Q22 for staff). All faculty respondents provided answers to this prompt; 9 of 13 staff respondents provided answers to this prompt. In decreasing order of frequency, respondents mentioned: time management; workload and balance; money and finances; professional clarity; and family and health. Nearly every respondent mentioned the challenge of time management or scheduling as a distinct stressor (11 of 12 faculty; 7 of 9 staff). Most also mentioned workload, balance, divided focus, or boundaries as a distinct stressor (6 of 12 faculty; 7 of 9 staff). Money and finances were the third most frequently cited concerns (4 of 12 faculty; 6 of 9 staff). Many respondents also mentioned either issues of professional clarity, such as perceptions/stigma, unrecognized competencies, and career steps (3 of 12 faculty; 2 of 9 staff) or the cluster of concerns about family, personal life, and health (3 of 12 faculty; 2 of 9 staff), though no one mentioned both.

Students participating in the series of focus group meetings also provided insight on bivocational stressors. Over the span of six sessions, they mentioned a variety of challenges facing bivocational students: balancing family, school, and ministry; setting boundaries, staying healthy, and delegating ministry tasks; finances (both personal and church); congregational expectations; and how the COVID-19 pandemic changed the way people work and relate to each other. Several mentioned high expectations for pastors in African American and Latino communities to be available for all major events and to be present in every community function. One Latino student observed that it is disrespectful to have an outsider or an associate pastor perform the duties of the lead pastor. An African American student noted that because pastors are often the most educated persons in the community, the congregants value the pastor's input. These expectations place tremendous pressure on pastors, most of whom are bivocational, when serving these communities. The expectation to perform to high standards was perceived among all racial and ethnic groups. One student admitted, "Some of us want to take on the 'Old School responsibilities,' to do it all as we were taught by our pastors and not to delegate to others." Another student observed differences in expectations based on the size of the congregation. "Larger churches have various leaders, different roles/positions and the structure is passed down to the next leaders. Larger church members do not express the same level of need as those of small churches." As a group, these students evidenced keen awareness of the challenges and contextually specific expectations of bivocational ministry.

Programs at Lancaster Theological Seminary

Opinions were mixed regarding Lancaster Seminary's current efforts to meet the needs of bivocational students. Students, staff, faculty, and trustees were surveyed about the seminary's current efforts. Additionally, staff and trustees were asked whether the seminary should improve its efforts in the same areas. Of all the groups, trustees were the most reluctant to disagree with statements about the seminary's positive efforts and the most willing to acknowledge that the seminary should improve the way it meets the needs of bivocational students. A majority of staff and trustees agreed that the seminary should improve its efforts in all of these areas, with only one respondent disagreeing with any of these questions.

Lancaster Seminary seems to offer helpful scheduling choices for bivocational students, with room for improvement. Most respondents agreed that "Lancaster Seminary already does a good job catering to the needs of bivocational students through scheduling choices" (Q15). Trustees believed this more than other groups: 75% agreed and none disagreed. Among faculty, two in three agreed, and only 15% disagreed. Staff and students showed a wider variety of opinions, though only 25% disagreed. When asked whether the seminary "should improve the way it meets the needs of bivocational students through scheduling choices" (Q19 to staff and trustees), staff and trustees responses aligned: over 50% agreed, and none disagreed.

Opinions varied widely regarding the current academic curriculum, with most responses neutral, though many felt the seminary should improve in this area. About 30% of faculty and staff agreed that the seminary "already does a good job catering to the needs of bivocational students through academic curriculum" (Q14); less than 20% of students and only one trustee agreed (figure 7). Among all respondents, 24% disagreed to some extent. Faculty were decidedly mixed in their opinion of the academic curriculum: four disagreed; four were neutral; two agreed; and two strongly agreed.

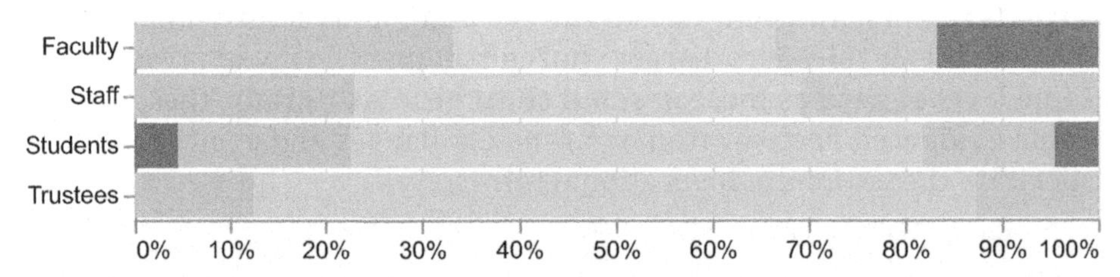

Figure 7: "I believe Lancaster Seminary already does a good job catering to the needs of bivocational students through academic curriculum" (Q14). 2% strongly disagree; 22% disagree; 53% neutral; 18% agree; 5% strongly agree.

Staff and trustees overwhelmingly (over 70%) agreed that the seminary "should improve the way it meets the needs of bivocational students through academic curriculum" (Q18 to staff and trustees); none disagreed (figure 8).

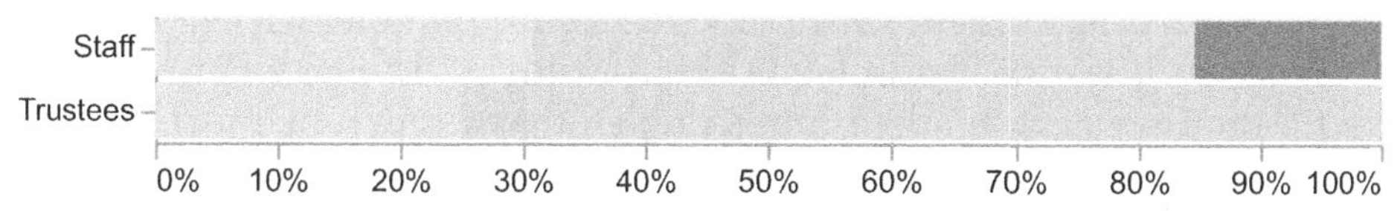

Figure 8: "I believe Lancaster Seminary should improve the way it meets the needs of bivocational students through academic curriculum" (Q18 for staff and trustees). 0% strongly disagree; 0% disagree; 29% neutral; 62% agree; 10% strongly agree.

In a multiple-choice inquiry, faculty indicated that they "currently prepare students for bivocational ministry" (Q21 for faculty) through various means, checking all options provided with approximately equal frequency: case studies, assigned readings, assignments, classroom discussion, academic advising, Comprehensive Vocational Review, and "scheduling, deadlines, and expectations for completing classroom and academic requirements." No faculty respondents utilized the open-ended "other" option for this question.

Regarding co-curricular offerings, again, opinions varied widely, most responses were neutral, and there was a general perception that the seminary should improve in this area. Faculty and trustees rated the seminary's efforts more positively than did staff and students. About 35% of faculty and trustees agreed that the seminary "does a good job catering to the needs of bivocational students through co-curricular offerings" (Q17); just over 10% of staff and students agreed. Staff expressed the most disagreement (about 30%) and the least agreement. A majority of staff and trustees agreed that the seminary should improve in this area (Q21 to staff and trustees); only one person disagreed.

Staff and faculty seemed to have difficulty naming specific examples of current co-curricular support for bivocational ministry. When asked to "name three co-curricular experiences supportive and modeling of bivocational ministry" in an open-ended response (Q20 for faculty), only 3 of 12 faculty responded with examples (adjunct faculty; chaplains, preachers, and presiders in chapel; field education); three responded that they did not know or were unsure; six offered no response. The same open-ended inquiry was posed to staff (Q24 for staff): one respondent stated, "our adjuncts provide good models for this"; another answered, "Our co-curricular offerings are bare because we have not yet found a way to get students to participate in them"; nine persons replied "not sure" or provided no response.

Regarding student services, once again opinions varied widely. Separate questions addressed current student services and the need for improvement. Students rated the seminary's current efforts more positively than did the other groups: 27% of students agreed that the seminary "already does a good job catering to the needs of bivocational students through student services" (Q16); only 12% of other respondents agreed. About 22% of all respondents disagreed or strongly disagreed; 60% of responses were neutral. Staff and trustees were asked an additional question about the need for improvement. A majority of staff and trustees agreed that the seminary should improve in this area (Q20 to staff and trustees); none disagreed.

Faculty and staff named many specific examples of student services supportive of bivocational ministry. In an open-response question, 50% of faculty and staff offered substantive examples of "advising and student support services for bivocational ministry" at the seminary (Q19 for faculty; Q23 for staff). Both groups named the following examples: seminary chaplains, academic [faculty] advisors, field education, Comprehensive Vocational Review, financial counseling and debt reduction program, and after-hours library access. Faculty also named: the dean, other students, library e-resources, Saturday worship, and faculty availability outside standard hours. Staff also named: writing center, four-year [weekend] Master of Divinity program, denominational advisors, registrar, and flexible [staff] schedule. The most-often-mentioned student support services by the 25 faculty and staff respondents were: seminary chaplains (7); faculty academic advisors (5); field education (3); and student debt reduction program (3). In a multiple-choice inquiry, staff were asked, "How do you currently contribute to the preparation of students for bivocational ministry?" (Q25 for staff): respondents checked all options provided except "lowering my expectations." The most frequent responses were "shifting my work hours and availability" and "transforming the way I do my job with bivocational students in mind." No staff respondents utilized the open-ended "other" option for this question.

Distinct Viewpoints Shared

Each of the four constituencies—staff, faculty, students, and trustees—offered distinct viewpoints on bivocational ministry and the seminary's efforts. Survey respondents were given the opportunity to voice additional observations, opinions, questions, or concerns in an open-response format (Q26 for staff; Q22 for faculty; Q18 for students; Q26 for trustees). The following discussion characterizes the responses received by each constituency. Analysis of student responses is augmented with detailed feedback from the student focus group participants. Analysis of trustee responses is reported in conversation with trustee responses in other parts of the survey.

Staff

Staff observed that the concept *bivocational* is not consistently understood even as they affirmed its relevance and posed challenging questions about the seminary's current programs. One staff person recognized ambiguity in the way the term is often used:

> The term *bi-vocational* is still confusing to me in our seminary context. In many ways, it sounds like *bi-vocational* is used to describe people working in ministry and get[ting] a degree at the same time. At the same time[, it] could be understood as people who want to have two careers after seminary.

Another staff person also expressed a desire for definitional clarity. Their concerns are warranted. The literature on bivocational ministry reveals a wide range of uses for the term as well as many other related terms. Researchers, many working on behalf of judicatories or theological schools, often begin with an exploration of the range of definitions and terms (Bentley 2018; Deasy 2018; Samushonga 2020; Stephens, chapter 1 in this volume).

Nevertheless, the term *bivocational* held sufficient valence for staff to express opinions and concerns. Another staff person remarked, "*Bivocational* implies ministry and one other job whereas in different cultures and context the resources for the ministry are vastly different such that the two jobs (ministry and other) can very well be several jobs with full-time demands." Culture and context are indeed significant for the practice and prevalence of bivocational ministry, particularly when race, gender, and ethnicity are considered (Bentley 2018, 148; Deasy 2018, 66, 69; MacDonald 2020, 8–9; Perry and Schleifer 2019). The staff person who is quoted above about definitional confusion also spoke frankly about economic need: "In some cases, bi-vocational ministry is not a choice but rather an unfortunate reality of economic inequality." The same person also raised the issue of vocational coherence and integrity. "Integrating bi-vocational ministry into our seminary[, we] should be asking questions [such as,] How can a Pastor/Faith leader/Social activist always be that in all spaces?" This person also questioned the ability of existing degree programs to meet the needs of bivocational students, citing the limited number of electives, the high cost of a Master of Divinity degree, as well as the need to explore dual programs in social work, law, non-profit leadership, and so forth.

Faculty

Faculty responses indicated a spectrum of attitudes, ranging from complacency to avoidance to defense, revealing no concerns about the existing curriculum. One observed, "Many aspects of an LTS education are applicable to both single-vocational and bi-vocational ministry." Another admitted, "we at Lancaster Theological Seminary are still more focused on ministry as a full-time vocation than we are aware of bivocational ministry." In fact, despite a commitment to bivocational ministry preparation in the institution's strategic plan, one faculty person observed, "I do not recall this issue surfacing in faculty and/or staff meetings." Yet another confessed the complexity of bivocational ministry: "There are many variables in regard to this issue; it is almost impossible to generalize." These attitudes sat alongside other comments, which seemed to focus attention and responsibility elsewhere. One rued the difficulty of "maintain[ing] high pedagogical standards" with students struggling "to balance a full-time job with studies, ministry, and family responsibilities." Another cast attention on the church rather than the seminary:

> Sometimes bivocational ministry is how congregations and the wider church can benefit from the breadth of gifts that ministers bring to the table . . . the church recruits people to ministry for their gifts, and then promptly asks them to stop practicing that gift and "do ministry"

> instead. The church would best benefit by making room for the minister to serve the church as well as continue growing and practicing in their area of talent.

This may well be true of many churches. Yet, the observation deflected attention from the seminary and its role in supporting bivocational students and pastors. Missing from faculty comments was any discussion of what this institution of theological education might do differently to better educate for a thriving bivocational ministry.

Students

Students, more than any other group, defended the legitimacy of bivocational ministry and voiced appreciation to the seminary for raising the visibility of this form of pastoring. Of the seven students who offered a free response, three provided a justification for bivocational ministry. "Multi vocational ministry is a viable calling for serving the kingdom and maybe the way in which those who are called to serve can serve," commented one student. Another stated, "I believe it is another form of living out a call and isn't lesser than full time ministry—just different. I believe it can be in many different forms." Clearly, these students felt the need to defend bivocational ministry as "a viable calling" that is not "lesser than" univocational career paths. Yet another student remarked, "Bivocational ministry is not a new concept. While the term may have not been used in decades earlier, some ministers have always had two or more careers." This student drew attention to the fact that the newness is not the practice in the church but rather the awareness of this practice on the part of professional theological educators and the full-time, professional pastors they have trained over the years. Two students also thanked the seminary for its efforts in this area, and another indicated that the conversation about bivocational ministry was personally relevant to their professional discernment. As if to summarize the sentiments voiced by students, one remarked, "This should be an orientation topic for new students or prospective students."

Students participating in the focus group expressed a range of ideas for improving the way the seminary supports bivocational students and prepares them for bivocational ministry. Students identified several challenges, including the availability of student services, scheduling difficulties, field education placements, and boundaries between personal and professional realms. When asked about their needs as bivocational students, they mentioned the need for better communication about student workload and degree program expectations; transition support for second-career students and bivocational students; courses on finances, budgeting, entrepreneurship, and fundraising; and bivocational student advising. When asked how the seminary might better serve and equip future bivocational students, participants offered specific ideas: the importance of and need to incorporate practical experiences, such as mock weddings or baptisms, with some of the courses; not assuming that every student comes to seminary with church background and practical knowledge of congregational life; more availability of administrative staff on the weekends; early advisement on field education and Clinical Pastoral Education (CPE) options; and counseling, resources, and support for family members of bivocational students.

Trustees

Trustees showed a combination of caution and openness to institutional change. In open-ended comments, one expressed a need for more research to better understand the issue:

> As a member of the board of trustees, I realize I actually have very little information about how bivocational students and alumni feel about how LTS served them. I am unable to comment on recommended institutional changes without understanding better what we know about how we are currently doing with preparing students for bivocational ministry.

The approach is prudent; indeed, the very motivation for the present grant-funded project was to conduct research on these and other questions. Another trustee wasted no time in advocating for institutional change: "We need to raise the value of a pathway to ministry as a bivocational option. LTS could work with judicatories to create the training for these roles just like they did for alternate paths to ordination." This response requires some knowledge of institutional background for interpretation. Regarding training, the trustee drew a comparison to the seminary's new program of lifelong learning, which was created in response to recent changes in the United Church of Christ that allow candidates for ordination to fulfill educational requirements without earning a Master of Divinity degree or attending seminary. Thus, this trustee was suggesting that the institution think outside of current degree program offerings as it educates persons for bivocational ministry

Trustees were also given an opportunity through other parts of this survey to express their opinions about prioritizing specific institutional changes to promote and support bivocational ministry at the seminary. Exactly 50% agreed that the seminary should "create a program designed with the needs of bivocational students in mind" (Q23 for trustees) and "encourage students to consider a bivocational career path in ministry" (Q24 for trustees). Only one trustee disagreed with these statements. Furthermore, 75% agreed that the seminary should "raise the profile of bivocational ministry as a legitimate and vital form of leadership for the church" (Q25 for trustees), and 25% strongly agreed with this statement. However, ambivalence surfaced when trustees were asked about recruitment. Only 25% agreed that "Lancaster Seminary should prioritize institutional changes in order to recruit bivocational students" (Q22 for trustees); the remaining respondents were neutral.

The trustees presented a complicated picture of institutional response. On the one hand, they agreed that the institution should encourage bivocational career paths and bolster the legitimacy of this path. On the other hand, they implied that the seminary should do so outside of its existing degree programs. Would this combination of sentiments explain why trustees responded so affirmatively to institutional improvements yet expressed reluctance to recruit bivocational students?

Educating for a Thriving Bivocational Ministry

The preceding data and analysis provide a fine-grained picture of perceptions, attitudes, and opinions about bivocational ministry and seminary education according to four groups of constituents at Lancaster Seminary. This picture closely aligns with the existing literature, helping theological educators to understand the challenges and opportunities facing bivocational students and students preparing for bivocational ministry. These findings are indicative rather than definitive, inviting further research involving more schools and a larger set of respondents.

Perceptions of and attitudes about bivocational ministry were characterized by ambivalence. Many recognized the need for bivocational ministry even as they expressed no desire to be bivocational. All constituencies surveyed valued bivocational ministry as a distinct and legitimate form of ministry with vocational integrity. However, many expressed personal ambivalence about being bivocational. Students expressed the entire range of responses when asked if they were intentional about pursuing bivocational ministry. Nearly 70% of all constituents surveyed viewed bivocational ministry as the future of pastoral ministry; yet faculty and trustees overwhelmingly preferred the model of fully funded ministry. What does it mean that so many acknowledge the importance of a form of ministry that is different from their preferred form of leadership? Students and staff were less certain about this preference; were they just being more realistic than faculty and trustees about the employment options available to seminary graduates?

Theological educators seeking to respond to an increasing need for bivocational ministry preparation, training, and support will have to address ambivalence directly. Intentional efforts to expose existing negative perceptions and to destigmatize bivocational ministry are needed to validate and support students in bivocational ministry. These efforts must address attitudes internal to the institution, as well. If faculty and trustees harbor a full-time bias, the school should not be surprised if its students express ambivalence about bivocational ministry as a preferred career option. The bias against part-timers runs deep in higher education, as any contingent faculty member can attest. While one staff person suggested that adjunct professors provide a positive model of bivocationality, it is no secret that adjuncts suffer from significant institutional injustices (see, for example, Gaudet and Keenan 2019). This implicit curriculum must be changed if schools desire to promote bivocational ministry as a valued pathway for ministry. Significantly, students evidenced a need to defend the legitimacy of bivocational ministry in their survey responses. They also expressed appreciation to the seminary for raising the issue through this research. Though student focus group participants were paid a small stipend, it was clear that they valued the experience for more than the money. The focus group became a support group for students experiencing and exploring bivocational ministry. Through both the focus group and the survey instrument, the research itself seemed to fulfill a need for students, validating them in a form of ministry that holds distinct challenges and stresses.

This research confirmed the challenges and stressors most often cited in the literature on bivocational ministry, sometimes heightened by the seminary experience. Those surveyed mentioned financial pressures, inadequate professional support, negative perception and stigma, and the importance of intentionality and fit, balance and vocational integration, and renegotiating congregational expectations. At least two staff persons shared keen observations about economic inequality, the difficulty of vocational integration and pastoral identity in multiple spheres, the relevance of cultural context, and the need for definitional clarity of the term bivocational. Addressing intentionality and fit is also important to health and flourishing of the bivocational pastor (Watson et al. 2020, 18). However, as implied by the survey data, it is difficult to be intentional about a future vocation for which one feels tremendous ambivalence. The ability to discern a unique and appropriate fit for the individual in bivocational ministry is premised on bivocational ministry being valued and supported as a preferred career option.

The stresses of bivocational ministry are evident throughout the seminary experience. Students face these challenges not only in future bivocational ministry positions but also as students balancing schoolwork, family, jobs, and churchwork. In addition to pressures relating to the practical matters of finances, scheduling, and workload, seminary students actively seek vocational clarity while participating in an intense process of spiritual formation and discernment. Participants in the student focus group also revealed that many of these stressors are exacerbated by differences in privilege due to race, gender, and class. As do many ATS programs, this school provides programmatic guidance for vocational discernment, integration, and review. However, if bivocational ministry is not an explicit part of this structured experience, bivocational students may perceive these programmatic features of the degree program as irrelevant or antagonistic to bivocational integration and clarity.

Survey respondents named stressors and challenges more readily than the skills needed to address them. One item in the literature not evident in the data collected was the need for different pastoral leadership styles in bivocational congregations as contrasted with congregations that employ a full-time pastor. Knowing this difference is a matter of leadership skill. Based on the 2017 ATS Graduating Student Questionnaire, ATS researcher Jo Ann Deasy posed the following questions regarding skills development:

> The growing number of graduates going into bi-vocational ministry raises several questions about theological education. . . . What are the unique skills needed to prepare someone for bi-vocational ministry? Are there particular ways of thinking that need to be cultivated? Are there ways to help students develop a portfolio of skills that will allow them to structure a bi-vocational life that can support them financially? Should theological schools develop part-time programs that intentionally teach students how to live and think bi-vocationally as they balance work and school? (Deasy 2018, 70)

Deasy's questions about skills development remain only partially addressed by the current research. Distinctive skills and mindsets helping to structure a successful bivocational ministry can only be inferred from the survey data. Furthermore, bivocational ministry as such is under-researched; outside of this volume, there is a paucity of scholarly literature on the skills needing cultivation.

Survey data revealed wide disparity in opinion about this school's current academic curriculum as it pertains to bivocational ministry. Of several aspects of this school's programming, academic curriculum stood out as the area in most need of improvement, according to those surveyed. While the survey responses exhibited a general sense that the academic curriculum should be changed to support bivocational ministry, the survey was not designed to elicit ideas about how it should be changed. Disparity of opinion among the faculty about the academic curriculum combined with their overall preference for full-time ministry portend difficult conversations about the desirability of reshaping academic offerings to support bivocational ministry. One staff person questioned the ability of the current degree program to address the challenges faced by bivocational students. Furthermore, trustees voiced reluctance to prioritize recruiting bivocational students even though this seminary already offers a weekend schedule for its Master of Divinity curriculum, designed for students holding a job while attending school. Trustees were, however, in favor of creating a program with bivocational students in mind. There may be a significant number of faculty and trustees who consider bivocational ministry preparation more appropriate for this school's non-degree program of life-long learning than for its master's-level degree programs, as suggested by one trustee. This is an important conversation to pursue.

Lancaster Seminary is well-positioned to address Deasy's last question, about part-time programs of theological education. Most survey respondents agreed that the school supports bivocational students through scheduling choices, and most staff and trustees agreed that the seminary should improve in this area. This seminary's "weekend" track for the Master of Divinity degree has been successful enough to overshadow the more traditional, three-year "weekday" option; however, more effort is needed to meet the needs of bivocational students. The weekend program could be improved, in Deasy's words, by "intentionally teach[ing] students how to live and think bi-vocationally as they balance work and school" (Deasy 2018, 70). It is not enough merely to change the schedule to accommodate working students; bivocational ministry preparation requires intentional reflection on the schedule and what it means for students vocationally. Only about 10% of staff and students agreed that this seminary's co-curricular offerings meet the needs of bivocational students. The need to address bivocational ministry intentionally is evidenced in the difficulty staff and faculty had in naming specific examples of current co-curricular support of bivocational ministry. Scheduling and time constraints come into play, as one staff person noted, when students do not show up for the co-curricular activities the seminary offers.

Theological schools will need to explore Deasy's questions in partnership with students and practitioners as they develop ways to meet the needs of bivocational students and pastors. All constituencies surveyed agreed that student services should be improved. Faculty and staff could name many specific examples of existing student services supportive of bivocational students, and students, more so than any other group surveyed, seemed to think this seminary was already doing a good job at this. For example, Lancaster Seminary provides a program of financial literacy and coaching; this research underscores its importance and suggests an expansion of the program may be helpful. The wide array of existing student services and varied opinions about their efficacy indicate that this is an area of this seminary's offerings that is in generative flux; innovating and refining student services may be an opportunity for creative partnership as this school learns how to teach students to live and think bivocationally.

Conclusions

Theological educators seeking to improve the preparation, training, and support of bivocational students will have to find ways to address distinct challenges and stressors as well as skills development and perception. Cultivating more positive attitudes and perceptions about bivocational ministry is foundational. The current research inadvertently functioned in this capacity, promoting and legitimating bivocational ministry within this seminary community, suggesting that increased visibility is an important form of support for bivocational students. To be intentionally supportive of bivocational ministry, theological educators must reshape academic curricula to meet the needs of bivocational students. An increasing awareness of the need for bivocational ministry preparation, training, and support should prompt theological schools to partner with students, reflective practitioners, and churches to shape the curriculum in meaningful ways. Not of least importance, the full-time bias within higher education creates a strong implicit curriculum disfavoring bivocational pathways. Can schools that marginalize their contingent faculty promote bivocational ministry with integrity? Furthermore, is bivocational ministry preparation an integral part of degree programs in theological education, or does it belong more appropriately in non-degree programs of life-long learning? ATS member schools will need to decide whether bivocational ministry preparation is an essential or ancillary aspect of their mission as degree-granting institutions as they prepare to educate for a thriving bivocational ministry.

Works Cited

Aleshire, Daniel O. 2008. *Earthen Vessels: Hopeful Reflections on the Work and Future of Theological Schools.* Grand Rapids, MI: Eerdmans.

———. 2010. "Theological Education in North America." In *Handbook of Theological Education in World Christianity: Theological Perspectives—Regional Surveys—Ecumenical Trends,* edited by Dietrich Werner, David Esterline, Namsoon Kang and Joshva

Raja, 502–13. Regnum Studies in Global Christianity. Oxford: Regnum.

———. 2011. "The Future has Arrived: Changing Theological Education in a Changed World." *Theological Education* 46, no. 2: 69–80. *ats.edu/files/galleries/2011-theological-education-v46-n2.pdf.*

———. 2021. *Beyond Profession: The Next Future of Theological Education.* Theological Education between the Times. Grand Rapids, MI: Eerdmans.

Association of Theological Schools in the United States and Canada (ATS). n.d. "Total School Profile Reports." Accessed January 2, 2022. *ats.edu/resources/student-data/total-school-profile-reports.*

Bentley, Kristen Plinke. 2018. "Perspectives of Bi-Vocational Ministry: Emerging Themes in Bi-Vocational Ministry Research at Lexington Theological Seminary." *Lexington Theological Quarterly* 48: 115–51. *lextheo.edu/wp-content/uploads/2021/09/j-4-Perspectives-of-Bi-Vocational-Ministry.pdf.*

Bickers, Dennis W. 2007. *The Work of the Bivocational Pastor.* Valley Forge, PA: Judson.

Carroll, Jackson W., and Becky R. McMillan. 2006. *God's Potters: Pastoral Leadership and the Shaping of Congregations.* Grand Rapids, MI: Eerdmans.

Chapman, Mark D., and James W. Watson. 2020. *Canadian Multivocational Ministry Project: Educating Multivocational Leaders—White Paper. ureachtoronto.ca/wp-content/uploads/2020/11/Educating-Multivocational-Leaders White-Paper.pdf.*

Chaves, Mark, Joseph Roso, Anna Holleman, and Mary Hawkins. 2020. "National Congregations Study: Waves I–IV Summary Tables." Duke University Department of Sociology, Durham, NC. Last modified January 11, 2021. *sites.duke.edu/ncsweb/files/2021/01/NCS-IV_Summary-Tables_For-Posting.pdf.*

Christian Reformed Church in North America. 2020. "Study of Bivocationality Task Force." October 30. *faithaliveresources.org/Products/830135/study-of-bivocationality-task-force.aspx.*

Deasy, Jo Ann. 2018. "Shifting Vocational Identity in Theological Education: Insights from the ATS Student Questionnaires." *Theological Education* 52, no. 1: 63–78. *ats.edu/files/galleries/2018-theological-education-v52-n1.pdf.*

Earlham School of Religion. n.d. "Bi-vocational Ministry Project Resources." Accessed May 31, 2021. *esr.earlham.edu/community-resources/economic-challenges-facing-future-ministers/bi-vocational-ministry-project-resources.*

Edington, Mark D. W. 2018. Bivocational: Returning to the Roots of Ministry. New York: Church Publishing. *bivocational.church.*

Gaudet, Matthew J., and James Keenan, SJ, eds. 2019. Special Issue on Contingency and Catholic Colleges. *Journal of Moral Theology* 8. *jmt.scholasticahq.com/issue/1798.*

González, Justo L. 2015. *The History of Theological Education*. Nashville: Abingdon.

———. 2020. "There's No Theological Education Pipeline Anymore." *Christian Century* 137, no. 27. *christiancentury.org/article/how-my-mind-has-changed/there-s-no-theological-education-pipeline-anymore.*

Grand Rapids Seminary. 2018. "Bi-Vocational Ministry: Balancing Dual Roles." Audio. *soundcloud.com/grand-rapids-theological-seminary/bi-vocational-ministry-balancing-dual-roles.*

Lancaster Theological Seminary. 2020. "Student Body Statistics (as of October 15, 2020)." *lancasterseminary.edu/about/lancaster-seminary-at-a-glance.*

Lindner, Cynthia G. 2016. *Varieties of Gifts: Multiplicity and the Well-lived Pastoral Life*. Lanham: Rowman & Littlefield.

MacDonald, G. Jeffrey. 2020. *Part-Time is Plenty: Thriving without Full-Time Clergy*. Louisville: Westminster John Knox.

Miller-McLemore, Bonnie J. 2008. "Spinning Gold from Straw: A Matter of Multiple Vocations." In *From Midterms to Ministry: Practical Theologians on Pastoral Beginnings,* edited by Allan Hugh Cole Jr., 164–78. Grand Rapids, MI: Eerdmans.

Perry, Samuel L., and Cyrus Schleifer. 2019. "Are Bivocational Clergy Becoming the New Normal? An Analysis of the Current Population Survey, 1996–2017." *Journal for the Scientific Study of Religion* 58: 513–25. *doi.org/10.1111/jssr.12593.*

Samushonga, Hartness M. 2019. "A Theological Reflection of Bivocational Pastoral Ministry: A Personal Reflective Account of a Decade of Bivocational Ministry Practice Experience." *Practical Theology* 12: 66–80. *doi.org/10.1080/1756073X.2019.1575040.*

———. 2020. "On Bivocational Ministry-focused Training in British Theological Schools: Dialoguing with British Theological Educationalists." *Practical Theology* 13: 385–99. *doi.org/10.1080/1756073X.2020.1787006.*

Scharen, Christopher, and Sharon Miller. 2016. "Bright Spots in Theological Education: Hopeful Stories in a Time of Crisis and Change." *Auburn Studies* 22. *auburnseminary.org/report/bright-spots.*

Stephens, Darryl W. 2021. "Preparing to Educate for a Thriving Bivocational Ministry: A Seminary Case Study." *Religions* 12, no. 8: 592. *doi.org/10.3390/rel12080592.* Supplementary materials available online at *mdpi.com/article/10.3390/rel12080592/s1.*

Watson, James W., Wanda M. Malcolm, Mark D. Chapman, Elizabeth A. Fisher, Marilyn Draper, Narry F. Santos, Jared Siebert, and Amy Bratton. 2020. "Canadian Multivocational Ministry Project: Research Report." *canadianmultivocationalministry.ca/master-report.*

Yamada, Frank M. 2020. "Living and Teaching When Change is the New Normal: Trends in Theological Education and the Impact on Teaching and Learning." *Wabash Center Journal on Teaching* 1: 23–36. *doi.org/10.31046/wabashcenter.v1i1.1580.*

Endnotes

1 This research was funded by Lancaster Theological Seminary and a matching grant from the In Trust Center for Theological Schools. This chapter was originally published under a CC-BY license as Stephens, Darryl W. 2021. "Preparing to Educate for a Thriving Bivocational Ministry: A Seminary Case Study." *Religions* 12, no. 8: 592; *doi.org/10.3390/rel12080592*. I would like to thank researcher Nilda Roman for facilitating the student focus group meetings, Mwat Asedeh for bibliographic research assistance, and Zeke A. Stephens for preparing the data tables.

2 Questionnaires and raw data are available online at *mdpi.com/article/10.3390/rel12080592/s1* (Supplementary S1: Survey instruments; Supplementary S2: Survey Data).

3 Based on the ATS Graduating Student Questionnaires from 2013–2020, 31% of this seminary's graduates reported plans to serve bivocationally, compared to 30% of all ATS member school graduates (ATS n.d.); however, fewer of this seminary's graduates ruled out bivocational ministry compared to ATS member school graduates overall: 39% versus 51%, respectively (ATS n.d.). Based on 2020–2021 data, Deasy (chapter 15 in this volume) suggested, "two-thirds of master's graduates from ATS schools are either planning on or considering serving in multiple positions."

CHAPTER 15

The Multivocational Plans of Students in Graduate Theological Education

JO ANN DEASY

Since 2013, the Association of Theological Schools (ATS) has tracked the bivocational plans of entering and graduating students who attend graduate theological schools in the United States and Canada. The data have taught us quite a bit about bivocational ministry, particularly how it factors into student plans for ministry when they enter seminary and at graduation. The data have also revealed demographic differences among those pursuing bivocational ministry, including a significantly higher percentage of Black students planning to serve or already serving in such positions. In 2019, ATS began a process of revising the student questionnaires. My own experience as a bivocational minister, the experiences of my peers, and research undertaken as part of an initiative funded by the Lilly Endowment on the Economic Challenges Facing Future Ministers suggested that our current questions related to bivocational ministry were too narrow in scope. New questions were added to help us better understand the nature and scope of bivocational ministry. This chapter explores what we have learned from students at ATS-member institutions through the questionnaires. This knowledge is expanding our understanding of bivocational ministry, prompting us to embrace a complex multivocational reality that includes both paid and volunteer ministry.

History of Bivocational Ministry in the ATS Student Questionnaires (mid-1990s to 2013)

In the mid-1990s, the Association of Theological Schools created a set of questionnaires to gather information on students as they enter and graduate from member schools. The first questionnaires assumed that students would be planning on a single full-time job at graduation. However, by the first revision in 2001, a part-time response option was added. This change may have been due to the recession that hit the United States and Canada around that time. It may have been due to growing concerns about the ability of graduates to find full-time placement in congregations. It may also have been in recognition of those students planning to work part-time for a number of reasons, including the desire to balance work and family life, those serving in retirement, and the growing number of students entering graduate theological schools from traditions that historically hire bivocational pastors.

Data from 2001 suggested that this concern was unwarranted. Over 94% of graduates reported plans to work full-time. However, that percentage dropped to 87% the next year and over the next ten years steadily declined until it reached a low of 74% in 2012. During that decade, there was a growing awareness that many students planned to serve in bivocational ministry upon graduation. In 2013, ATS added a new question during a third revision of the questionnaires: Do you anticipate holding another paid position in addition to your ministerial work after graduation? Students were given the option to respond with yes, "unsure about being bivocational," no, or "no plans to do ministerial work."

While the question provided some information about the bivocational plans of students, it lacked clarity. First, it did not define ministerial work or clarify whether that ministerial work would be paid.

Second, it did not clarify whether the paid position would be full- or part-time and it assumed that a student would only have one other position. Finally, it assumed bivocational ministry meant one ministerial job and one "non-ministerial" job. It is likely that, when the question was crafted, there was an assumed model of bivocational ministry as one part-time paid ministry position and one part- or full-time paid non-ministry position.

A second question from the revised student questionnaire provided additional insight into the bivocational nature of students' work plans. The questionnaire asked students to indicate a single position they would be working in after graduation—a clear assumption that students would work in one primary job. They were first asked to indicate whether or not that position would be in a congregation and then whether it would be full-time or part-time. In 2013, there was a slight change to the question. Rather than asking students where they would be working after graduation, they were asked where they "anticipated" working after graduation. This change brought an increase in those planning to work full-time from 74% in 2012 to 81% in 2013. That percentage remained fairly steady, fluctuating between 80% and 82% over the next seven years.

When we compared the question on bivocational ministry with the question on what position a student anticipated serving in after graduation, we noticed that while approximately 80% of master's graduates planned to work in a single full-time position, 30% planned to serve in bivocational ministry. It became clear that students were not equating bivocational ministry with working part-time. Did this mean that students were working on one full-time paid position and then volunteering in ministry? Were they working one full-time paid position and a second or third part-time paid position? Our questionnaire was unable to capture the complexity of how students were navigating ministry, vocation, and paid work.

The Emerging Picture (2013–2019)

Over the next seven years, the Association of Theological Schools began looking closely at data on bivocational ministry among its students. Data clearly showed that bivocational ministry is impacted by various demographics, including race/ethnicity, age, and gender.[1]

This data also gives insight into ways the image of pastoral ministry has changed among ATS-member schools.

From 2013–2019, the ATS Entering Student Questionnaire asked students whether or not they anticipated holding another paid position in addition to ministry upon graduation. One quarter of entering master's students planned on bivocational ministry when entering seminary and another 40% were considering that possibility. These percentages remained quite steady over those seven years. That means that two-thirds of all students entering master's programs in graduate theological schools considered bivocational ministry a possible outcome of their degree. This statistic indicates a dramatic shift in the role of graduate theological schools, which historically focus on preparing students for full-time ordained ministry. As noted above, it was not until 2001 that the ATS student questionnaires even offered an option for graduates to indicate whether they would be working full-time, and bivocational ministry did not make it into the questionnaires until 2013. Bivocational ministry is not something on the margins but rather a central orienting image for a large percentage of those considering or engaged in pastoral ministry.

Do theological schools impact bivocational identity?

While bivocational ministry is a central image, some of those considering bivocational ministry as entering students changed their minds at graduation. The 2013–2019 ATS Graduating Student Questionnaires asked students whether or not they anticipated holding another paid position in addition to ministry upon graduation. Responses were consistent over those seven years. Figure 1 compares the answers of entering and graduating students, showing the total percentage of all respondents from 2013–2019. Among graduates with master's degrees, 30% anticipated holding another paid position; 20% were unsure; 41% did not plan on holding another position; and 8% reported no plans to serve in ministry.

Do you anticipate holding another paid position in addition to your ministerial work after graduation?				
	Yes	Unsure	No	No plans for ministry
2013–2019 Entering Students	25%	39%	30%	6%
2013–2019 Graduating Students	30%	20%	41%	8%

Figure 1: Comparison of bivocational plans among entering and graduating students (ATS 2020).

Graduate theological schools seem to help some students clarify whether or not they want to serve in bivocational ministry. Upon entering seminary, 39% of students were unsure about bivocational ministry. That percentage dropped to 20% at graduation, indicating that almost 20% of students gain clarity about bivocational ministry during seminary. That clarity is reflected in the increase among those not planning on bivocational ministry from 30% to 41% and among those planning on bivocational ministry from 25% to 30%. It is unclear from ATS data how and why students are making these decisions. Does graduate theological education acculturate students towards a particular form of ministry? Do students gain clarity about the realities of ministry jobs available while in their programs? Does a master's degree cause them to aspire to a full-time position or to serve in communities that cannot afford a full-time pastor? Do students graduate with educational debt that prevents them from considering part-time positions? Additional research is needed to clarify exactly how graduate theological schools influence student plans for bivocational ministry.

How do demographics impact bivocationality?

Data from the questionnaires showed significant differences in plans for bivocational ministry based on a number of different demographics, including the country where they attended school, their age, and their race or ethnicity. Perhaps surprisingly, there were only slight differences by degree program or gender. The various differences suggest that bivocational ministry is impacted by a variety of factors.

From 2013–2019, there was a slight decrease in the percentage of graduates from ATS schools in the United States who planned on bivocational ministry, and, while percentages fluctuated, the general trend of graduates from Canadian schools was slightly upwards (figure 2). Until 2019, graduates from schools in the United States were more likely to plan on bivocational ministry than graduates from Canadian schools. This may be due to differences in the ways ministry is structured and funded in Canada, different expectations of seminary graduates, the fact that Canadian seminary students are less likely to pursue ministry in a congregation, or a number of other factors. The data does beg the question whether or not there were external factors in Canada in 2015 and 2019 that impacted graduates' plans for bivocational ministry or whether shifts in the composition of schools participating in the questionnaires impacted the data.

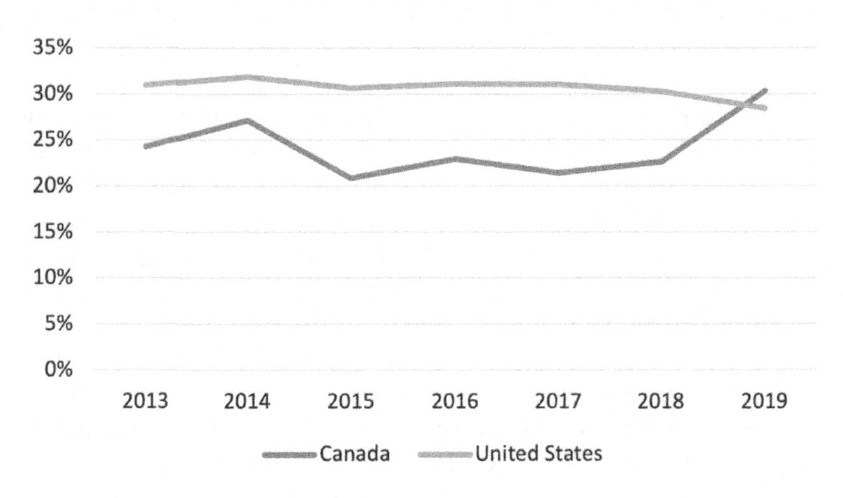

Figure 2: Graduates' plans for bivocational ministry in the United States vs. Canada (ATS 2020).

When looking at master's graduates by age, students aged fifty or older were more likely than younger students to plan on bivocational ministry, with a differential of 10%. Given the fact that many older students attend seminary to pursue a second career or to prepare for retirement, it makes sense that a higher percentage would plan to serve bivocationally. However, one quarter of students in their 20s and 30s also planned on bivocational ministry (figure 3).

	20-29 years	30-39 years	40-49 years	Age 50 or older
% planning on bivocational ministry	24%	26%	33%	35%

Figure 3: 2019–2020 bivocational ministry by age (ATS 2020).

When viewed by race and/or ethnicity, the differences in plans for bivocational ministry are even greater. Figure 4 shows the percentage of 2019–2020 master's graduates planning to serve in bivocational ministry by race/ethnicity. When ATS first started gathering data on plans for bivocational ministry in 2013, 58% of Black/non-Hispanic master's graduates planned on bivocational ministry versus only 25% of White/non-Hispanic. Graduates from 2019–2020 reported similar percentages with just over 50% of Black/non-Hispanic graduates planning on bivocational ministry versus 25% of White/non-Hispanic graduates. For Black/non-Hispanic students, bivocational ministry reflects the lower economic status of many Black congregations and communities as a result of historical financial inequities in the United States and Canada. A Pulpit & Pew study from 2003 found that 41% of Black pastors earned less than $13,000 per year and that Black pastors' salaries were about two-thirds of their White counterparts (McMillan and Price 2003, 14–15). The economic inequities faced by Black students are also evident in data related to educational debt. In 2019–2020, over 70% of Black graduates reported taking out student loans while in seminary versus 40% of White graduates, and the average debt of Black graduates was approximately $42,700 compared to $31,200 for White graduates (ATS 2020).

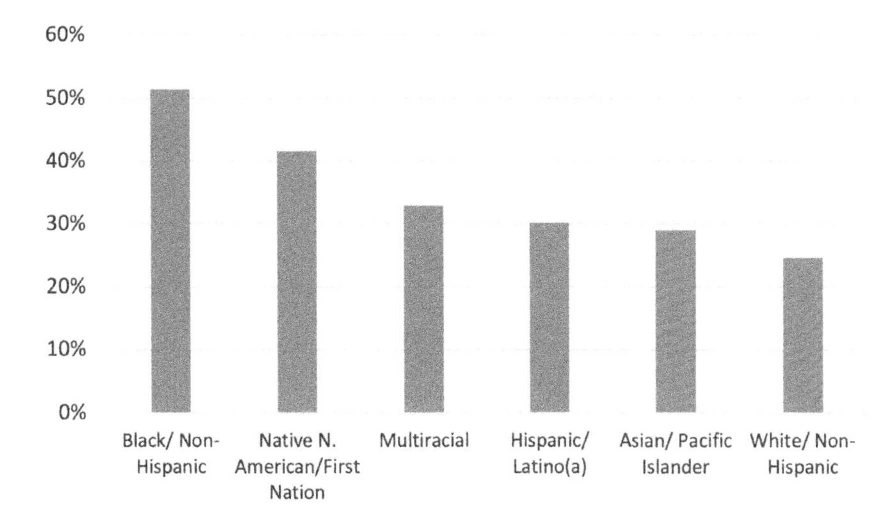

Figure 4: Bivocational ministry by race/ethnicity, 2019–2020 (ATS 2020).

The data raise questions about the financial impact of graduate theological education on students who plan to serve in bivocational ministry. Is the preparation received in seminary worth the cost of the degree? Should there be a different model of educating and forming those pastors who intend to serve in bivocational ministry? If different models are adopted, will they be comparable in terms of education and value within the denominational systems? Will such an approach further class divides or help overcome them?

In what positions do bivocational ministers serve?

The 2013–2019 ATS Graduating Student Questionnaires provided data on the positions students anticipated after graduation. By correlating data on bivocational ministry and anticipated position, the questionnaires revealed information on the types of bivocational ministries graduates planned to pursue. The questionnaires allowed students to provide data on only one anticipated ministry position.

Data gathered from 2013–2019 suggested that about 20% of bivocational graduates planned to serve as pastors, priests, or ministers of congregations. Another 40% planned to serve in staff ministry positions, including associate or assistant pastor, youth ministry, church planting, and minister of Christian or religious education. Just under 15% planned to serve in ministry outside the church, including hospital or military chaplaincy, campus ministry, social justice ministry, or missionary service. Men going into bivocational ministry were much more likely than women to plan to serve as senior or solo pastors (28% versus 13%). This is likely due to ecclesial differences among ATS schools, some of which are related to denominations that do not allow women to be ordained.

A Shift Towards Multivocationality

The Association of Theological Schools gathered seven years' worth of data on bivocational ministry between 2013–2019. During that time frame, the Association also undertook two different but related initiatives. In 2013, ATS began coordinating an initiative funded by the Lilly Endowment entitled, "The Theological School Initiative to Address the Economic Challenges Facing Future Ministers." This initiative included grants of up to six years awarded to 67 theological schools to address the economic challenges of their students through research, education, institutional changes, and collaborations. Several schools in the initiative began to look more closely at bivocational ministry and its impact on the financial wellness of both pastors and congregations.[2] Research focused on the shape of bivocational ministry, which we learned was incredibly diverse in terms of structure and motivations, and its financial impact on pastors. Meanwhile, a parallel initiative, also funded by the Lilly Endowment, focused on denominations and other organizations that support pastoral leaders. The denominational initiative sponsored several research projects, documenting a growing number of pastors serving in bivocational ministry throughout the United States (Hadaway and Marler 2017 and 2019).

The data gathered, both through the questionnaires and through the Lilly initiatives, contributed to a new revision of the questionnaires, launched in fall 2020. This new revision shifted the language from bivocationality to multivocationality. The questionnaires also sought to clarify the relationship between ministry and salaries. Were students working one or more jobs so that they could do ministry for free? Were they working to earn additional money while serving in congregations that could not afford to pay them a living wage?

ATS first began thinking about multivocationality after engaging the research of Charisse Gillett and Kristine Bentley at Lexington Theological Seminary (Bentley 2019; Bentley, chapter 7 in this volume). Their research revealed a variety of ministry and vocational configurations among those who might be considered bivocational. Some held multiple ministry positions. Others balanced ministry with secular jobs. Still others held a single paying job and volunteered in ministry. The *bi-* portion of *bivocational* was not always accurate. While some clergy understood themselves as having multiple vocations, many felt they had a single vocation—a call to ministry—which was financially supported in several different ways.

Their research echoed my own experiences in ministry. Just prior to joining the staff at ATS, I served as a bivocational pastor. I was the part-time pastor of a small church just outside of Chicago. It had never been my intention to serve as a bivocational pastor, but finding work in the church or academy in 2010 was difficult. So, I took a part-time position at the church and worked in a variety of other jobs in order to pay the bills, including jobs such as bookkeeping, children's ministry, adjunct teaching, and consulting. I had a single vocation but worked multiple jobs to allow me financially to fulfill that call. Several colleagues also served in multiple configurations of work and ministry. One shifted his pastoral position to part-time and took a job as a football coach because he felt called to live out his vocation both in the church and the world. Another served three small rural congregations in northern Minnesota. Others were professors who also pastored local churches or parents who chose to work part-time in order to spend more time raising young children. Still others were full-time business leaders who stepped in when their church needed a pastor. The language of *bivocational* was inadequate to describe the multiple ways we were living out our calls to ministry and financial stewardship.

The Current Landscape (2020–2021)

During the 2020–2021 academic year, ATS gathered its first data with the new revisions of the questionnaires. To capture the complexity of multivocational ministry, we asked graduates the following questions:

Upon graduating from this program, do you anticipate holding multiple paid positions?

- ☐ Yes
- ☐ Yes, and one or more positions will be ministerial work
- ☐ Unsure, but one or more positions will be ministerial work
- ☐ Unsure
- ☐ No

Upon graduating from our school, what types of positions do you anticipate having? (Check all that apply)

- ☐ Congregational/parish ministry
- ☐ Teaching or educational setting
- ☐ Health care chaplain or counselor
- ☐ Faith-based nonprofit
- ☐ Other

Do you anticipate holding a volunteer/unpaid ministerial position after graduation?

- ☐ Yes
- ☐ No
- ☐ Unsure

Graduates were also asked if they planned on multiple positions five years after graduation and the types of positions in which they anticipated serving. While the responses clarified some aspects of the work configurations of graduates, they also raised several questions about how graduates interpret the relationship between work, vocation, and ministry.

What percentage of graduates plan to serve in multiple positions?

The 2020–2021 survey had two questions related to the positions students would be serving in after graduation. The first question was quite direct: "Upon graduating from this program, do you anticipate holding multiple paid positions?" Just over 30% of graduates were planning to work in multiple positions. Another 33% were unsure about serving in multiple positions. Just over one-third (35%) were not planning to work in multiple positions. This response was similar to data from previous years. Also similar to previous years, Black/African American/African Canadian graduates were most likely to plan on serving in multiple positions (46%) followed by Hispanic/Latino(a)/Latin@ students (38%). Asian descent/Pacific Islander, Native North American/First Nation/Indigenous, and White/Caucasian students were least likely to plan on serving in multiple positions (approximately 27% each).

The second question was less direct: "Upon graduating from our school, what types of positions do you anticipate having?" Students were given the following options and asked to check all that apply: congregational/parish ministry, teaching or educational setting, health care chaplain or counselor, faith-based nonprofit, and "other." Overall, the second question revealed that 40% of graduates anticipated serving in multiple types of positions at graduation with a small percentage (4% overall) planning to serve in four or five positions at graduation. This was higher than the 32% who indicated in the first question their plans to serve in multiple paid positions. Why the difference in responses between these two questions? It may be due to differences in wording. The first question specifically asked about paid positions: "Do you anticipate holding multiple paid positions?" The second question simply asked, "What types of positions do you anticipate having?" It is possible that some students were not differentiating between paid and volunteer positions in the second question. It is also possible that students who indicated they were unsure about serving in multiple positions in the first question selected multiple "anticipated" positions in the second question.

This connection between being unsure and anticipating multiple positions arose again when we compared it to data related to placement. The percentage of graduates who anticipated serving in multiple positions in the second question was higher (50%) for students who did not yet have a position at graduation or who planned on further studies after graduating with their master's degree. This connection between lack of placement and multivocationality seems to be confirmed by data from the first question, which allowed students to indicate that they were unsure about working in multiple paid positions. Among those who did not have placement at graduation, over 50% were unsure about working in multiple positions and an additional 26% planned on multiple positions. Regarding placement, two other groups had significant percentages of students (45% each) who said they were unsure about multiple positions: those who were not seeking placement because they attended seminary for personal enrichment and those who planned on further graduate studies. Interestingly, only 2% of those students who attended for personal enrichment indicated certainty about serving in multiple positions versus one-third (33%) of those planning on further graduate studies.

When students are struggling to find placement at graduation, many imagine the need to seek multiple positions. For some, this may be a result of a particular call to multivocationality or to serve congregations that cannot afford a full-time pastor. For others, working in multiple positions may be a way to meet financial obligations when a full-time position is not available. That was certainly the case for me after I completed my doctoral degree. Faced with a challenging job market, I pieced together any work I could find in order to pay off student loans, a mortgage, health insurance, and other living expenses. For some, the path of multivocationality simply reflects how they currently understand the job market in the United States and Canada. More and more people are operating in a gig economy where work consists of multiple, part-time, permanent or short-term "gigs" that are pieced together to make a living wage.

What percentage of students serving in multiple positions plan to serve in ministry?

The data show that just over half of those unsure about and planning on serving in multiple paid positions are planning on serving in a paid ministry position. Prior to 2020–2021, data from the ATS student questionnaires assumed that those students serving in multiple positions were planning to serve in ministry. In 2020–2021, those graduates who indicated that they were considering multiple paid positions (unsure) or were definitely planning on multiple paid positions (yes) were asked to clarify if one of those multiple positions would be in ministry. The data revealed that only about half of those planning to serve in multiple paid positions would be serving in ministry. Figure 5 shows the percentage of graduates planning to work in one paid position, which may or may not be in ministry, those who were unsure about working in multiple paid positions, and those who definitely planned to work in multiple paid positions. Data on graduates who were unsure or planning on serving in multiple paid positions is further broken down by those who planned on working in at least one paid ministry position and those who did not plan on any paid ministry positions.

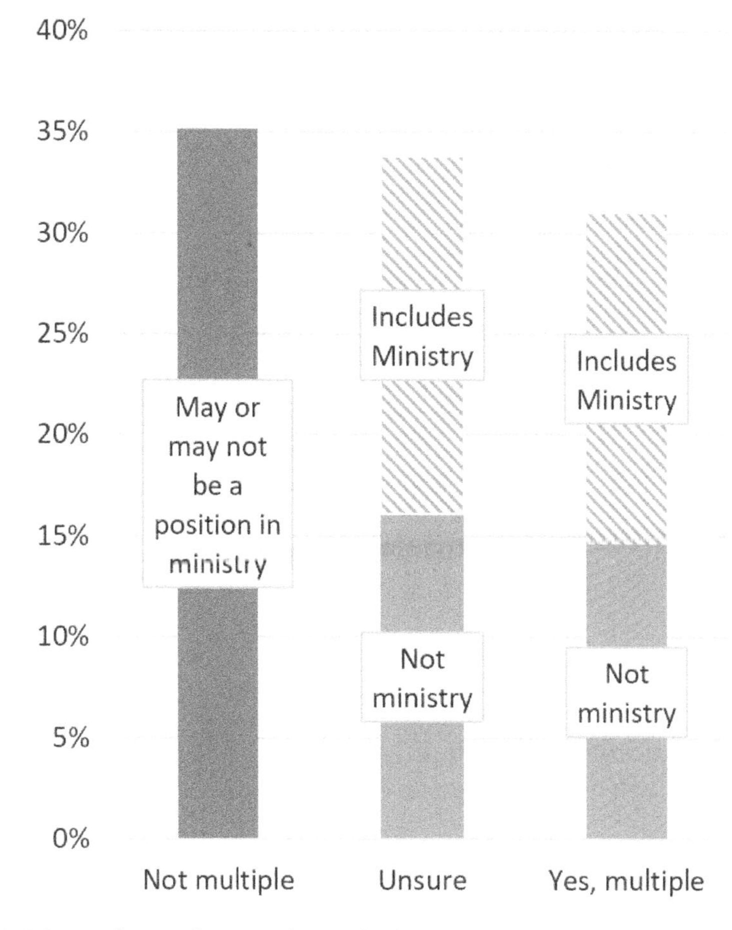

Figure 5: Do graduates plan to work in multiple positions? (ATS 2021)

In figure 4, we noted that a greater percentage of Black/non-Hispanic graduates (compared to other demographics) were planning to serve in multiple positions. Data from 2020–2021 showed a similar high percentage for Black/African American/African Canadian graduates, with 46% planning to serve in multiple paid positions (figure 6). In 2020–2021, a higher percentage of Hispanic/Latino(a)/Latin@ graduates planned to serve in multiple paid positions (38%, figure 6) than in previous years (30%, figure 4). Percentages for Asian descent/Pacific Islander and White/Caucasian students were similar to previous years, between 25% and 30%. Figure 6 shows that, in almost every racial/ethnic category, about half the graduates planning to serve in multiple paid positions were planning on one of those positions being in ministry. There was one exception: Native North American/First Nation/Indigenous graduates. The number of respondents in this racial/ethnic category was quite small. Further data will be needed to understand if this is an anomaly or a trend for these graduates.

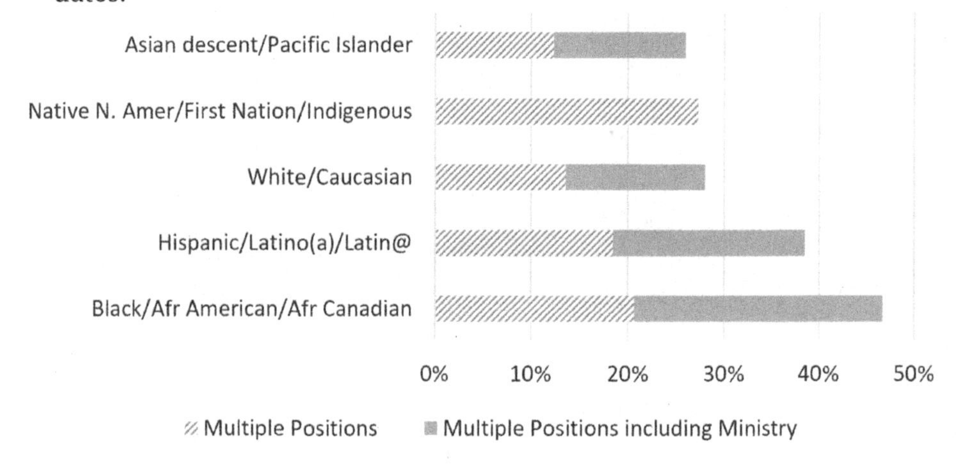

Figure 6: Plans for multivocational ministry by race/ethnicity, 2020–2021 (ATS 2021).

Data from this question focusing on multiple paid positions seems to indicate that, while a large percentage of students are planning on serving in multiple positions, far fewer are actually planning on serving in multivocational ministry. If these students are not planning to serve in ministry, where are they planning to serve?

Where will multivocational graduates be serving?

Multivocational graduates plan to serve in a wide-variety of settings, many of them within congregations. However, the data also raise questions about how respondents were interpreting the survey questions. In the first question, when asked specifically if they would be working in multiple paid positions that included ministry (figure 5), just over half chose, "Yes, and one of those positions will be in ministry." In the second question, when these same respondents were asked what types of positions they anticipated holding after graduation, 61% indicated plans to work in a congregation or parish, work that would likely be considered ministry. In addition, 39% indicated plans to work in teaching or educational settings, 26% in healthcare chaplaincy or counseling, 31% in a faith-based non-profit, and 25% in some other setting. Of the 26% who planned to work in healthcare or counseling, about a third indicated in a later question that they planned to serve as chaplains. It is possible that graduates were not entirely sure where they would be serving after graduation, resulting in conflicting data. This would suggest that further research among alums would provide better data on multivocational ministry among graduates of theological schools. It is also possible that the slight difference in wording—the addition of "paid" position in the first question—skewed the data. Respondents may have interpreted the second question more broadly to include volunteer as well as paid positions.

Are Volunteer Ministers Bivocational?

In 2020–2021, the ATS questionnaires added specific questions about volunteer ministry. While volunteer ministry is rarely considered a form of bivocational or multivocational ministry, earlier data from the questionnaires suggested that volunteer ministry is much more prevalent among female students and certain racial/ethnic groups (see also Young Brown, chapter 4 in this volume). This trend was confirmed in the new questionnaire.

Approximately 25% of all master's graduates plan to volunteer in a ministry position after graduation. Percentages are about the same for those planning to serve in one position or in multiple positions, including those multivocational graduates planning on a paid position in ministry. Similar to multivocationality, percentages of students planning on volunteering in ministry varies by race/ethnicity. Comparing data from 2019–2020 (figure 4) to data from 2020–2021 (figure 7) on the impact of race/ethnicity on plans to serve in multiple positions, we see that Black/African American/African Canadian graduates are still the most likely demographic to plan on serving in multiple paid positions. They are also most likely to plan on volunteering in ministry after graduation. In 2020–2021, a greater percentage of Hispanic/Latino(a)/Latin@ graduates planned on serving in multiple positions than in 2019–2020. This may have been due to slight changes in the wording of the question about serving in multiple positions or changes in the question related to race/ethnicity that allowed graduates to select all that apply. It may also be related to fluctuations in the schools that participate in the questionnaire. More longitudinal data related to these new questions may help provide clarity.

Important to note in figure 7 is the relationship between multivocationality, volunteer ministry, and race/ethnicity. Black and Hispanic graduates had the highest percentage of respondents planning to serve in multiple positions and the highest percentage planning to volunteer in ministry. Multiracial graduates and White/Caucasian graduates were less likely to plan on multiple paid positions and also the least likely to plan on volunteering in ministry after graduation. Native North American/First Nation/Indigenous graduates and Asian-descent/Pacific Islander graduates were the least likely to plan on serving in multiple paid positions but more likely to plan on volunteering in ministry than their White and multi-racial colleagues. This data suggests that there are various ways graduates are negotiating the relationship between multiple paid positions and volunteer ministry. In some cases, such as among Black and Hispanic students, there seems to be a possible correlation between multiple paid positions and volunteering in ministry. Both racial/ethnic groups had high percentages of graduates planning to work in multiple positions and high percentages of graduates planning to volunteer in ministry. Among Asian students, the opposite seems to be true. While Asian students had the lowest percentage of graduates planning to work in multiple positions, they had the second-highest percentage of graduates planning to volunteer in ministry.

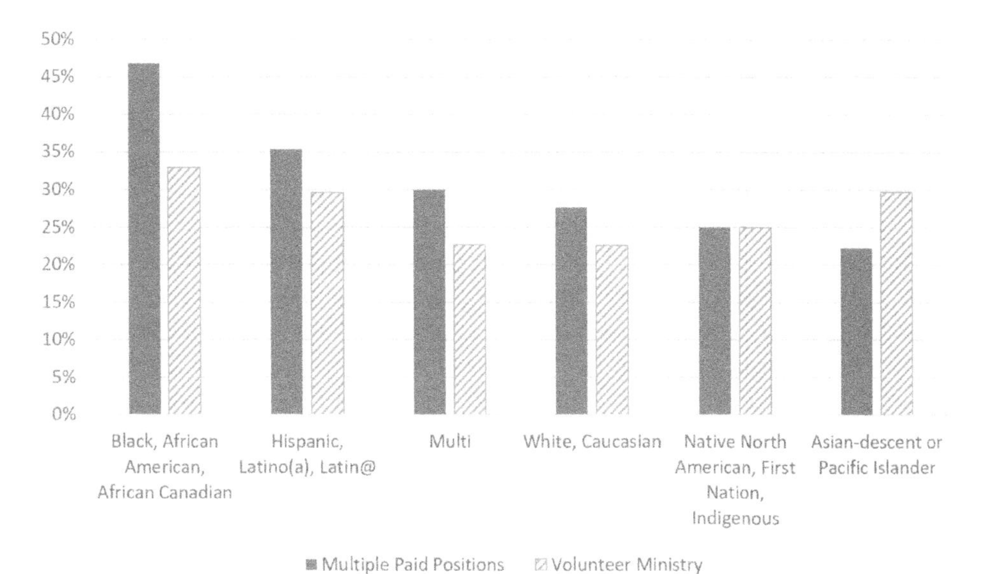

Figure 7: Percentage of 2021 graduates by race/ethnicity planning to serve in multiple paid positions and/or volunteer in ministry (ATS 2021).

Why the differences? Is it due to cultural expectations related to service, community, or ministry? Is it impacted by socio-economic status? How is it impacted by power and privilege in church and society? The data suggest that more research is needed in order to develop a definition of multivocational ministry that embraces various racial/ethnic expectations of work, service, and ministry.

Gender also has a significant impact on volunteer ministry. In every racial/ethnic category, female students were more likely to volunteer in ministry than male students. Differences were slight for White graduates, where 2% more females than males reported plans to serve in volunteer ministry. Differences were more pronounced for Asian (5% more), Hispanic (8% more), Black (9% more), and Native North American, where 40% of female graduates were planning on volunteer ministry in 2020–2021 compared to none of the male graduates. In fall 2020, "other" was added as a new gender category in the questionnaire, but there was not yet sufficient data to determine the percentage of those who identify as "other" who plan on volunteering in ministry after graduation. The higher percentages of women planning to volunteer in ministry may be related to ecclessial and theological barriers in some denominations to women serving in certain positions within the church. It may also be related to the way gender roles, work, and ministry intersect in the lives of female graduates. Female graduates are more likely to take a part-time position or volunteer in ministry while raising children. Female graduates of color are more likely to struggle with the dual economic inequities associated with both gender and race that may shape how they navigate work and ministry.

Discussions about bivocational ministry often leave out volunteer ministry in an attempt to focus on professional definitions of ministry as defined by credentials or a paid position. While this might be appropriate in some cases, this omission does not recognize the number of volunteer ministers who invest time and money in a graduate degree in order to serve their congregations. Often, these ministry leaders volunteer because their congregations cannot afford to offer them a salary. This is particularly true among communities and person groups that have lower socio-economic status or have been historically impacted by financial inequities in society. Young Brown (chapter 4 in this volume) argued that to leave these unpaid ministers out of our conversations about professional and multivocational ministry is to neglect a group of ministry leaders who play a critical role in the everyday functioning of the church. Volunteer ministers are active and visible leaders and must be included in the definitions of ministry that shape our research, practices, and policies.

Conclusion

Data from the ATS student questionnaires over the last decade reveal a complex landscape of multivocationality. This landscape is impacted by historic inequities and cultural differences among various racial/ethnic groups as well as broad changes in cultural approaches to church and work. The data also reveal the prevalence of multivocational ministry among graduate theological students. The data suggests that two-thirds of master's graduates from ATS schools are either planning on or considering serving in multiple positions.

Why is this the case? ATS does not have data to answer that question, but there are several possibilities. The first is related to the decline in church attendance and church funding, contributing to a growing number of congregations that cannot afford to pay a full-time salary. Many graduates are aware of the needs of these churches and hope to serve in ways that will not be a financial burden. A second possibility, though, is that this generation of graduates thinks about employment in terms of a gig economy, which relies on short-term contracts and freelance work. A third possibility is that a growing number of students enter graduate theological education from ministry cultures that assume multivocational ministry, whether in congregations or non-profit ministries. With almost two-thirds of graduates planning on or considering multivocational ministry, the Association of Theological Schools and other educational institutions must take into account the implications of multivocationality for graduate theological education and the preparation of ministers.

What is the best way to prepare and support multivocational ministers? Our educational models often assume a full-time student or a student who is able to take off work to attend intensive courses. We often ask students to prioritize education over all the other parts of their life. While there is certainly value in this type of education, the reality is that many of our students are not able to dedicate such time to graduate theological education. They are multivocational students juggling work, family, ministry, and their studies in an attempt to follow God's call to lives of meaning and service.

Theological schools must look more deeply at the reasons why so many students are multivocational. Many are related to the reasons cited above as to why graduates are deciding to work in multiple positions, but there may be other reasons more directly related to theological education. ATS data on educational debt suggests that cost might be one reason students are choosing to be multivocational students. There are increasingly more students who do not receive financial support from denominations or congregations to pay for the cost of seminary. In some cases, this is due to financial struggles in these organizations. Often these financial struggles are related to socio-economic inequities impacting the broad ecology that supports students. In other cases, lack of financial support is due to the growing number of students who come to seminary without any formal denominational affiliation.

ATS data also suggests that age and life-stage may impact the choice to be multivocational. More students are waiting until they are older to come to seminary. While they bring with them rich experiences that enhance their educational experience, they also often bring with them added responsibilities in terms of finances, family, and work. It is more difficult for older students to disentangle themselves from their numerous responsibilities and callings to attend seminary full-time. They may be selling homes, moving families, and quitting jobs that provided health insurance and retirement benefits.

In my experience as a dean of students at a seminary, I encountered students who chose to be multivocational for a number of other reasons as well. For some, it was not so much about finances as about mission and vocation. They did not feel released from the places they were serving to attend school full-time. They felt that the needs of the congregation or community they served were too great to step away. For some, it was an educational decision. They learned best when they had some place to immediately apply their learning. They were not able to focus as full-time students and needed the balance of work to help them succeed. For others, it was a cultural decision. They recognized that the seminary did not understand their particular ministry and cultural context. They wanted to receive a solid education but not lose themselves and their culture in the process. They needed mentors within the community to help them integrate what they were learning in seminary. Theological schools need to learn more about why students choose to be multivocational in order to create solutions that best help students and schools achieve their missional goals.

The multivocational reality of students provides a challenge but also an opportunity for theological schools. Theological schools are no longer just preparing students for ministry. They partner with students in a journey of life-long learning that includes preparation as well as on-going professional development. Too often, theological schools teach students how to think deeply about various topics but do not give them the tools needed to do ministry well in the bounded spaces that are part of a multivocational reality. Multivocational students give theological schools a great opportunity to explore educational models that can prepare their graduates, not just with a foundation but also with the tools to continue learning throughout their lives and ministries. How does one learn best with limited time and resources? How does one balance a life of reflection and action? How does a pastor prepare for a sermon in a week during which there is also a wedding, a death, and a spiritual crisis? How does a pastor develop a theological and pastoral response to a community crisis when juggling two jobs and a family? What does it mean to live a life of discipleship ministry with such limited time constraints? How can theological schools prepare their students for this reality? What research is needed to find practices that help with this integration—practices that do not force pastors to choose between the practical and spiritual? In order to best serve and prepare students, theological schools and others who train people for ministry will need to find ways to meet these students where they are and give them tools to thrive in the multivocational ministries they have been called to.

ATS data reveals a complex landscape of multivocational students and alums who are navigating work, ministry, vocation, and education in a wide variety of ways. Theological schools have responded by offering part-time degrees, reduced credit hours, evening and weekend courses, and online courses. In many cases, they have lowered tuition and increased scholarships. All of these responses have made theological education more accessible and more affordable, but they have often required students to fit theological education into the margins of their multivocational lives. By looking more closely at the lives of multivocational ministers and students, theological schools have the opportunity to rethink their educational models in ways that focus more on integration and life-long learning. They have the opportunity to rethink the broad financial ecology of ministry. And they have the opportunity to create a more just system of theological education that is not just accessible but is also designed to equip and support those preparing to serve in multivocational and volunteer ministry roles.

Works Cited

Association of Theological Schools (ATS). 2020. "ATS Entering and Graduating Student Questionnaires (Version D) Multi-Year Datasets, 2013 to 2020." Some of the data is available in the annual total school profile reports available on *ats.edu*.

———. 2021. "ATS Entering and Graduating Student Questionnaires Total School Profile Dataset, Revision E. 2020–2021." Some of the data is available in the annual total school profile report available on *ats.edu*.

Bentley, Kristen Plinke. 2019. "Perspectives of Bi–vocational Ministry: Emerging Themes in Bi-vocational Ministry Research at Lexington Theological Seminary." *Lexington Theological Quarterly* 48: 115–51. *lextheo.edu/wp-content/uploads/2021/09/j-4-Perspectives-of-Bi-Vocational-Ministry.pdf.*

Deasy, Jo Ann. 2018. "Shifting Vocational Identity in Theological Education: Insights from the ATS Student Questionnaires." *Theo-*

logical Education 52: 63–78. *ats.edu/files/galleries/2018-theological-education-v52-n1.pdf.*

Hadaway, C. Kirk, and Penny Long Marler. 2017. "Economic Challenges Facing Pastoral Leaders: Report on NEI Planning Grant Research, 2015–2016." June 30. *web.archive.org/web/20210817180054/https://www.ecfpl.org/wp-content/uploads/2019/01/ECFPL-Hadaway-Marler-Research-Report.pdf.*

———. 2019. "What Pastors Get Paid, and When It's Not Enough." *Christian Century.* June 6. *christiancentury.org/article/critical-essay/what-pastors-get-paid-and-when-it-s-not-enough.*

McMillan, Becky R., and Matthew J. Price. 2003. "How Much Should We Pay the Pastor? A Fresh Look at Clergy Salaries in the 21st Century." *Pulpit & Pew Research Reports* 2 (Winter). Duke Divinity School.

Endnotes

1 The language of "race/ethnicity" comes from the Association of Theological School's Committee on Race and Ethnicity. These particular words were chosen to try and embrace the breadth of diversity within ATS schools, which include a wide range of Judeo-Christian denominations as well as schools in both the United States and Canada.

2 Schools looking at bivocational ministry included Austin Presbyterian Theological Seminary, Calvin Theological Seminary, Earlham Theological Seminary, Grand Rapids Theological Seminary, Iliff Theological Seminary, Lancaster Theological Seminary, Lexington Theological Seminary, New Orleans Baptist Theological Seminary, Payne Theological Seminary, Trinity Evangelical Divinity School, George W. Truett Theological Seminary, and University of the South School of Theology.

CHAPTER 16

Preparing to Teach a Bivocational Ministry Seminary Course

PHIL BAISLEY

During my first pastoral experience, as director of children's ministries at a church in north central Pennsylvania in the mid-1980s, I was busy but never felt overworked. Honestly, I loved my job. With almost one hundred children, preschool through sixth grade, involved in various programs—approximately one-third of the congregation—I felt my ministry was vital to the entire church. Unfortunately, church politics led me sadly to resign my position after only two years.

During an exit interview with the church's governing body, an elder remarked, "You certainly worked hard these past two years, but we always wondered why you never got a second job anywhere."

"Why would I?" I asked. "I had a full-time job right here."

"Yeah," the elder answered, "but we were only paying you for half-time."

In more than three decades of pastoral ministry, those were the only two years I was not bivocational, even though, as it turned out, I was still only paid "half-time." Bivocational ministry, also known as tentmaking, less-than-fully-funded ministry, and part-time pastoring, has been a way of life for me and for many others.

When I applied to teach pastoral ministry at Earlham School of Religion, I proposed a class to encourage and assist pastors in self-care, focusing on maintaining spiritual, mental, physical, emotional, and social health when deeply involved in ministry. I included a unit on bivocational ministry because I wanted seminary students to understand the fiscal realities of twenty-first century pastoring. I also wanted them to feel that there was no shame in pronouncing a benediction and asking, "Would you like fries with that?" on the same day of the week.

I got the job. Within weeks of accepting the position, I received a call from the presiding clerk of a small Quaker meeting I had pastored for one year shortly after graduating from seminary. They heard I was moving back to Richmond and asked me to be their pastor again. And I was back to being bivocational.

During my first few years at Earlham, I included units on bivocational ministry in the originally proposed course—Pastoral Spirituality—and another course—Work of the Pastor. Much of what I taught was based on my own experiences delivering pizzas, working in a hardware store, and substitute teaching while pastoring congregations in Ohio and Indiana. I assigned *The Tentmaking Pastor* by Dennis Bickers (2000) as my primary text, along with Michael F. Coughlin's article, "Full-time Pastor, Part-time Pay" (1991). Since my experience jibed with that of Bickers and others, I assumed mine was typical for bivocational ministers.

After 14 years of teaching about bivocational ministry and seeing more and more of my students graduating to less-than-fully-funded pastorates, I proposed an entire course on bivocational ministry and received grant money to study how best to teach it. In the following pages, I present the research behind the first syllabus for that course, what I have learned through my teaching, and my recommendations for other theological educators creating a syllabus for a bivocational ministry seminary course.

Gathering the Data

Before creating my first bivocational ministry course syllabus, I set out to gather as much data as would be useful in discerning what contemporary bivocational pastors need to know to have an effective ministry. I employed a student assistant with experience in designing surveys to create questionnaires for pastors and congregational leaders. She beta-tested the questionnaires via telephone interviews with a few churches. After sharing her collected data with me, we tweaked the questions.[1] I then set out to conduct in-person interviews with pastors and congregants from a sampling of churches in denominations that provide most of Earlham's students: Friends (Quakers), Metropolitan Community Church, Church of the Brethren, and the Episcopal Church. After contacting judicatory leaders in each of these traditions, as well as receiving some Baptist recommendations from Dennis Bickers, I arranged interviews with representative churches in Pennsylvania, Ohio, Indiana, Iowa, Colorado, and Oregon. Those interviews informed the course syllabus.

Expectations Based on Practical Wisdom

Having been a bivocational pastor for 24 years prior to beginning my research, I brought with me certain assumptions about bivocational ministry and certain expectations as to what the research would reveal. For example, I thought there were only two forms of bivocational pastoring. The first is when the minister's full-time job finances their pastoral service. Almost my entire teaching career I have served some local congregation as their pastor. The desire to minister and keep a congregation afloat, not the meager financial compensation, motivated me. My career financed my ministry. The second type is when a part-time job, such as delivering pizzas, supplements an inadequate ministry income. I had a lot of experience with this kind of bivocational ministry as well. I also assumed that most bivocational ministers enjoy the often unusual ministry opportunities afforded them through their work outside the church.

I certainly appreciated those unexpected ministry moments that came my way while "on the job." For example, while pastoring in Ohio, I worked at a Domino's Pizza. It was during the time when a number of big-name television preachers were getting into all sorts of ethical trouble. That was a topic of much joking at work, so I asked my boss why they were saying such cruel things about these preachers, but they did not include me in their jokes. He said, "Because you're not like them. You're the preacher who lives down the street. We know you." I will never forget that comment. Some months later that same store manager, late one night as we were closing, said,

> Phil, it's not like I have anything against the church, it's just that churches aren't open when I can go. I work 'til 4:00 a.m. every Saturday night, and I have to be there to open the store at four o'clock on Sunday afternoon. If there was a church open at 4:30 in the morning, I'd be there, and I bet the other store managers would be there too.

So I replied, "All right, starting next Sunday we'll have church at 4:30 in the morning. The lights'll be on and the doors'll be open. I'll remind you Saturday night."

For the next year and a half, I met with two to ten Domino's workers at 4:30 a.m. every Sunday for a Bible study based on the sermon I would preach later in the morning. One assistant manager's wife and kids started coming to Sunday school and the regular morning worship. It was a great feeling when, the next summer, the folks at the main church changed the time of their annual church picnic from right after Sunday worship (11:30 a.m.) to early afternoon (1:00 p.m.) so the Domino's employees could come right before opening their stores in the afternoon. That day our two "congregations" had joint fellowship for the first time.

A few years later, I worked the opening shift at a Hardee's restaurant. My manager, who was not a church attender, lived with her boyfriend on a nearby military base. One evening a gas explosion tore through their building. Both received severe burns; her partner's were more extensive. For weeks, I visited them both in the hospital. My manager recovered and eventually returned to work. Her boyfriend did not. I was honored to participate in his military funeral and to welcome her into our church family.

These ministry experiences led me to believe that my research would be filled with stories of folks whose careers financed their ministry or of pastors with second jobs to make ends meet, all of whom would have opportunities to minister inside and outside of church doors. While the research revealed some similarities between my experiences and those of other bivocational ministers, I had no idea of the full depth and breadth of bivocational ministry.

Interpreting the Data

As it turns out, my experience was more the exception than the rule. I quickly learned that my way of doing bivocational ministry, while similar to that described by Bickers, was far from the only way of doing it. Among the churches I visited, I found a wide variety of ways of being bivocational: a pastor whose primary occupation was stay-at-home dad, pastors who shared two half-time pastorates with their spouse, pastors who shared one part-time position by dividing the responsibilities according to their personal skill sets, and pastors who used multiple sources of retirement income to support their meager church remuneration. Through questionnaires and interviews, I also found many commonalities among bivocational pastors and congregations.

Pastors felt overworked but were not complaining

Most bivocational pastors worked more hours for their churches than those for which they were paid. Add those hours to their other job, and it would seem bivocational ministry is only for the workaholic. However, they saw it as a reality that cannot be helped. Most of the pastors said their "ideal" would be not to work a second job.

Self-expectations were higher than congregational expectations

The main reason bivocational pastors felt overworked at church was high self-expectations. They wanted to give as much of themselves as possible to the church. Congregation members, however, were quick to recognize that their pastor can only do so much. While most congregants wished their pastor could be full-time, the vast majority did not expect more than part-time work from their pastor.

Congregations were very supportive of the pastor's need for self-

care and time off

All of the pastors interviewed expressed gratitude for congregations, particularly oversight boards and committees, that encouraged—sometimes demanded—self-care, including taking days off and spending time with family. While most churches preferred a full-time pastor, all were very supportive of their pastor's self-care. This seemed extremely important to the congregations participating in this study. Time and again, pastors and congregants told me about how the congregation encouraged their pastor to take time off and keep family time. One Midwestern Baptist church, when they found out their pastor and his wife had never had a real honeymoon and were planning a trip to Hawaii, asked for all the receipts from the trip and reimbursed them so the pastor could have a completely free and much-needed vacation. Bivocational pastors must be particularly attentive to self-care.

Pastors in a committed relationship considered communication with their partner essential

Because of the busyness of two jobs and the tendency of those jobs to supplant family time, the bivocational pastors who were in a committed relationship said they had to maintain a high level of communication with their spouse or partner. None believed they did it perfectly, and the few spouses I spoke with indicated it was an ongoing struggle. Nevertheless, they were committed to supporting their partner's ministry vision.

Congregations were only somewhat aware of their pastor's other job and time spent pastoring

Congregants knew generally what the pastor did outside of ministry but not necessarily how many hours they worked in their secular job. As for pastoral hours worked versus perceived hours worked, the data were evenly divided between pastors who worked more hours, fewer hours, and about the same number of hours the congregation thought they did. Furthermore, nearly two in three congregants responding could not think of any conflicts between their pastor's jobs.

Congregations were willing to work with the pastor to keep time conflicts to a minimum

Negotiating potential time conflicts in bivocational ministry required flexibility and transparency. Flexibility in both jobs was key for bivocational ministry to be successful, and the only way for flexibility to work was through transparency. For one pastor, "transparency" meant that as long as both employers knew what the possible conflicts were, they could work around them. I found this true in my own experience as well as in those I interviewed. Most pastors interviewed admitted occasional conflicts between jobs, often worked out due to flexibility by both parties. One pastor worked out occasional conflicts with an understanding employer but felt some tension with other employees who had to work regular Sunday rotations while he was given Sunday mornings "off" to pastor.

Congregants felt bivocational ministry enhanced their church's overall ministry

Many responding congregants felt bivocational ministry enhanced their church's overall ministry. They saw their pastor as more aware of what was going on in the community. Respondents referred to the financial advantage—almost every congregation brought up finances at some point in the interview. A typical response was, "We couldn't make it if we had to pay a full-time salary and benefits."

Some interview respondents mentioned how bivocational ministry makes more people active in the church because the pastor is not expected to do everything. Other responses indicated perceptions that bivocational pastors use time more efficiently. Being bivocational shows the pastor "really wants to be here," and part-time ministry has the potential of becoming full-time.

Overall, pastors saw more advantages than disadvantages to bivocational ministry

Perceived advantages varied from person to person. Nearly half the pastors interviewed said that having a secular job informed their ministry, citing "real world" experience, meeting people outside of their church, and so on. This sentiment was echoed by every bivocational pastor I spoke to during this study, including a rabbi I interviewed early in 2015 in preparation for this research.

"Daniel" (not his real name) was an associate rabbi at the time. He also managed a fast-food outlet. Prior to my interviews with Christian pastors, I asked him the survey questions. He told me of numerous times when employees and customers who knew he was a clergyperson asked for spiritual help. Some wanted a listening ear. Others asked to be remembered in prayer. Daniel expected to be named senior rabbi at his congregation upon the retirement of the current rabbi and said he would miss the ministry opportunities his secular job gave him. He added that he hoped to do some volunteer work with a social service agency to keep "one foot in the real world."

My own experience echoes Daniel's thoughts. I teach my seminary students to be aware of—but not seek—job-related ministry opportunities. I believe ministry opportunities are the result of trust between the bivocational minister and the public or other employees, not aggressive evangelism.

Among other advantages mentioned by interviewees were: flexibility of schedule, being forced to be honest about their abilities (what they can and cannot realistically do), freeing up money for outreach ministries of the church, and spreading ministry opportunities among the congregation.

One pastor contrasted the way their secular job suited their results-oriented personality with their church ministry, which was rewarding in ways not associated with measurable results. "Cal" (not his real name) pastored a small church in Iowa. Most of his income came from managing a bowling alley about twenty-five miles from the church. Cal described himself as "results-oriented," which did not always match up with pastoral ministry. He told me he loves people, but he knows that nothing about them is ever finished; they're always in-process. The bowling alley was a different story. If a lane broke down and a bowler reported it, Cal would send a technician to fix it almost immediately. This suited the results-oriented part of Cal's personality perfectly, allowing him to minister effectively among people whose problems are not likely to be "fixed" with a phone call. Cal only regretted that the church was too far away for his bowling customers to attend. Still, some customers occasionally sought his advice as a pastor and not just as the guy behind the counter.

Regarding the disadvantages of bivocational ministry, most respondents mentioned their pastor's lack of time for church activities. Other responses included concern about the amount of time the pastor spends with family, wishing they had a full-time pastor, worry about stress on the pastor, and lower pastoral expectations. Almost all disadvantages identified by pastors had to do with time management and stress, affecting family time, personal time, and a desire to do more for the church. The comprehensive nature of this stress is indicated by the fact that no one gave me specific incidents. They just looked at me as if I would understand. In my own experience, I remember having to think twice before telling a parishioner I needed to be "at work" or telling my son his mom would have to drive him to 4-H because I had to be at the church.

Preparing for Bivocational Ministry

I concluded each interview by asking for suggestions as to what Bible colleges and seminaries could do to help prepare students for the realities of bivocational ministry. Both pastors and congregants offered clear answers.

The pastors interviewed asked first and foremost for educational institutions to give students a reality check on what they can expect in the world of congregations. To do so, they suggested inviting actual bivocational pastors as guest lecturers. Schools should emphasize that being bivocational does not mean the minister is a failure. The second most common response was emphatic: self-care. Seminaries should encourage students to create support systems for themselves, especially when preparing for bivocational ministry. Schools should also provide suggestions or tools to help students create such systems. Bivocational pastors also wanted seminaries and colleges to teach practical skills adaptable to the "outside world." Some suggested that schools encourage students to work at an other-than-ministry setting while attending seminary. Pastors interviewed felt that seminaries should teach their students how to craft a résumé emphasizing the skills ministers acquire and develop. In the event a second job is needed, students should be ready to get that job. Lastly, due to the amount of work expected of them by multiple employers plus personal and family needs, bivocational pastors looked to their educational institutions for time management tools. As long as there are a finite number of hours in a day, the need will exist to use those hours effectively, not just for employers but for the sake of their own health and those closest to them.

Time management was the first thing congregants mentioned in education for bivocational ministers. While congregants approved of how their current pastor was managing time, many felt that pastors needed more training in using time wisely, due to the immensity of two jobs. Congregants also expressed the ideas labeled earlier as "transparency" and "flexibility." They felt that seminaries and colleges should emphasize these communication skills to build stronger relationships between bivocational pastors and their constituencies. No one wishes to overwork their pastor to the point of burnout. The only way to avoid this, according to congregational representatives, is to have regular dialog about time and responsibilities and expectations. Congregants surveyed did not see this as adversarial but as informative and preemptive of future problems.

Since bivocational pastors have limited time to spend among their constituents, church members felt their pastors needed to learn how to understand their congregation's geography and demography more rapidly and more intentionally than fully funded pastors would. A traditional pastor has more hours and more days to spend getting to know their parish; they can work at this slowly and deeply. Bivocational pastors do not have that luxury. To be effective they must "read" their congregations quickly and adjust their ministry, if they are able, to meet their needs.

A few congregants suggested that theological education for pastors should include internships that are not ministry-based. They felt that, in addition to doing the traditional field education in ministry that is part of the Master of Divinity degree, students should do an internship in the "real world" by working retail, driving a school bus, delivering pizza, and so on. Further discussion around this response led to suggestions that pastors be able to reflect theologically on their secular job the way they do their church job. This makes a lot of sense in terms of knowing one's congregation because the typical congregant has only a secular job on which to reflect. For a pastor to effectively encourage church members to be faithful believers on the job, they must understand what it is like to experience God within those jobs.

Creating a Syllabus

My research confirmed that I had a lot to learn from other bivocational pastors and congregations. While I am still learning, I believe I discovered some significant findings that will help seminaries prepare future bivocational ministers. Bearing in mind the suggestions of both pastors and congregants, I advise instructors to include the following topics in a bivocational ministry course. For each topic, I have provided suggested resources beyond the chapters of this volume. Many of these topics, though not unique to bivocational ministry, are especially critical to the success of bivocational ministers.

Validity of bivocational ministry

Begin by looking at historical and current attitudes toward bivocational ministry. Bring out statistics about the percentage of pastors in bivocational ministry, even explaining the difficulty of obtaining accurate figures because denominations seem to downplay their increasing use of bivocational pastors. Emphasize a theme throughout the course: bivocational ministers are not "part-time help." They are not second-class pastors. They are, in fact, vital to the success of the twenty-first century church. Resources include Bickers (2000); Coughlin (1991); Edington (2018); Grand Rapids Seminary (2018); MacDonald (2020); New Leaf Learning Centre (2020); Rainer (2016); Small (2018); and Watson et al. (2020).

Congregational awareness

Consider the importance of learning who a congregation is—their demographics and their culture. Bivocational pastors have less time to do this than fully-funded pastors. This topic requires tools to gain congregational awareness effectively within a limited timeframe. Students need to learn the art of looking at a congregation anthropologically—that is, learning the culture via observation, questioning, and paying particular attention to language, artifacts, spaces, and rituals unique to their congregation. Craig Storti's *The Art of Crossing Cultures* (2021) and Patty Lane's *A Beginner's Guide to Crossing Cultures* (2002) can be helpful in this process (see also Frank 2000).

Nancy L. Eisland and R. Stephen Warner (1998, 40, 43) called this kind of congregational research an “ecological perspective” and introduced a tool I recommend to my classes—the congregational timeline. If a new pastor can create the space and time for such a congregation-wide activity, the depth of knowledge can be immeasurable. Creating a congregational timeline also helps the bivocational pastor to focus their energy on things that really matter to the congregation.

Self-care and family care

Examine ways of keeping oneself and one’s family from becoming victims of ministry burnout by emphasizing physical, mental, spiritual, and social health. In my classes, I ask students to create self-care plans touching on each of these areas. Former students often tell me that they return to this exercise, even after seminary, as their lives and ministries change. I have also used David Olsen and Nancy Devor’s *Saying No to Say Yes* (2015) and Bruce Epperly’s *A Center in the Cyclone: Twenty-first Century Clergy Self-care* (2014) to reinforce this topic. See also Grand Rapids Seminary (2018); Stephens (n.d.); and Watson et al. (2020).

Time management

Time management is vital to successful bivocational ministry. Assist students in finding a means of managing their time that works for their personality type and ministry setting. Time management systems were always mystifying to me. I once worked for a company that expected everyone to use a Day-Timer religiously. I found myself wasting potentially productive time just keeping track of time. I discovered a hidden gem that I share with my classes: Soorej Gopi’s *The Time Management System: The Secret to Productivity that Lasts a Lifetime* (2017). The ambitious title belies a simple system that helps the user discover their own best plan for time management. When students find time management tools that work for them, encourage them to share with their peers. Bivocational resources include Grand Rapids Seminary (2018); New Leaf Learning Centre (2020); and Stephens (n.d.).

Creating a support system

Bivocational ministers cannot go it alone, even though they often feel that way. It is important to cultivate needed support through a network of friends, mentors, and colleagues. One means of support is to find another bivocational minister with whom they can meet regularly to reflect theologically on aspects of their secular employment. Drawing on the pattern of weekly supervisory sessions experienced during field education, participants should reflect on cases or incidents that take place outside of their traditional ministry. These peer meetings can include mutual sharing, since both ministers have experience in the church and in the larger world.

Transparency, vulnerability, and trust

Transparency about job expectations for both the pastor and congregation, as well as honesty about what the non-church job entails, is vital to the success of bivocational ministry. This kind of vulnerability plays a significant part in the relationship between bivocational pastor and congregation. Students need to understand how vital vulnerability is when ministering bivocationally. The trust level needs to be high when a pastor is not always readily available to the congregation. I use a chapter in Mandy Smith's *The Vulnerable Pastor*, titled "Learning to Like the Mess: How Vulnerable Pastors Create Culture," to demonstrate how pastoral vulnerability can lead to the kind of transparency in congregations and ministers necessary for effective bivocational ministry (2015, 103–20; see also Grand Rapids Seminary 2018).

The "other job"

Getting the proverbial "second job" is harder than one might think. Raise students' awareness of current hiring practices to help them find and attain a second means of financial support beyond pastoring. A key component is creating an effective contemporary résumé based on one's ministry, life experience, and academic curriculum vitae (CV). Looking into business practices concerning the interview process is another worthwhile component of the class. Representatives from the human resource departments of local businesses have been guest lecturers in my classes. Students have been very keen to learn just what hirers look for in the interview process.

Finances

Since finances are usually the reason clergy are bivocational in the first place, I suggest spending time studying church finances. Record-keeping and budgeting are often weak areas for small congregations. These topics, along with capital maintenance planning, are worthwhile to include in a course syllabus. A discussion of and resources for health insurance, often the missing component in bivocational ministry compensation, is also very helpful. Resources include: Faith and Money Network (2021); Jamieson and Jamieson (2009); and Small (2018).

Experience-related lectures

Invite practicing bivocational pastors to guest lecture. Students appreciate the opportunity to "pick the brains" of people with various kinds of bivocational experience. For example, in 2019, I invited a bivocational pastor as a guest lecturer who not only shared his experiences but also gave the students tools for equipping the laity for ministry. This was greatly appreciated since the bivocational church relies on laypeople to do much of the work traditionally done by the fully-funded pastor. Resources include: Grand Rapids Seminary (2018); New Leaf Learning Centre (2020); Samushonga (2020a; 2020b); Small (2018); and Stephens (n.d.).

Conflict transformation

While this topic did not come up in my research, conflict transformation skills are critically important for bivocational pastors, who often fail to see the conflict present in their churches because they do not spend as much time with the people. Familiarizing students with tools for dealing with conflict in ministry need not be an exhaustive study, as most students and pastors have access to more in-depth conflict transformation courses at the seminary or workshops presented by various church agencies. See Grand Rapids Seminary (2018).

Ongoing Pedagogical Challenges

A persistent challenge in teaching bivocational ministry is that, for most seminary students, bivocational ministry is not their first choice of career path. Even among the pastors I interviewed, almost all would have preferred a fully funded ministry over bivocationality.[2] Assuring students of the necessity for and validity of bivocational ministry must permeate every class. Celebrate the future minister who chooses bivocational ministry. Their numbers will most likely increase as a new generation experiments with creative ways of doing and financing ministry. For those who follow a call to ministry that they hope to be full-time, make sure they understand how the future in which they find themselves is as much in divine hands as the future they wish for themselves.

Because my research was conducted within the continental United States and because I had no international students prior to 2017, I had not given much thought to the ramifications of bivocational ministry for pastors outside of the United States. However, two students from Kenya attended my second Bivocational Ministry class in 2019. They represented a point of view I was barely aware of and had not included in the syllabus—that of African pastors who are grossly underpaid and yet are told by their churches that they are not being true to their pastoral calling if they try to supplement their income with outside employment. I plan to research this further to see if this perspective goes beyond Kenya and to include my findings in future iterations of the Bivocational Ministry course. Resources include Forster and Oosterbrink (2015) and Samushonga (2020b).

Learning and Ministry Continue

Bivocational ministry is here to stay. The Apostle Paul's example of self-financing ministry was not an aberration in the first century and may still be the norm in the twenty-first. Even as I tried to identify bivocational ministers to interview, some of the denominational executives with whom I corresponded expressed doubts that I would find many among their congregations.[3] The pastors themselves told a different story. And while bivocational ministry is commonplace among non-White congregations in the United States, too many leaders in White-majority denominations are reluctant to accept this reality. Nevertheless, theological institutions have a responsibility to prepare their students for the kind of ministry they will actually face, not just the dream job we wish them to find. As theological educators, we must help them thrive in that ministry.

Works Cited

Bickers, Dennis W. 2000. *The Tentmaking Pastor: The Joy of Bivocational Ministry*. Grand Rapids, MI: Baker.

Coughlin, Michael F. 1991. "Full-time Pastor, Part-time Pay." *Leadership* 12, no. 2: 111–3.

Edington, Mark D. W. 2018. *Bivocational: Returning to the Roots of Ministry*. New York: Church Publishing. *bivocational.church*.

Eisland, Nancy L., and R. Stephen Warner. 1998. "Ecology: Seeing the Congregation in Context." In *Studying Congregations: A New Handbook*, edited by Nancy T. Ammerman, Jackson W. Carroll, Carl S. Dudley, and William McKinney, 40–77. Nashville: Abingdon.

Epperly, Bruce. 2014. *A Center in the Cyclone: Twenty-first Century Clergy Self-care*. Lanham, MD: Rowman & Littlefield.

Faith and Money Network. 2021. *faithandmoneynetwork.org*.

Forster, Dion A., and Johann W. Oosterbrink. 2015. "Where is the Church on Monday? Awakening the Church to the Theology and Practice of Ministry and Mission in the Marketplace." *In die Skriflig/In Luce Verbi* 49, no. 3: 1–8. *doi.org/10.4102/ids.v49i3.1944*.

Frank, Thomas Edward. 2000. *The Soul of the Congregation: An Invitation to Congregational Reflection*. Nashville: Abingdon.

Gopi, Soorej. 2017. *The Time Management System: The Secret to Productivity that Lasts a Lifetime*. CreateSpace Independent Publishing Platform.

Grand Rapids Seminary. 2018. "Bi-Vocational Ministry: Balancing Dual Roles." Panel discussion moderated by Julián Guzmán, director of the Urban Church Leadership Center. Panelists: Khary Bridgewater, Angel Ortiz, Elizabeth Conde-Frazier, and Chris DeBlaay. *soundcloud.com/grand-rapids-theological-seminary/bi-vocational-ministry-balancing-dual-roles.*

Jamieson, Janet T., and Philip D. Jamieson. 2009. *Ministry and Money: A Practical Guide for Pastors.* Louisville, KY: Westminster John Knox.

Lane, Patty. 2002. *A Beginner's Guide to Crossing Cultures: Making Friends in a Multicultural World.* Downers Grove, IL: InterVarsity.

MacDonald, G. Jeffrey. 2020. *Part-Time Is Plenty: Thriving Without Full-Time Clergy.* Louisville, KY: Westminster John Knox.

New Leaf Learning Centre. 2020. "Multivocational Resources." *newleafnetwork.ca/multivocational-resources.*

Olsen, David C., and Nancy G. Devor. 2015. *Saying No to Say Yes: Everyday Boundaries and Pastoral Excellence.* Lanham, MD: Rowman & Littlefield.

Rainer, Thom. 2016. "The New Marketplace Pastor." *Church Answers.* January 26. *churchanswers.com/podcasts/rainer-on-leadership/the-new-marketplace-pastor-rainer-on-leadership-193.*

Samushonga, Hartness. 2020a. "The Bivocational Pastor." Interview with Dennis Bickers. December 12. *youtu.be/6-te8hNaXhM.*

———. 2020b. "Ministry Beyond the Church." Interview with Shingi Munyeza. December 12. *youtu.be/4_JApYecBmw.*

Small, Holly. 2018. "Resources From the Bivocational Ministry Gathering Last Month." *The Network, Christian Reformed Church in North America.* May 24. *network.crcna.org/pastors/resources-bivocational-ministry-gathering-last-month.*

Smith, Mandy. 2015. *The Vulnerable Pastor: How Human Limitations Empower Our Ministry.* Downers Grove, IL: InterVarsity.

Stephens, Darryl W. n.d. "Bivocational and Beyond." *darrylwstephens.com/bivocational-and-beyond.*

Storti, Craig. 2021. *The Art of Crossing Cultures*. Third Edition. Boston: Nicholas Brealey.

Watson, James W., Wanda M. Malcolm, Mark D. Chapman, Elizabeth A. Fisher, Marilyn Draper, Narry F. Santos, Jared Siebert, and Amy Bratton. 2020. "Canadian Multivocational Ministry Project: Research Report." *canadianmultivocationalministry.ca/master-report*.

Endnotes

1 Interview questions for pastors and congregations can be found at *esr.earlham.edu/community-resources/economic-challenges-facing-future-ministers/bi-vocational-ministry-project-resources*.

2 For a more positive view toward bivocational ministry as a first choice of career path, see Bickers (2000); Edington (2018); Grand Rapids Seminary (2018); MacDonald (2020); New Leaf Learning Centre (2020); Rainer (2016); Samushonga (2021a; 2021b); Small (2018); and Watson et al. (2020).

3 MacDonald (2020, 5–7) encountered similar responses in his research.

CHAPTER 17

A Mentored Practice Approach to Bivocational Ministry Education

RONALD W. BAARD

The church in the twenty-first century is changing, and thus the way it educates and forms ministers is also changing. Due to decreased attendance, the culture of church and ministry has shifted in parishes of the United Church of Christ (UCC) in northern New England (Maine, New Hampshire, and Vermont). Many—if not most—small churches can no longer afford to employ a full-time minister with a Master of Divinity degree from an accredited theological seminary. Consequently, many clergy serving small churches in our region are bivocational or even multivocational, holding two or more jobs simultaneously, where one job is a church ministry position and the other a secular employment of some kind. This way of working in ministry is as old as the Apostle Paul, who supported himself as a "tentmaker" while engaging in his apostolic and ministry endeavors (Acts 18:1–3, NRSV). Furthermore, prospective clergy are seeking alternatives to seminary for ministerial formation. The

Maine School of Ministry—a regional theological educational program of the Maine Conference United Church of Christ—provides one such path.

To nurture the gift to the wider church that is unique to bivocational ministry, the Maine School of Ministry utilizes both academic study in a classroom context as well as a "mentored practice" approach to formation and preparation for ordained leadership. A mentored practice experience provides the benefit of increasing competence and confidence on the part of the pastoral intern in the "doing" of ministry in a parish ministry setting. The mentored practice approach counts on the accrued wisdom of life experience of the student pastor, or pastoral intern,[1] as a critical factor as they experience the great joy of doing ministry with and for others in a real context, including preaching, teaching, providing spiritual guidance, and working for justice in various settings. To observe the increase in competence across a semester of experiential learning is a thing of beauty. It is very fulfilling for the pastoral intern as well as for the congregants of their teaching church committee and for the mentor-pastor.

Important ministerial and pastoral education and formation occurs through the mentored practice experience, a type of apprenticeship. William Sullivan, in his *Introduction to Educating Clergy: Teaching Practices and Pastoral Imagination*, wrote of the importance of the apprenticeship model:

> Future clergy do a good deal of their preparation learning in classrooms, reading and studying texts and being assessed. . . . Still . . . educators of clergy generally work hard and creatively at linking this cognitive or intellectual apprenticeship with the demands of future clergy practice. (Sullivan 2006, 7)

In terms of preparation and study for pastoral ministry, this approach requires "integration"—classroom work in church history, systematic theology, ethics, biblical studies, and pastoral studies all come together in the practice of embodied ministry in a particular context. Sullivan described the way seminaries teach this integration as "the second apprenticeship,"

> in which students learn by engaging in the actual activities of clergy practice. Simulations, case studies, field placements, and clinical pastoral education are common . . . the skills developed in the apprentice-

> ship of practice . . . are the essential completion and complement of the cognitive capacities developed in the intellectual apprenticeship. (Sullivan 2006, 7)

Thus, integration happens when the student minister practices the art of ministry joyfully in a setting that demands their all. It happens when, in a given instance of ministry, a student truly sees the various dimensions of academic study reflected in the act of ministry. The Maine School of Ministry provides integration through a mentored practice approach. For bivocational ministry students in particular, the mentored practice approach to formation provides deep personal and professional integration, as well as wisdom, through service in the church as a parish pastor.

This chapter discusses some of the strengths of a mentored practice approach to the formation and education of prospective UCC ministers in Maine. I write as the dean of the Maine School of Ministry—a role in which I help to educate bivocational candidates for ministry. I begin with a brief synopsis of the current context of church and ministry in the state of Maine. I then provide a short sketch of the recent and impactful closing of Bangor Theological Seminary, which served for nearly two centuries as the only accredited seminary in northern New England. The closure of this seminary affected ministry candidates as well as the congregations they served, particularly those congregations dependent on student ministers. Responding to this need, the Maine School of Ministry provided a new context for both the academic study necessary to ministry education and formation and a mentored practice approach, illustrated by two extended case studies. I believe the gifts and graces of the bivocational pastor for ministry are best developed through an acknowledgement of their accrued life wisdom and brought to full fruition through mentored practice.

The Context of Church and Ministry in Maine

Since the case studies presented in this chapter are set in Maine churches, it is important to provide some contextual background and analysis on the unique features of this New England state. Viewed from within, some claim there are "two Maines," by which they mean 1) greater southeastern Maine from Kittery to Portland to Brunswick and westward towards the border with southern New Hampshire, and 2) inland, northern and "downeast" Maine. Actually, I have found it is far more accurate to talk of "three Maines," the third being coastal Maine (Baard 2017, 143).

Coastal Maine has by far the most resources economically. In recent decades, more and more persons of means from out of state have bought land parcels up and down the midcoast of Maine (as well as other parts of Maine) and farther north, up the coast of Maine, thus driving up real estate values. This dynamic makes it harder for "real Mainers" to keep up with property taxes and the general cost of living. Inland, northern and "downeast" Maine present another picture, one that is more rural and agricultural, characterized by diminished resources and a slower economy. Maine is still over 90% forest, and the economics of the lumber business in this huge geographic region go up and down. Thus, the economies of many northern Maine communities follow in the wake. In some counties in northern Maine, the regional dynamics are similar to small communities in Appalachia. Portland and southern Maine provide yet another picture, for they share in the energy and vitality of the economy of Boston, northern Massachusetts, and southern New Hampshire, where the culture tends to be much more cosmopolitan and urban (Baard 2017, 143–44).

The churches in this Maine context differ widely. Larger churches are located in Bangor, Brunswick, and Portland, as well as on the coast in Camden and Bar Harbor. Small and very small churches are alive in every other nook and cranny across the Maine landscape, many in fairly isolated areas. Fully two-thirds of churches in the Maine Conference of the United Church of Christ are small (defined as 50 members or less) or very small (defined as 15 to 20 members or active participants—often less). This fact is directly related to the geography of the state of Maine, which is so richly varied. It is primarily these smaller churches that are ideally suited for participation in the mentored practice program. Many of these small churches require the utilization of an off-site mentor-pastor to fulfill the mentoring needs of the pastoral intern serving them. This means, especially in the era of COVID-19, that most of the mentoring meetings are accomplished virtually and remotely through use of online platforms like Zoom.

The Closing of Bangor Theological Seminary and the Opening of the Maine School of Ministry

Bangor Theological Seminary closed its doors in June of 2013, after 199 years of admirable service in the work of forming and educating ministers for service in the parishes of Maine and northern New England and beyond. Bangor Theological Seminary was one of seven closely related seminaries of the United Church of Christ. It held its final graduation service in June of 2013. The closing of the seminary was painful for all involved. The grief for everyone, including staff, students, alumni(ae), faculty, and board members was immense. The tradition of providing theological students to serve as student pastors to small churches across the region was, in many respects, a mainstay of the identity and mission-driven esteem of the seminary. Thus, for decades in the twentieth century and into the twenty-first century, this mutually beneficial relationship of service-driven contextual education enhanced the life of students, the seminary, and the parishes they served.

In his anecdotal, reflective, and eminently practical account of his work as director of field education from an earlier period in the life of Bangor Theological Seminary, Walter Cook—a predecessor to my current work with the mentored practice program—wrote of how important and powerful the formation of pastoral identity was for both the student ministers and for the sense of mission these teaching churches lived into.

> For I often see how much faithful lay people can do to help a pastor. When a student learns he [sic] can count always on the labor, friendship, counsel and prayers of a dozen staunch church members he [sic] can become a real power for God. (Cook 1978, 152)

The churches in northern New England experienced a vacuum with respect to the closing of their seminary. Over the years, these churches formed a strong sense of mission and identity around "forming" theological students who served as student pastors while completing their formal theological education at the seminary.

> *The loss of a role or of one's accustomed place in a social network is experienced as role loss.* The significance of the role loss to an individual is

directly related to the extent to which one's sense of identity is linked to the lost role. (Mitchell and Andersen 1983, 42, original emphasis)

> *Systemic loss is a concept that forced itself upon us as we studied what our informants told us. To understand it, we must first recall that human beings usually belong to some interactional system in which patterns of behavior develop over time . . .* When those functions disappear or are not performed, the system as a whole, as well as its individual members may experience systemic loss. (Mitchell and Andersen 1983, 44–45, original emphasis)

In addition to providing worship and faith-deepening opportunities to their members and friends in the community, these congregations understood a major part of their identity for mission and service to be in the loving, nurturing, and teaching relationships formed with their student pastors. When the seminary closed, this was a huge and sudden loss for many small churches across the landscape, resulting in significant disorientation and grief.

The Maine School of Ministry—an educational program of the Maine Conference United Church of Christ—rose to fill the void that this systemic loss created.

> Schools of ministry are cropping up and growing largely for the purpose of strengthening lay roles in congregations. In Maine, for instance, a void emerged in [2013] when Bangor Theological Seminary (BTS) closed due to the same declining enrollment dynamics that are challenging so many other freestanding institutions. With the BTS closure, northern New England was left with no mainline training ground for church leaders, but the void gave rise to something new. The Maine School of Ministry was founded by the Maine Conference of the UCC to provide low-cost training in specific areas for lay people and future clergy. (MacDonald 2020, 115)

The Maine School of Ministry is a regional school of ministry under the wider umbrella of the Maine Conference United Church of Christ. It was formed in the fall of 2013 in response to the closure of Bangor Theological Seminary, and it held its first classes in 2014. It offers various certificate programs for ministry education and formation, as well as continuing education events for clergy and laypersons.

Mentored Practice

The Mentored Practice Course—a form of field education or supervised ministry—provides experiential learning and constitutes one of the last steps in the formation and education process in the Christian Studies and Pastoral Leadership certificate program offered by the Maine School of Ministry.

The mentored practice experiential learning process begins with the naming of clear learning goals for the pastoral intern, shaped in conversation with both their mentor-pastor and the church being served. This Learning Goals Covenant, completed together by the pastoral intern, mentor, and host congregation, specifies a commitment to one hour a week of mentoring conversation. The Covenant also includes a "teaching church committee" of three laypersons who meet with the pastoral intern several times during the semester for feedback and support. As the semester moves to completion, the student writes a thorough self-evaluation, the mentor writes an evaluation of the pastoral intern, and the teaching church committee works together to write a careful evaluation of the semester with their pastoral intern. The pastoral intern's self-evaluation at the end of the term is a key source of learning in mentored practice.

Mentored practice, as it is expressed through the Maine School of Ministry, emphasizes the significant role of the mentor in the process of both education and formation. The word *mentor* comes from the character Mentor in Homer's *Odyssey*. In that story, Mentor—a friend of the protagonist Odysseus—was entrusted with providing the education of Telemachus, Odysseus's son (O'Donnell 2017). The role of the mentor involves both deep responsibility and the evocation of trust and goodwill in the mentoring relationship (see Fain, chapter 12 in this volume).

Mentors for student pastors are carefully selected. They need to have years of experience in congregational leadership and their skills in supervision must be well honed. The mentor-pastor's commitment to their student's growth means that they each spend an hour a week in conversation with their chosen pastoral intern. These mentoring conversations are intended to focus squarely on the pastoral intern's professional development and professional practice for ministry. This is different from a focus on personal growth, such as might be accomplished in a therapeutic process, or a focus on spiritual growth, as would be the goal in spiritual direction. While it may indeed happen that both personal and spiritual growth are evident in a pastoral intern's experiential learning in the mentoring process across a semester, in a sense they must be viewed as byproducts of their growth in professional practice (see Connelly, chapter 10 in this volume). A supportive infrastructure for the mentors, required as part of the overall program, consists of several gatherings of the participating mentor-pastors with the dean of the school for the purpose of support, accountability, and theological and spiritual reflection on the deeper meanings and impacts of the mentoring process.

The mentored practice program is illustrated here through the vocational journey stories of two different mid-life ministry students: Debbie and Travis.[2] Both of these students studied at the Maine School of Ministry in the Christian Studies and Pastoral Leadership curriculum for several years with the goal of becoming authorized ministers in the United Church of Christ. Both served as pastoral interns by engaging with a congregation in the Mentored Practice course. These case studies were chosen to illustrate the formative impact that the mentored practice approach to ministerial education and formation can have on the wider church in the twenty-first century, both in terms of its impact on student ministers and on the congregations they serve in their supervised ministry practice.

Formed as a people of mercy

The case of Debbie at Inland Lake UCC, located in a rural yet recreational area of Maine, illustrates how a mentored practice context and experience can serve as an educational vehicle for both the pastoral intern and the teaching church in which they are practicing ministry. This case emphasizes the essential components of empathy and compassion that are alive between the pastoral intern, the mentor-pastor, and the teaching congregation. In this case study, the congregation itself was transformed in its engagement with their pastoral intern as their hearts were turned toward mercy, empathy, and compassion.

A bivocational ministry student in her mid-50s, Debbie worked for many years as a fitness coach and trainer at a local branch of the YWCA USA, Inc., with a special interest in the health and well-being of senior citizens. She felt a call to serve in ministry over many years and began taking classes at the Maine School of Ministry from its inception. She completed many semesters of required courses, including two semesters of Mentored Practice at this small church in rural Maine.

Working with her mentor (who was also the congregation's pastor), Debbie named three learning goals: "1) Learn how to use technology as a tool for ministry; 2) Gain experience in church administration; and 3) Gain experience in developing children's ministry in a small church context." Quotations from Debbie's self-evaluation illuminate some of the struggles and highlights of the final semester of her mentored practice at Inland Lake UCC.

During the year-long mentored practice assignment, Debbie experienced health challenges that impacted her ministry. Debbie's work with the chairperson of the Christian education committee on behalf of the children was exemplary and creative. Her devotion to and learning in her third goal, to "gain experience in developing children's ministry in a small church context," came through clearly, despite her obstacles.

> When I started the spring semester, I had some health challenges to deal with. But I was fortunate to have a wonderful and patient teacher, Pastor Carol, to help me through the semester. She was understanding and patient. She had me participate in the areas I was comfortable with, in small steps, retraining me in areas that used to be familiar. Without this support, it would have been difficult to finish this internship. Words cannot express my thanks and appreciation.

Her mentor-pastor began the work of interpreting to the congregation the nature of these struggles in the weekly church newsletter as well as from the pulpit. With this sort of leadership and encouragement from their pastor, the church community did not see Debbie as fungible because she was having some difficulty performing all assigned duties. Instead, this experience was formative for the congregation as they learned to live more deeply into becoming a people of mercy.

As she acknowledged, Debbie's health challenges, due to the lingering effects of an accident in the fall semester, were indeed significant and challenging for her ongoing ministry practice. In turn, these challenges raised the mentoring bar for her mentor-pastor and for the whole church.

> During this semester, I continued to help develop the weekly Orders of Worship as I did in the fall semester. I also continued to put togeth-

> er the weekly Children's Moments to coincide with the scripture that Sunday or with the lesson that the children received from Christian Education. I continued to record weekly audio Bible lessons and upload them to SoundCloud so the Christian Education Committee could email the lessons to the families. I enjoyed working with [the] chairperson of the Christian Education committee as we selected and put together the last seven weeks of lessons that finished out the school year on June 13th. I also kept in touch with the Sunday School children by sending them seed crosses and coloring pictures for Easter, and Certificates of Achievement with stickers for the end of the school year. The certificates were also sent to teachers and administration staff to let them know Pastor Carol and I appreciated their hard work during this past school year.

Debbie, her mentor, and her church rose to meet these challenges in a beautiful way, demonstrating Christian love and patience at each step of the journey.

Debbie's struggle with certain health challenges as she worked her way through each week of the mentored practice semesters became a focus for learning and growth both for her and for the Inland Lake UCC church members. While she learned increased patience and grace with herself in her desire to overcome her health obstacles, her mentoring and teaching church community was on the same learning curve, learning and re-learning the Christian faith practices of mercy, patience, empathy, perseverance, and compassion.

How does the work of pastoral/theological formation continue when health issues arise and interfere with the practice of ministry? What is the hidden curriculum at work here? In Micah 6:8 we learn of the biblical and prophetic imperative to "Do justice, love kindness, walk humbly" (Mic. 6:8). Both Debbie and the church members were stretched in all these ways of doing justice, loving kindness, and walking humbly as they navigated each turn in the road of mentoring and being mentored. Especially impressive in this case was Debbie's mentor's ability to guide both Debbie and the congregation through these challenging turns. Frequently in the weekly church newsletter, the pastor offered words of compassion to keep everyone on track. Debbie received excellent evaluations from her mentor-pastor and her three-member teaching church committee at the conclusion of each of her two semesters of mentored practice.

Maturing in ministerial formation

This case of Travis at Coastal Maine UCC, located in mid-coastal Maine, demonstrates how personal, professional, and spiritual growth can occur in a pastoral intern. During the mentored practice experience, Travis was challenged to mature in ministerial formation when conflict with a congregant arose.

A bivocational student in his mid-40s, Travis is consistently sought after as a guest preacher for congregations in and near the area he resides. He worked in a management position for a railway company for many years while pursuing his formational studies at the Maine School of Ministry and completed many semesters of required courses before moving into his first semester of mentored practice at this suburban church in Maine. Travis named three learning goals: "1) Grow my understanding and participation in the role of missions within the local church; 2) Gain insights and learn ways of working with people whom I feel are difficult or people with whom I disagree; and 3) Gain a greater understanding and appreciation of the role and importance of social justice within the UCC." Travis's mentor-pastor arrangement was unique in that he worked with a team of three mentor-pastors instead of only one. This approach to mentoring was an experiment in the program, and, in Travis's case, it worked well and produced significant professional growth in his ministry practice.

Travis's goal of learning more about mission and outreach at Coastal Maine UCC broadened his awareness of the church's many areas of investment and involvement in the community. This awareness also blossomed in his mentoring process as he participated in a program offered through the Maine Council of Churches to expand his awareness and abilities as a church leader in this outreach area even further.

> The semester more than sufficiently allowed me to meet my learning goals. Beginning with missions, I spent time with our Chair of Missions learning about areas of focus for Coastal Maine UCC. I was not aware of the broad areas of involvement and how the church has impacted many lives. Coastal Maine UCC is involved with as many as nine different organizations or programs throughout the year. This really opened my eyes even more to the need of missions and made me realize I should be doing more.

All of this has made a positive difference in Travis's professional formation as a pastoral intern. Perhaps this area of Travis's growth is best described as new skills development. He was grateful for expanding his awareness and developing new skills in the outreach and missions area of ministry.

One core issue that Travis struggled with in his ongoing formation for ministry was how to work in a church with persons he disagrees with or dislikes.

> The second goal focused on two people as it relates to difficult people or with whom I disagree. The growing edge in this area was the awareness that these people are beloved children of God despite exhibited behaviors that can be challenging to me. One was a retired clergy member who, discreetly and unknown to me, was asking about my Member in Discernment (MID) status, my covenant with the local UCC Association and with Coastal Maine UCC and questioning my theological thoughts on a text and sermon. I found it to be offensive to learn he was doing this.

Travis was given some insight into how to deal with this situation by his reliable team of mentor-pastors who opened up for him different avenues of approach. He learned essential skills in his mentored practice semester about how to work with congregants who offend him or whose behaviors he felt were out of line.

> With encouragement from my advisors, I initiated contact to get to know this member better. I learned how to better navigate someone like this. I learned that he, perhaps, feels the need to be a mentor or wants to be looked upon as a source of great advice and wisdom. I quickly saw a change when I positioned myself as a seeker of his advice and gave him the opportunity to feel he was in an advisor role.

Through this experience, Travis learned new attitudes and approaches to conflict management in parish ministry. Travis had to face conflict directly and honestly. He learned to utilize a team of mentor-pastors to expand perspectives. This process requires a strong commitment to growth for all involved.

This kind of experiential learning can only come in practice. This is especially highlighted when Travis said, "I quickly saw a change when I positioned myself as a seeker of his advice and gave him the opportunity to feel he was in an advisor role." The command of Jesus to "love your enemies" (Matt. 5:38–48) is at play here. This is sometimes not so easy in the real world of lived practice of ministry in a local church setting, Yet Travis made great strides experientially, and he gained some ground by finding and experimenting with new approaches to stubborn problems in the life of the church. In that same way, his work in this spiritually challenging area was mirrored by his team of three mentor-pastors as they and Travis worked to overcome some similar obstacles and some occasional conflict in the mentoring process across the weekly meetings.

Travis's case reveals another dynamic of the mentored practice process: the interplay between the two sides of bivocational work life. On the one hand, in his church work, through the help of his mentors, Travis opened himself to a problem of education for social justice. On the other hand, in his management work for the railroad company, Travis advocated for employees within his company.

> The greatest highlight of the semester was around the church's role in social justice. At the suggestion of Rev. Smith, I enrolled in a four-part advocacy series hosted by the Maine Council of Churches. At the same time, my employer was just announcing a new LGBTQ+ Business Resource Group. I was incredibly moved by the first Advocacy Series, which led me to apply to be the chair or vice chair of the new group. I was ultimately named chair of this group and realized my potential and need to be an advocate for LGBTQ+ employees within the company, as well as how my pastoral leadership can help guide the group. I gained a greater appreciation of advocacy needs within the UCC, and I look forward to becoming more involved in causes.

Each endeavor enriched the other. This interplay constituted real professional formation advances for Travis, both in his secular work and in his ministry practice. Travis received excellent evaluations from both his team of three mentor-pastors and his teaching church committee at the conclusion of his first semester of mentored practice with Coastal Maine UCC Church.

Final Reflections

Mentored practice, as it is offered through the curriculum of the Maine School of Ministry, is an essential element in the formation of bivocational ministers as they pursue the goal of ordained ministry in the United Church of Christ. Both Debbie and Travis demonstrated invaluable experiential learning and growth gained through mentored practice ministry formation. This approach borrows from the wisdom of the early church—the wisdom of tent-making and apprenticeship. The emerging church in this new day needs to open its heart to new ways of forming ministers that challenge the still dominant residential seminary-based pathway model. A mentored practice model offers many strengths and much potential if widely considered and utilized in a variety of ministry education and formation settings.

Works Cited

Baard, Ronald W. 2017. "Some Benefits of Using Technology in Supporting and Nurturing Student Ministers in Field Education." *Reflective Practice: Formation and Supervision in Ministry* 37: 142–51. *journals.sfu.ca/rpfs/index.php/rpfs/article/view/474/458*.

Cook, Walter L. 1978. *Send Us A Minister . . . Any Minister Will Do.* Rockland, ME: Courier-Gazette.

MacDonald, G. Jeffrey. 2020. *Part-Time Is Plenty: Thriving Without Full-Time Clergy.* Louisville: Westminster John Knox.

Mitchell, Kenneth R., and Herbert Anderson. 1983. *All Our Losses, All our Griefs: Resources for Pastoral Care.* Louisville: Westminster John Knox.

O'Donnell, B. R. J. 2017. "The Odyssey's Millennia-Old Model of Mentorship." *Atlantic*, October 13. *theatlantic.com/business/archive/2017/10/the-odyssey-mentorship/542676*.

Sullivan, William M. 2006. "Introduction." In *Educating Clergy: Teaching Practices and Pastoral Imagination*, by Charles R. Foster, Lisa E. Dahill, Lawrence A. Golemon, and Barbara Wang Tolentino, 1–16. San Francisco: Jossey-Bass.

Endnotes

1 In this chapter, the terms *student pastor* and *pastoral intern* are used interchangeably. Also, the terms *mentor* and *mentor-pastor* are used in a similar way.

2 These persons and the congregations they served have been de-identified to provide confidentiality. Quotations used by written permission of the participants.

CHAPTER 18

Seeking Information Mastery in Multivocational Ministry

> *Pastor Sondra told us she thought one of the "greatest resources" she received in her seminary education "was how to use information, how to find it, and how to discern the information," especially when she was preparing a sermon.*
>
> – Eileen Campbell-Reed (2021, 46)

SUSAN J. EBERTZ

When I read this sentence in *Pastoral Imagination* by Eileen Campbell-Reed, I was struck by the fact that the "greatest resource" was learning about information and not learning information or facts. It was not what I was expecting. Learning to find true information can feed us and help us to continually learn. The world we live in is in constant flux. Anyone called to ministry today can expect to face ever-new and evolving challenges. To respond to these challenges, those in ministry must be continual learners. Programs that prepare students for ministry are important, and learning must continue beyond the institutions that house these programs. Effective ministry requires continual learning and personal development. It requires that those in ministry be able to find, analyze, and apply the information they need to respond to those they serve and to the world in general.

In this chapter, I begin by adopting a model of learning by Hubert Dreyfus and discussing the importance of continual learning to achieve mastery in an area. I then turn to the need to find time for learning. Learning is too important to allow the urgent to displace it. I then discuss how to determine what information is needed, where to find it, and how to evaluate it. I then invite the reader to share what is learned with their congregations, ministry colleagues, and community. Such collaboration brings one in contact with diverse voices, promoting innovation and allowing for creativity in thought and practice. Through careful and efficient research and collaboration with others, multivocational ministers can continue their learning in ways that support effective ministry.

A Model of Learning

My father installed air-conditioning equipment in large hotels and businesses. He learned his trade at a technical college. His two-year degree taught him not only the practical "how-to" but also the "why" so that he could safely do what he was taught to do. His work history included the usual steps of apprenticeship, journeyman, and master in his profession. I remember once being at the mall with my father. A man walked up to him. The man, who worked for a competing company, asked my father for advice on how to install an air-conditioning unit. Because of my father's education, experience, and continued reading on the subject, he was able to offer an innovative solution to his friend's problem.

This everyday example illustrates an important model of learning. Hubert Dreyfus, in his book *On the Internet* (2009, 27), described a process in which "a student learns by means of instruction, practice, and, finally, apprenticeship, to become an expert in some particular domain and in everyday life and what more is required for one to become a master." Dreyfus named six stages to this learning process: 1) Novice, 2) Advanced Beginner, 3) Competence, 4) Proficiency, 5) Expertise, and 6) Mastery.

In the *Novice* stage, the student learns the mechanics of the task and "is then given rules for determining actions on the basis of these features, like a computer following a program" (Dreyfus 2009, 27). The student also needs to understand "the context in which that information makes sense" (28).

In the *Advanced Beginner* stage, the student begins to learn what the relevant contexts are and "to attempt to use the maxims that have been given" (29).

In the *Competence* stage, the student becomes overwhelmed by the number of different situations and struggles to know which skill to use for each situation. Many create general plans for how to respond to various situations, but it is common for the learner to feel uncertainty in deciding which plan to use for a particular situation. The student must figure out which plan is appropriate given the details of the case (30–34).

According to Dreyfus, "*Proficiency* seems to develop if, and only if, experience is assimilated in this embodied, atheoretical way. Only then do intuitive reactions replace reasoned responses" (emphasis added).

Concerning the *Expertise* stage, Dreyfus wrote, "The ability to make more subtle and refined discriminations is what distinguishes the expert from the proficient performer" (35). A variety of experiences "allows the immediate intuitive situational response that is characteristic of expertise" (36).

In the *Mastery* stage, the student desires to go beyond being an expert. "The future master must be willing and able, in certain situations, to override the perspective that as an expert performer he intuitively experiences" (41). In a sense, the student reaches an innovative capacity.

Dreyfus's model shows the need for continuing education for ministry. Looking at the example of my father, his professional training led him through a learning process of progressing from novice, advanced beginner, and competence to eventually achieving proficiency, expertise, and mastery. His trade's levels of certification of apprenticeship, journeyman, and master included not only different experiences but also supervisors to help him learn about different situations and to integrate different types of installations depending on the building. For my father to achieve mastery and offer an innovative solution to his friend, my father, as a foreman who no longer had a supervisor on location, needed to find other sources of information, such as continued reading (one of his favorite magazines was *Popular Science*) in order to see situations from different perspectives.

Many multivocational ministers learn in context much as some air-conditioning installers learn their trade through doing and working with a supervisor. My father was able to exhibit mastery to "override the perspective" and present an innovative solution to his friend's problem. The friend then was able to grow in his learning by talking with my father, who served as a temporary mentor. Continual learning on the part of the friend was an important part of doing the job well and helped him in growing toward his own mastery of the trade. My father's friend was not afraid to seek more information, even from someone who worked for a competitor, in order to learn how to deal with a new situation. Though the friend might not be at the mastery level, he at least could create another plan to add to his collection while in the competence stage. In a similar way, continual learning is important for those in multivocational ministry. When a new situation arises, a multivocational minister will want to seek more information not only to find a solution to a particular problem or situation but also to develop more mastery that can be applied to other situations.

Continual education is important for multivocational ministers no matter their educational background. For example, Christian Scharen, in his chapter in *For Life Abundant,* modified Dreyfus's learning model for seminary education. In seminary, a student may grow through the novice and advanced beginner stages. At these stages, students learn theories and philosophies of the subjects included in the curriculum and how to use them in particular situations. Understanding theories and applications gives students background to later make decisions that may go beyond what has been taught in seminary. This then becomes the basis for learning and integrating new situations and knowledge into practical skills. Applying Dreyfus's stages to ministry, Scharen (2008, 277) observed that "the competent stage occurs during the period when students are making their transition from seminary into full-time leadership in congregational life." Multivocational pastors who have attended seminary are, of course, not transitioning to full-time leadership in a congregation but to many part-time roles, each of which may be full-time in terms of expectations of the job or of others.

In the development of mastery, graduation from seminary or multiple pathways of theological education is not the end of learning. Classroom theological education is a process of helping students gain foundational knowledge and understanding that will feed later growth. Thus, Scharen (2008, 277) stated that the transition from competence to proficiency would take place four to six years after finishing seminary. The student, now minister, still has several years of learning before achieving mastery. Scharen also mentioned that a change to new contexts can move a person backwards in skill proficiency (274). The timeline that Scharen suggested for later stages can apply to all multivocational ministers no matter their educational pathway. Movement through Dreyfus's stages can take longer than some may expect. Thus, continual education is important for all multivocational ministers.

Making Time for Learning

One of the biggest challenges for anyone in ministry is finding time. Our lives are busy. We do not have the time to spend seeking more or better information. We barely have time to deal with the many vocations of our life. There is seemingly no time to add learning and educational growth to our schedule or to stop, learn, and reflect. However, the easiest way to find information may not provide the best information for what we need.

It would seem, at first glance, that it is easier than ever to find information. With virtual home assistants and chatbots becoming ubiquitous, information is available on almost any topic. Speak a question aloud and receive an instant answer. Type in a chatbox, and artificial intelligence finds the meaning of an array of medical symptoms, for example. Even in areas such as theology and biblical studies, a simple Google search will find many websites that provide quick and easy answers. Those involved in multivocational ministry may be tempted to go with such apparently time-saving solutions to meet their information needs. But discovering good and reliable answers for ministry questions takes a bit more work. One must know what kind of information one is looking for. And finding that information requires digging deeper than easy answers and necessitates critical thinking skills to evaluate it.

Most of us turn to search engines when we seek information. This may result in an overwhelming number of hits. In a 2016 report, *How Today's Graduates Continue to Learn Once They Complete College*, Alison Head told the story of what one graduate did to find out information.

> Without a second thought, she grabbed her iPad, did a Google search, and visited the sites she usually frequented, like YouTube, Pinterest, and Hipmunk. She also turned to a trusted friend for advice. These are the tools for lifelong learning in the 21st century, a flood of Internet-

> and human-mediated sources that help recent graduates solve basic to complex information problems. (Head 2016, 2)

Continuing her analysis of information gathering, Head (2016, 32) commented on the increased volume of information available today and the time necessary to wade through this information to get what is desired. Learning sources for personal life included search engines (89%), friends (79%), social networking (79%), family (77%), news (72%), books (70%), and videos (67%) (Head 2016, 23). Sources of workplace related information included coworkers (84%), search engines (83%), supervisor/boss (79%), books (51%), and professional conferences (49%). Friends and family fall lower on the scale for workplace information gathering. In both settings, books are still considered a source of information. While seminary students and multivocational pastors may be older and have more life experience than the undergraduate students in this report, their results would likely be similar. I have found, in my conversations with seminary students, that they also normally use search engines and people for finding information.

There is an ever-increasing number of sources a person needs to sort through to get accurate and reliable information, and time is at a premium for those in multivocational ministry. Most seminary students have had information literacy courses or instruction. These sessions, geared to the novice, foster skill development in finding information. Because the multivocational minister may not have developed the skill further than the advanced beginner stage, searching may still not be intuitive. Adding to the difficulty for multivocational pastors who have completed their formal training is the fact that research databases that students learn to use for their academic work, such as exegesis papers and research in church history and theology, are sometimes no longer available to them. Thus, finding information can be a daunting task. Those in ministry may not find the time to start such research or make a habit of doing thorough research on a regular basis.

Some pastors might think, "all I really need to know about ministry I learned in seminary." This attitude on the part of the seminary-trained pastor indicates that, once they acquire their degree, the pastor may think that they will have the tools and knowledge for ministry. I have heard students anticipating graduation from seminary talking as if they will not need any more education. While it may be true that they do not need any more advanced degrees, it does not follow that they should stop learning. Other pastors, who learned through an apprenticeship model, may feel that once they have completed their apprenticeships, they no longer need to learn anything anymore. However, the world changes and so must those in ministry. Learning to use a slide rule to solve complicated calculations may have been adequate in the past, but to think that such knowledge is enough—or even necessary—appears absurd in our day when we perform mathematical calculations on our phones.

Continued learning is essential because formal theological education and apprenticeships are just the beginning of learning and growth to mastery, taking the learner from the novice to advanced beginner or competence stage as seen in Dreyfus's model. For those who were seminary educated, it is less and less true that seminary education covers all the subjects necessary for ministry. As seminary curricula become shorter and shorter, some subjects necessarily appear only as footnotes in courses. Even courses in core subjects merely introduce students to their subject matter. In the same way, those who have learned through an apprenticeship model may assume that all subjects and situations have been learned, since they are now a pastor. This is not the case. Learning beyond the basics is essential for growth to mastery.

Even if we realize that we need to learn and that finding good information for learning takes time, it may still be difficult to make time for learning. Early stages of novice, advanced beginner, and competence may take more time, but, with practice, the skills involved in finding reliable information will be easier to apply each time. As stages are reached, and with practice, the learner will take less time to find information. In the proficiency stage, for example, the learner has come to trust favorite sites, as we saw in Head's story of the woman doing iPad searches. However we judge her favorite sites of quality information, this graduate has decided that the sites do provide answers to her questions and quickly goes to them when they appear in her results. Time has been saved.

Finding Reliable Information

There are a number of ways to continue growth toward mastery of finding reliable information for ministry. A first step in the search for information is to sit down and think through just what kind of information one is looking for. Is it in preparation for a sermon and looking for quality materials to help interpret the Bible text? Sometimes a member of the congregation may raise a theological question or need help in understanding a particular situation through a theological lens. Perhaps the search is for information on pastoral ministry. Second, after deciding on what kind of information is needed, it is helpful to jot down some keywords that help to identify the topic. Synonyms or different ways of saying something may produce different results. Communion, Eucharist, and Lord's Supper are three different ways of naming a particular Christian ritual. Noting that these three terms may be used in different webpages is helpful in finding reliable results. Third, make a list of colleagues, mentors, former teachers and supervisors, and others who may be able to guide the search for information. Who can point the way to key information? Who might mentor? My father's friend recognized at the mall that there was an opportunity to learn more. Who might help to set up situations in which contextual learning can take place? Are there workshops available? Are there resources, such as libraries and librarians, that may be of help? By taking time to ask a few questions like these, the search can be focused and time is saved. Keeping a list of possible resources will help in future seeking.

The internet is not the only source of information, but it is one source we all use. So how can we use it most wisely? The graduate who grabbed her iPad is like most in the competence stage. She has a plan for looking for information. Search engines and friends are her two top resources. Hopefully, she has learned how to evaluate the hits that would be most helpful and weed out those that are biased or irrelevant. With this skill, she can quickly scan the results for quality, relevance, and truth, avoiding disinformation (see Owens, chapter 13 in this volume). Once we understand how to evaluate search results on the internet, time becomes less of a problem. For example, I talked with a student who heard about Brené Brown and was curious to know more about her. He googled "Brené Brown" and received a number of hits. The next step was to evaluate which of the hits to examine first. I suggested that the best way to find out what Brené Brown says is to hear what she says about herself. The link to Brown's website was the first site we looked at. Information about Brown and her views were on her site. Some of the other distracting search results included advertisements for Brown's books and blogs quoting her work. Some of the other sites may be interesting but would be a rabbit hole in finding good information quickly.

Brown's website provided a podcast she had done explaining some of her main points. Honing in on the needed information and ignoring extraneous information can save time in searching.

In considering the use of search engines, it is important to note that a search engine tailors its results to each enquirer; the selection of links the search engine lists will be different for each searcher. This occurs because search engines use algorithms to analyze an individual's search habits, including which sites an individual user has visited in the past. As the search engine gathers more and more information about a particular user, software enables the computer to predict what kind of information each searcher wants to see. In a sense, the more one searches, the more the artificial intelligence learns what one looks for. For example, I live in Dubuque, Iowa. Recently I was searching for a particular restaurant in Dubuque. The search box finished my search term by offering the restaurant name then adding "Dubuque." The search engine had learned that I often look for this restaurant. The restaurant also appeared at the top of my search results. This may be helpful in terms of time saved, but it may not increase the usefulness of searching for more quality information. Some search engines do not gather information as much as others. For example, at the time of this writing, Duck Duck Go advertised on its search page, "We don't store your personal information. Ever." They differentiate themselves from other search engines by promising privacy in searching. Google also has a privacy setting enabling Private Google, which uses a different kind of algorithm.

The machine learning involved in some of the algorithms may simply produce confirmation bias, or verification for what we already think. For example, if I am searching for information about gun violence and the search engine had concluded from my search history that I supported greater gun control measures, the search engine would provide links to sites that reinforce this view. On the other hand, if I am a staunch defender of free and uncontrolled gun ownership and have a history of reading websites that criticize any form of gun control legislation, then the search engine will provide links that reinforce this view. This is one of the reasons our nation, as well as our churches, has become so polarized. Information sources feed us what we want to hear. It becomes harder for us to find information on both sides of an issue when we have trained artificial intelligence with a particular viewpoint. Another example can be found in the book *Race After Technology*. In it, Ruha Benjamin posits that technology reinforces White supremacy.

> Such findings demonstrate what I call 'the New Jim Code': the employment of new technologies that reflect and reproduce existing inequities but that are promoted and perceived as more objective or progressive than the discriminatory systems of a previous era. (Benjamin 2019, 5)

Whether you agree with Benjamin or not, the evidence provided in her book shows an interesting correlation with search results that show bias. In short, looking for information by "just googling it" or asking Siri or Alexa can produce biased information. Given the way search engines work, it is easy to see how they could easily reinforce racism and bias or a one-sided view of a topic. We stunt growth from the competence stage to proficiency when we limit our information through algorithmic bias.

How can one counter this search bias? It is probably not possible to avoid it completely, but it is possible to be wary of search results and to look for other views. Since search engines can pick up on "trigger words" used by supporters of various positions, it can be helpful to find non-trigger synonyms to search instead. It also helps to go beyond the first page of hits. Seeking out differing voices, both online and in other resources, can broaden one's perspective. Books, articles, blogs, and podcasts may provide guidance and new ideas as well as different perspectives. New voices challenge us and open us to new ways of thinking, sparking new ideas. Outside input can also help us to pivot quickly when the context changes by teaching us new plans for new situations, helping us move from competence to proficiency to expertise. We no longer try to fit a particular plan to a new situation but can intuitively respond to the new situation.

So, there are ways to try to counter the inbuilt bias of search engines. But one should also go beyond search engines to gather information online. A growing number of open access (OA) academic articles and books (such as this one) are available via reliable sources. Seminary libraries have curated lists of these as well as other freely available articles. These lists have usually been vetted by the seminary librarian and may be trusted. Most seminary librarians and faculty members are happy to help in finding good, academically sound sources on the internet. Many seminaries also allow pastors to access library resources. Public libraries and denominational agencies and offices also provide good print and online resources.

The graduate who grabbed the iPad to find information also sought the advice of a trusted friend. Like a trusted website, a trusted friend can provide good information. When seeking recommendations or advice from friends, we often think about who would give us the best information. For example, if I am looking for a good restaurant, I would probably ask someone who has similar tastes to mine. If I am looking for a contractor, I would ask a friend who just had work done on their house. In my father's case, his friend sought his advice to figure out the best way to install the air-conditioning unit in a challenging situation. In a similar way, when looking for information, we could ask a friend or an expert in the relevant area, perhaps a colleague or former professor or mentor.

"Trustworthy" and "knowledgeable" are two very important criteria for evaluating a source of information, whether this is a website, a friend, a book, or an article. In determining whether a source of information is trustworthy, we need to know what we believe and why we believe it. Some of this is learned through studies in theological doctrine and biblical studies or in apprenticeship programs with a mentor or supervisor. Our core theology is our foundational belief and becomes important in discerning whether information is helpful to us. When we learn new information, we balance the new information with the foundational beliefs that we have. If the new understanding is coherent with those foundational beliefs, then it would make sense to incorporate the new learning into our lives. If the new understanding is not coherent, then the question is whether to discard the new learning as false or to modify our foundational beliefs or, even more drastically, to decide our foundational beliefs are wrong. For example, diversity, equity, and inclusion are currently important issues in many churches and communities. Whether the diversity concerns race or gender identification, emotions may run high. When seeking relevant information, it is important to consider one's core theology in evaluating information discovered in the search. This will help to steady us in looking at important issues.

Mentoring is another source of growth in both knowledge and wisdom as one moves through the stages toward mastery (see Fain, chapter 12 in this volume). Mentorships may be formal relationships with someone who will guide and advise as needed. The mentor can provide not only "how-to" information but answer the questions of "why." The mentor can teach and demonstrate. Colleagues may serve as mentors by becoming conversation partners in new or challenging situations, perhaps sharing experience in similar circumstances. Colleagues may offer insight or be a listening ear or ask the right questions to help with creative ideas or solutions.

Becoming Both Learner and Teacher

There is a sense in which we are both learners and teachers as we travel together along Dreyfus's stages of growing in our skills and abilities. Multivocational ministers may lack time and perhaps feel marginalized for not being full-time in ministry. Yet working collaboratively with others who are similar but different not only helps with a sense of belonging but also sharpens thinking and perspective. Collaboration can also help in our motivation to keep learning. Weekly groups to study the lectionary text or to test out preaching ideas can be good sources of information and insight. Book clubs, writing groups, and beer and theology groups can be good places for discussion and learning and may be excellent means of encouraging us to learn and think and see things from a different perspective. It may increase our "ability to make more subtle and refined discriminations" (Dreyfus 2009, 35) and thus move us to the expertise stage.

Finding ways to implement "continuous improvement"—an idea taken from business—can help us learn new things to apply in ministry situations. Evaluating the congregation on a regular basis may reveal, for example, that the Sunday School program is no longer helping students learn. Observation might show that the students are restless during sessions and that there are increased absences. Evaluation may point out why the program is not helping students learn. This may be a situation when more information is needed to determine why the usual way of dealing with a situation is not working and what improvement is needed. Figuring out what kind of information is needed, deciding how to find the information, and using appropriate researching skills will help one advance through the stages of learning. Our search to find reliable information to improve the program may include looking at successful Sunday School programs and seeing why they do what they do. It may also involve others in the congregation or in churches nearby. Perhaps we may bring in experts in childhood education (temporary mentors) or read a book with others (collaboration with colleagues). Evaluation and looking at the context may point to a need for incremental change or a major change in the Sunday School program. Striving for continuous improvement also fosters growth in skill and knowledge toward mastery in multivocational ministry.

Along a similar line, one can look for opportunities to commit oneself to learning in new areas. I often submit proposals for professional development sessions based on what I want to learn rather than what I already know. I find that this helps me do research on something that is important to me. It motivates me to study and to learn. Some ministers offer to lead sessions at professional conferences; others may lead an Advent or Lenten study to encourage their own continued learning. Preaching a series on a particular topic may provide the same kind of motivation. As we are both learners and instructors, it is important to share what we have learned. Information and skills become more embedded in our lives when we share, promoting growth from expertise to mastery.

I opened this chapter with a quote from Pastor Sondra, who considered one of her greatest resources learning to find information. This skill was not only for ministry-related study. Later, Campbell-Reed observed,

> Learning about how to use resources went beyond preaching and teaching. She [Sondra] says her "personal study" and "personal devotion time" became essential to nourishing her well-being as a minister. Referring to her spiritual nourishment, she says, "You know, I can go eat, too, and I can eat well." (Campbell-Reed 2021, 46)

Continually learning and finding reliable information are not just for works of ministry but also for feeding our souls. We are whole people when we make sure that we are well-fed, not just for mastery of multivocational ministry but also for our own spiritual growth and formation.

Works Cited

Benjamin, Ruha. 2019. *Race after Technology: Abolitionist Tools for the New Jim Code*. Cambridge, UK: Polity.

Campbell-Reed, Eileen R. 2021. *Pastoral Imagination: Bringing the Practice of Ministry to Life*. Minneapolis, MN: Fortress. *doi.org/10.2307/j.ctv17vf3w9*.

Dreyfus, Hubert L. 2009. *On the Internet*. 2nd ed. Thinking in Action. New York: Routledge.

Head, Alison J. 2016. "Staying Smart: How Today's Graduates Continue to Learn Once They Complete College." *Project Information Literacy Research Report*. January 5. *doi.org/10.2139/ssrn.2712329*.

Scharen, Christian. 2008. "Learning Ministry over Time: Embodying Practical Wisdom." In *For Life Abundant: Practical Theology, Theological Education, and Christian Ministry*, edited by Dorothy C. Bass and Craig R. Dykstra, 265–88. Grand Rapids, MI: Eerdmans.

CHAPTER 19

Reimagining Theological Education with a Multivocational Mindset

DARRYL W. STEPHENS

Bivocational ministry is more than holding down another job to make ends meet. This much should be clear to readers having ventured to the end of this book. Intentional bivocational or multivocational ministry is a theological mindset with material implications for how we live and work together. A multivocational mindset is a helpful—perhaps necessary—way to reimagine theological education in light of challenges facing the church in North America today.

A multivocational mindset respects the partially funded pastor as much, or even more, than the fully compensated pastor—for all ministry is full time. In the body of Christ, each member is an individual with distinct spiritual gifts. A multivocational mindset is an intentional missional strategy as well as a calling—an approach to ministry that shares more in common with Cynthia Lindner's (2016, 115–17) description of "multiple-mindedness in ministry" than her all-too-accurate depiction of the way denominational leaders, ministry committees, and theological educators often foist "bivocational ministry" on vulnerable candidates, "plac[ing] the burden of congregational life support on clergy, asking them to look elsewhere for employment that will supplement the church's shrinking budget." In contrast, intentional multivocationality attends to Lindner's concept of multiplicity as well as the idea of unique fit as pastors learn to live out their calling within and beyond the church (Watson et al. 2020).

A multivocational mindset has implications for the renewal of graduate theological education in North America, prompting theological educators to consider: What role does theological education play in cultivating this mindset, nurturing the gifts of all Christians, and recognizing a calling to bivocationality or multivocationality? How can theological educators best equip leaders for a thriving multivocational ministry? What are the justice implications of adopting a multivocational mindset? Multivocational ministry is both a challenge and an opportunity for institutions of theological education as well as the leaders and churches they serve.

In this chapter, I adopt a bivocational and multivocational mindset as a way of renewing graduate theological education in North America. I predominantly use the term bivocational because the term multivocational is not yet prominent in the literature. The chapter begins by noting that preparation for bivocational ministry is rarely addressed by professional theological educators in North America; intentional bivocational ministry preparation occurs primarily—though not exclusively—outside of ATS-member institutions. Then, I offer observations about the changing context of predominantly White, Protestant churches in North America and their attitudes, perceptions, and experiences, establishing both the need for and the challenges to educating for intentional bivocational ministry. The work of Justo González on the history of theological education and Daniel Aleshire on the future of theological education serve as conversation partners in the task of reimagining theological education in light of bivocational ministry. Current institutional forms of higher education reveal significant obstacles to adopting a bivocational-friendly model of education, implying the need for institutional changes. Finally, I draw attention to both the necessity and the insufficiency of a multivocational mindset, which must be combined with antiracist and other justice-oriented commitments in order to reimagine and accomplish life-giving change within graduate theological education.

Against the Grain

Educating for bivocational ministry goes against the grain of established, professionalized, accredited institutions of graduate theological education in North America. Daniel O. Aleshire (2008. 137), then executive director of the Association of Theological Schools in the United States and Canada (ATS), observed, "How do schools and denominations continue to value theological degrees for those who can obtain them as the number of pastors without them increases? Will there be an increasingly double-tiered understanding of ministry?" In other words, can pastors be viewed as distinctive and equally valued, despite differences in formal education? Elizabeth Conde-Frazier (2021, 123) turned the question around, directing her gaze at the way we perceive theological educators who also serve the church. Recognizing "the importance of bivocational work," she drew attention to "the remarkable vitality of bivocational scholars and the communities they serve." Viewing bivocational scholarship as a gift—a charism in which "God is creating . . . a mix of many things"—she argued, "These 'mixed' or 'blended' vocations are not something to be outgrown. They are sources of strength and insight." That she felt compelled to defend bivocational scholars is indicative of the adverse climate for bivocational ministry currently found in institutions of theological education.

Bivocational ministry is often a null curriculum among educators discussing the state of theological education. ATS does not mention bivocational or part-time ministry in either its standards of accreditation or *Self-Study Handbook* (ATS 2020). Full-time, fully funded ministry functioned as the implied norm for the "common profession" of "diverse practices" examined in a study of clergy education sponsored by the Carnegie Foundation for the Advancement of Teaching, which made no mention at all of bivocational ministry (Foster et al. 2006). The topic was also absent from a special journal issue on "The Current and Future Directions of Theological Education" (Scharen 2019). Bivocational ministry also went unmentioned in a volume of essays in honor of Aleshire's tenure at ATS (Wheeler 2019). In a special issue of the American Academy of Religion's *Spotlight on Theological Education* on the theme, "Theological Education between the Times: Reflections on the *Telos* of Theological Education," only two contributors mentioned bivocational ministry (Cascante-Gómez 2017, 5–6; Wong 2017, 19–20).

Bivocationality does not fit comfortably within discourse about graduate theological education. Of the 95 contributors to the extensive *Handbook of Theological Education in World Christianity*, only three mentioned bivocational ministry, and then only in passing (Werner et al. 2010, 475, 511, 692). Of the three, Aleshire (2010, 511) provided the most engagement. He contrasted bivocational ministry preparation with the mission and purpose of the primary institutions of theological education in North America—ATS-member schools, all of which "grant graduate professional degrees for a variety of areas of ministry practice." As an aside, he observed, "Other [non-ATS] schools offer theological education at the baccalaureate degree level, and a growing number of educational programs offer non-degree study for bi-vocational and alternatively credentialed clergy." Clearly, he considered these "other" schools and programs offering bivocational ministry preparation as falling outside the scope of his chapter, "Theological Education in North America."

Bivocational ministry preparation cannot be ignored simply because theological schools and seminaries feel ill-equipped to meet this need. Aleshire (2008, 136–37) acknowledged that "alternative patterns for credentialing part-time and bi-vocational clergy are emerging rapidly" (see also Aleshire 2011, 72). This caused him to question how ATS-member schools might navigate this future: "Can theological schools continue to operate alternative educational models out of their back pockets as these models become increasingly dominant?" (2008, 137). At the time, Aleshire's questions implied a greater concern for maintaining the validity of a master's degree than meeting the educational needs of bivocational pastors. Changes in the landscape of ministry and education for ministry can be anxiety-producing for persons and institutions invested in the "standard model" of univocational clergy.

Noticing these changes is a necessary first step in reimagining theological education. Researchers at Auburn Seminary recognized a disjunction between seminary education and bivocational ministry preparation, observing "a whole world of theological education outside the ATS member schools," primarily serving students who are "bivocational and already in ministry, either lay or ordained, when they seek out theological education" (Scharen and Miller 2016, 8). They went on to say,

> Rather than certification for ministry, as in the old mainstream denominational model, these ministers are seeking deeper knowledge

and skills for ministries in which they are already immersed and which they usually continue to lead all through their coursework. This model of community-based, contextual theological education is a hallmark of the Bible Institute system and offers a way for other theological schools to rethink both curricular structure and pedagogy, which too often separates coursework from the practice of ministry. (Scharen and Miller 2016, 8)

The Bible institute, judicatory licensing school, and non-degree lifelong learning program each have something to offer to the theological education and formation of pastoral leaders. Likewise, the congregation is no less a contributor to the vocational formation of pastors, despite not having any accreditation as a school of theology. As these multiple pathways of education increase in influence in churches traditionally served by degree-bearing pastors, Aleshire's observation about the rise of "alternative patterns for credentialing" becomes even more relevant.[1]

Scharen and Miller's invitation to rethink, and perhaps redesign, "curricular structure and pedagogy" is a tall order for ATS-member schools. Complexifying this task are embedded, racialized dynamics, in which the "whiteness" (Jennings 2020, 9) of the "old mainstream denominational model" contrasts with the diverse forms of education arising from communities of color, immigrants, and others. Less difficult to name is the array of pragmatic hurdles. Assessing the 2017 ATS Graduating Student Questionnaire, Jo Ann Deasy (2018, 70) suggested that theological schools will need to address new questions relating to skills development for bivocational ministry (see also Deasy, chapter 15, and Stephens, chapter 14, in this volume). Needed is a discussion of bivocationality as a central part of the story of theological education.

Observations about Bivocational Ministry

Churches and schools are recognizing and responding to the needs of bivocational students and pastors in structured as well as improvisational ways. Before his retirement from ATS, Aleshire (2021, 108–9) recognized Wesley Seminary of Indiana Wesleyan University and Pittsburgh Theological Seminary as examples of ATS programs designed primarily for bivocational students. As discussed in this volume, Earlham School of Religion (Baisley, chapter 16 in this volume), Lexington Theological Seminary (Bentley, chapter 7 in this volume), and Lancaster Theological Seminary (Stephens, chapter 14 in this volume) are among the ATS schools turning their attention to bivocational ministry preparation. There are others, though these efforts have yet to be coordinated and reported in a comprehensive way. To inform these efforts, I offer observations about the changing context of predominantly White, Protestant churches in North America and their attitudes, perceptions, and experiences of bivocational ministry.

Changing context of the church

Bivocational ministry in North America is helpfully viewed within the context of churches undergoing tremendous change. Four observations provide a broad-brush description of bivocational ministry within this context. First, bivocational ministry is an umbrella term for many different arrangements of pastoral ministry combined with other paid and unpaid employments—arrangements that go by a variety of names. Second, bivocational ministry has been the norm for ministry across many cultures, denominations, and historical eras. It is "new" within the context of the White, North American mainline denominations that have professionalized ministry during the past 150 years, paralleling the historical emergence of ATS-member schools. Third, the norm of fully funded pastoral ministry is a structural feature of many predominantly White denominations, in which bivocational ministry is considered aberrant and exceptional by tradition, ethos, and polity. Fourth, when fully funded pastoral ministry declines as a statistical norm, expectations and structures no longer match demographic and financial realities within White mainline denominations. This situation creates systemic challenges to ministry.

Discrepancies between the way things used to be and the way things are indicate the need for change, contributing to already-present anxieties over declining membership rolls, congregational vitality, missional clarity, societal presence, and institutional clout (Stephens 2020). The increased visibility of bivocational ministry in recent years among Episcopalians, United Methodists, United Church of Christ, Lutherans, Presbyterians, Southern Baptists, the Christian Reformed Church in North America, and other predominantly White denominations signals a sea change in these churches' relation to society and self-perception. Simply put, the old White North American Christendom is over (Jones 2016).

Attitudes, perceptions, and experiences of bivocational ministry

It should be no surprise that an anxious church during a time of significant cultural change expresses a wide range of attitudes, perceptions, and experiences of bivocational ministry. Bivocational ministry challenges individualism and self-sufficiency within the pastorate and can contribute to a renewed missional vitality when the congregation becomes a partner in ministry (Edington 2018; MacDonald 2020; Stephens, chapter 1 in this volume). Bivocational ministry can also involve distinctive stressors. Factors that can reduce stress and increase satisfaction among bivocational pastors include: vocational integration, congregational receptivity, intentionality in employment, discerning a unique fit, and being psychologically prepared (Watson et al. 2020). Bivocational ministry thrives with whole-life integration of vocation, employment, ministry, family, and other aspects of our "multiplicity" (Watson et al. 2020; see also Lindner 2016). There is some evidence that younger generations are more open to partially-funded ministry as part of the new gig economy, particularly as enabled through digital technologies (New Leaf Network 2020).

Nevertheless, bivocational ministry is widely considered deficient compared to the fully-funded (White, middle class) ideal within aged, White mainline churches. This perception reflects discrepancies and anxieties embedded in denominational polities and ethos and cannot be disentangled from reigning social biases regarding race, gender, class, educational levels, financial success, marital status, and material realities in North American societies. Women, persons of color, immigrants, differently abled persons—these groups are more likely than others to be partially funded in ministry (Perry and Schleifer 2019). Percentages of bivocational pastors are much higher among immigrant and non-White communities. Women face greater hurdles balancing multiple demands and commitments vocationally and personally than men (for a brief discussion, see MacDonald 2020, 27; Deasy, chapter 5 in this volume).

Seminaries and churches adopting a bivocational mindset will encounter racialized and gendered constructs, generational differences, and tradition-bound practices even as they seek to create something "new." Bivocational ministry and contextually-originated training are hardly new approaches, given the two-thousand-year history of the church and its ministry and the proliferation of Bible institutes and non-degree certifications available in many non-White ministry contexts. It is graduate theological education that must be renewed and reenvisioned for the current day and age.

Reimagining Theological Education with Justo González

The task of reimagining theological education is helpfully informed by a consideration of the historical trajectory that brought us to this point. In his book, *The History of Theological Education* (2015), Justo González provided an overview of two millennia of Christian efforts to disciple and equip persons for ministerial leadership. Contrasting several models, González offered directives for reconstituting theological education for "the new times we are facing" (127), suggesting specific ways ATS-member schools can respond to these new challenges in light of the broader history of the church and its educational efforts. Reading González's insights through the lens of intentional bivocational ministry yields constructive ways of reimagining theological education.

Equipping leaders for a thriving bivocational ministry may require a new model of theological education. Learning from the rich history of theological education over many centuries, González (2015, 121–27) provided an assessment of two existing models of theological education and one suggested model (see also Wayman 2021). Existing models fail to address the challenges of bivocational ministry. The residential or "semimonastic" model of theological education cloisters students in a learning community for formation over several years. However, this model does not fit students with multiple responsibilities and demands on their time (González 2015, 122–23)—clearly not a good fit for the realities of bivocational ministry. A second model offers flexible scheduling arrangements: for example, weekend and evening classes, extension programs, and online instruction. This model allows students to remain in their community contexts as they learn. However, it carries the risk that "ministerial training tends to become a matter of instruction and not of formation" (123). While flexibility is important for bivocational students, this model does nothing to alleviate the parallel risk that bivocational ministry may become a matter of financial expediency or necessity and not of missional intentionality on the part of the minister or congregation. In contrast to these two models, González suggested building on innovations in technology (such as the internet) and contextual education ("supervised ministry") for "a radical revision in the curriculum" (127). In this new model, theological education consists of a continual spiral of praxis-theory-reflection-praxis, altering current methods of teaching, scholarship, and evaluation (126–27). These innovations would empower bivocational students by centering the practice of ministry in the learning environment and valuing the variety of life-skills they bring as an integral part of theological education.

Implementing this new model requires reconstituting theological education in specific ways. González enumerated seven directives for this new vision of theological education (2015, 127–29), each of which is potentially responsive to the realities of bivocational ministry. Viewed with a bivocational mindset, each directive addresses challenges of bivocational ministry. First, González suggested returning theological education to the church by locating learning in the community of faith (see also Wayman 2021). This directive enhances intentional bivocational ministry, which is most effective when it becomes the congregation's curriculum and laity are included in the educational process (Stephens, chapter 1 in this volume). Second, he suggested teaching and evaluating student achievement based on application within communities of faith. This directive enhances bivocational ministry formation by valuing the student's ministry context as a primary place where a student teaches, learns, and ministers. Third, González emphasized theological education as a life-long process; seminary is no longer considered an exceptional time of formation, after which one enters the real work of ministry. This directive resonates with formation in bivocational ministry, which often begins prior to formal theological studies, may or may not include seminary studies, and continues long after basic educational requirements are met. Fourth, he encouraged academic theological educators to partner with churches to address new and evolving challenges and circumstances. Intentional bivocational ministry is but one example of the kind of challenge implied by this directive. Fifth, González recognized that theological studies and the practice of ministry go in both directions and that they are not confined to pastoral ministry. Theological education can benefit those in vocations outside of pastoral ministry as well as those already in the practice of ministry. As a case in point, bivocational ministry is often a blending of these two directions in one person. Sixth, he suggested training mentors to lead theological reflection on not only pastoral ministry "but even more the pastoral practice of the entire community of faith" (129). This directive pertains directly to enabling the congregation to take on bivocational ministry as its curriculum. Seventh, González encouraged redefining the way faculty publications are evaluated, based on their relevance and usefulness to ministry. This directive would elevate the status of scholarship on practices of ministry; currently, there exists very little scholarly and peer-reviewed literature on bivocational ministry.

Embracing the above directives would require significant changes by ATS-member schools. González (2015, 138–39) suggested that "traditionally accredited theological education" must respond to current challenges by learning from the history of the church. He prescribed eight responses, each of which has implications for bivocational ministry. First, learn to view theological education as a continuum from catechesis to lay education to pastoral training to research and reflection. This prescription implies that, to equip persons for bivocational ministry, seminaries should allow multiple entry points to theological education. Offering only a standard, three-year master's degree is not a sufficient response to this need. Second, disrupt the idea that theory precedes practice. This prescription implies that the practices of bivocational ministry must inform our theology of mission and ministry and the way we teach in graduate theological education. Third, set aside institutional elitism. This prescription implies that, to equip persons for bivocational ministry, seminaries need to lower the bar to entry and participation. For example, is a bachelor's degree a necessary requirement for admission into theological studies? Fourth, realize that theological education and ordination are not necessarily coincident. This prescription implies that persons seek formal theological education for a variety of reasons. Educating for bivocational ministry will include laity, persons preparing for ordination, and those not preparing for ordination. Fifth, establish closer ties with immediate communities and their needs. This prescription implies that communities and congregations are essential partners in theological education. Bivocational education requires getting involved in the faith communities in proximity to the seminary. Sixth, accredited programs must encourage and acknowledge non-accredited programs of theological education. This prescription implies that non-degree programs are a necessary option for many people and should be valued as such. Bivocational ministry often relies on pastors educated through non-traditional, non-accredited programs of study. Seventh, seminaries must widen their ecclesiastical and denominational horizons. The need for and desirability of bivocational ministry transcends confessional and denominational differences. Eighth, González asserted that theological schools must "acknowledge the cultural captivity of much of our institutional and ecclesial life" (139). When the wisdom and experience of bivocational ministry emerges from the margins, the entire church and academy will benefit from those not previously centered in the fully-funded model of professional parish ministry.

Reimagining Theological Education with Daniel Aleshire

The task of reimagining theological education is also helpfully informed in conversation with those in charge of accrediting graduate degree programs. Daniel Aleshire served as executive director of ATS for nearly twenty years, 1998–2017. According to Aleshire, the goal of theological education is:

> the development of a wisdom of God and the ways of God, fashioned from intellectual, affective, and behavioral understanding and evidenced by spiritual and moral maturity, relational integrity, knowledge of the Scripture and tradition, and the capacity to exercise religious leadership. (Aleshire 2021, 82)

One key aspect of relational integrity, beyond how one relates to others, is how one relates to one's own complexity. Intentional multivocational ministry demands a kind of relational integrity within oneself, evidenced, practiced, and lived out across all of one's life activities. Equipping for a thriving bivocational ministry cannot be accomplished without attention to this aspect of relational integrity. Aleshire's assessment of theological education can inform the education and preparation of bivocational ministers—if it is read with a bivocational or multivocational mindset.

From the vantage point of his experience, Aleshire (2021, 140) recognized that theological education must be "right for its time." To meet today's challenges, he recognized that "formational theological education" will need to change, requiring both a "fundamental reorientation to higher education" as well as technical adaptations (136). He named three institutional changes needing closer examination: "the evaluation of students, the organization of student learning, and the partners that theological schools engage" (131). Each of these changes has implications for how ATS-member schools can better educate for a thriving multivocational ministry.

First, Aleshire (2021, 132) pointed out the need for schools to develop more qualitative forms of evaluating students. He asserted the need to find appropriate ways to evaluate a student's spiritual or moral maturity, if that "becomes a legitimate goal for theological education." In other words, if formation is a goal, how do we assess a student's adequate progress toward this goal? In a similar vein, theological educators might consider evaluation criteria for vocational clarity, integration, and balance. Successful bivocational ministry relies heavily on the ability of the individual to understand their own gifts and calling, to find ways to integrate their ministry into the wide range of activities comprising one's day-to-day life, and to achieve some sense of sustainable proportion among the various aspects of their life. Multivocational education is one way of intentionally tending to one's multiplicity as a minister and a human being—how will theological schools teach and assess the skills necessary to success in this form of ministry?

Second, Aleshire (2021, 134) recognized the need for an integration of academic disciplines in student learning. He observed that the structure of academic disciplines and subdisciplines does not match the way ministry is practiced. Ministry requires integration of knowledge and practice across disciplinary divisions. Aleshire asserted that the "tasks of integration . . . need to become the responsibility of theological schools," not just the individual student. Integration is not just a curricular issue; it is also an issue for multiple vocations. Multivocational ministry takes the task of integration one step further: not only must theological education equip the student to integrate knowledge through the practices of ministry, but theological education must also be integrated through the entire spectrum of one's life activities. How can theological education contribute to an integration of knowledge, practice, and individual multiplicity? An apprenticeship approach, such as promoted by the Carnegie volume

Educating Clergy (Foster et al. 2006), holds promise—if this approach were cognizant of and attentive to multivocational realities in the lives of students and ministers (see Fain, chapter 12 in this volume).

Third, Aleshire (2021, 134–35) observed the need for increased engagement with new partners to promote and nurture experiential learning. The kinds of "behavioral and affective learning" to which Aleshire alluded occur not only in formal ministry settings but also in the multiple locations in which one lives out one's call as a disciple and leader of other disciples. The wide, collaborative engagement suggested by Aleshire lends itself to multivocational preparation. Field education is one under-utilized way to do this, providing a natural site for exploration and learning about bivocational ministry. Other avenues of learning and partnership occur through informal interaction among one's peers in ministry and the congregations served. Multivocational ministry is most successful with the support of intentional partners who participate in one's ongoing, life-long formation and learning as a faith leader. How can theological educators partner with the student body to cultivate meaningful avenues for peer evaluation and support? And how can theological educators partner with congregations? Aleshire's observations about needed institutional changes lend themselves to a consideration of bivocational ministry, though he did not do so himself.

Present Obstacles

A multivocational mindset is a helpful—perhaps necessary—way to reimagine graduate theological education as "right for its time" today. Reimagining theological education in conversation with Justo González and Daniel Aleshire showed the resonance of their ideas with the demands of bivocational ministry as well as the necessity of bringing to their discussion a multivocational mindset in order to draw out implications for equipping persons for a thriving multivocational ministry. This mindset also reveals specific obstacles presented by current forms of theological education.

I offer the following observations and questions about theological education today, based on the above discussion and my own experience and research about educating bivocational pastors. First, many ATS seminaries mirror the design, purpose, prejudices, perceptions, and anxieties of the White, mainline churches they primarily serve. This observation is both consistent with and illustrative of the distorted formation resulting from "white self-sufficient masculinity" as described by Jennnings (2020, 5–9). Instead, can seminaries lead as change agents for the church, moving from existing models of residential and flexible scheduling arrangements to a truly contextual mode of praxis-based learning? Second, fully-funded, professionalized ministry is the norm around which most academic theological education programs are currently designed and implemented. What would it look like for seminaries to restructure their education programs with bivocational ministry as the norm, truly partnering with congregations? Third, current curricula are designed with full-time students as the norm, paralleling the challenges confronting part-time pastors. How can seminaries recenter their curricula around part-time, multivocational students as the norm? Fourth, current curricula are centered around degree programs to support credentialing in ministry. What would it look like for seminaries to partner with churches more seamlessly to provide theological education spanning the spectrum from catechesis to discipleship to credentialing to life-long learning—a drip hose rather than a pipeline (González 2020)? Fifth, the tenure model, including funding for academic research through sabbaticals and subsidized scholarship, does not directly support the vision of the future of theological education envisioned by González (2015) and others. When seminary faculty are hired on the basis of scholarly research, when faculty are not credentialed in ministry, and when faculty have little experience in or connection to churches, how does this impact the school's ability to prepare persons for bivocational ministry? Sixth, contingent faculty in theological education are treated in ways that implicitly devalue bivocational modes of employment, including bivocational ministry. When contingent faculty are marginalized in theological education, what does that imply about the relative value placed on bivocational pastors in church structures?

The tenure system and the marginal status of contingent faculty are deeply embedded in ATS-member schools. Tenure is a mainstay of research institutions, including university-embedded seminaries. The tenure model is unlikely to change anytime soon, though it is unsustainable in the long term. Can stand-alone seminaries continue to fund scholarly research in the same way as research institutions, even when this research is directly tied to programmatic improvements in student learning for ministerial leadership? Furthermore, fully-funded faculty are currently prioritized and honored in ways that implicitly endorse and reinforce fully-funded ministry as the norm. Does this dynamic not imply that full-time pastoring is to be more highly valued and prioritized than bivocational ministry in the church? Can ATS-member schools elevate bivocational ministry without also addressing their bias toward full-funded faculty? I think not.

For theological schools to promote intentional multivocational ministry as a legitimate and equal calling, they will need to address their own inequities regarding adjunct faculty. The unfair treatment of contingent faculty has been recognized as a deficiency of "a culture of ethics" (Keenan 2015), an inconsistency with church teachings (Keenan and Gaudet 2019), an "ethical deficit" (Thistlethwaite 2018), an "ethical debt" (Anonymous 2019), and a "scandal" (Keenan 2018). In a vocational retrospective, Kathleen Henderson Staudt (2015, 38) provided a detailed assessment of her experience as an adjunct, including the injustices she faced and what could be done to ameliorate the worst of them, drawing an explicit parallel to bivocational ministry. For ATS-member schools to equip students for careers of intentional, partially-funded ministry—and to do this well and with integrity—they must address the inequities of the partially funded faculty who occupy the same classrooms.

Self-standing seminaries may have an advantage over university-embedded schools of theology in addressing these issues. Independent seminaries have the potential to be more agile, responsive, and innovative when it comes to changing inherited models: for example, tenure, funding, and faculty status. However, the treatment of contingent faculty is an issue for every institution of higher learning, and self-standing seminaries are no less susceptible to classism than other institutions.

Implications for Theological Education

A multivocational mindset can assist ATS-member schools in reimagining graduate theological education in the midst of current challenges. There is great need for renewal. "If theological education was ever in peril, it is now," observed Benjamin Wayman (2021), referring to a rash of seminary and church-related school closures within the most recent five years. To assist in the task of "Imagining the Future of Theological Education," the title of his article for the *Chris-*

tian Century, Wayman interviewed Emilie Townes, Justo González, Rowan Williams, and Sam Wells. The future of theological education, he concluded, requires "shifting the center from the university to the church," providing a variety of offerings "that attend to the vocation of each person," and "challeng[ing] the *isms* that have long poisoned theological education" (Wayman 2021). In conversation with Aleshire, González, Wayman, and others, what if North American seminaries were to risk reinventing themselves by adopting a multivocational mindset?

A multivocational mindset can equip the seminary to respond to each of the ideas Wayman put forth. A focus on intentional multivocational ministry can shift theological education back to the church. As the church's curriculum, bivocational ministry is praxis-focused, vocationally motivated, and community-centered. A bivocational mindset can address the directives and prescriptions offered by González as well as the needs for curricular integration and wider collaboration raised by Aleshire. A focus on intentional bivocational ministry can also provide a practical structure and theological framework for increasing the modes and types of educational offerings required to "prioritiz[e] vocational learning over degree completion," as Wayman (2021) expressed it. Attention to less-than-fully funded ministry can also open doors to new initiatives and partnerships.

Some theological schools have already made significant strides to adapt degree programs to meet the emerging leadership needs of bivocational congregations. Positive features and changes include:

- creation of modular or flexible-schedule course offerings designed for students concurrently pastoring or holding other forms of employment;
- renovation of degree programs to accommodate remote learning opportunities;
- development of hybrid models of instruction, online teaching, and other uses of technology;
- emphasis on contextual education as a site of learning;
- student debt reduction programs;
- commitments to antiracism, social justice, and diversity;

- prioritizing cross-cultural learning as integral to theological formation;
- placing seminary education within a continuum of life-long theological education—for example, by developing and supporting non-degree learning programs both prior to and beyond seminary;
- exploring bivocational ministry as an emerging leadership need in churches and a potential paradigm for theological education;
- involvement of full-time faculty in church-related programs and activities beyond the seminary's degree programs.

Recognizing multivocational ministry as an existing and emerging need of the church and fully embracing multivocational ministry as a strategic priority in their educational programming, seminaries would need to explore and identify various changes and initiatives required to reform their curriculum, extracurricular offerings, programs, structure, and ethos around this priority. Example initiatives and programmatic ideas include:

- curriculum and co-curriculum assessment in light of bivocational needs;
- seamless integration of degree and non-degree offerings, reducing barriers to entry and participation, and moving from the pipeline to drip hose metaphor;
- creating crossover learning opportunities for master's, doctoral, and non-degree students;
- support for innovative approaches by faculty (full-time and part-time) to model and support bivocational ministry;
- providing parity among fully-funded and contingent faculty with regard to remuneration for courses taught, support for research and writing, professional development, job security, and institutional standing;
- degree and non-degree class offerings coordinated with and within church contexts;

- student career and vocational advising, including bivocational models of ministry;
- job search support for students, including electronic portfolios, identification of skills and credentials, and interview skills;
- support and training for bivocational mentors to accompany students at all stages of ministerial leadership formation.

New programs, such as those above, could begin as grant-funded initiatives and then, as appropriate, become fully integrated into the permanent operations of the school. The specific initiatives and programmatic ideas appropriate for a seminary will depend on the strategic priorities of the school, as discerned by its administration and trustees, based on their vision for theological education and their understanding the emerging needs of God's world, including the church. Whether multivocational ministry is situated at the center or the periphery of this vision is a matter for their discernment—and ours.

A Necessary and Insufficient Mindset

In this chapter, I have invited readers to reimagine graduate theological education by adopting a multivocational mindset. I have argued that the challenges of bivocationality are one key to understanding the changes required within seminaries and schools of theology for the present time. For example, I have drawn attention to shifting contexts and needs within predominantly White Protestant mainline churches and named bivocationality as a class issue complicated by racial biases. In particular, I have drawn attention to inequities among faculty employment in schools of theology and the growth of "alternative" pathways for education and credentialing, particularly among non-White communities. Can theological educators address the challenge of material inequalities in church and academy sufficiently to provide a credible and faithful witness to a future in which the multivocational minister is lifted up as an honored member in the Body of Christ? The future of graduate theological education may require it.

Yet a multivocational mindset is not enough by itself. It must be combined with antiracist and other justice-oriented commitments in order to reimagine life-giving change. For example, conversations about bivocational ministry often transcend common ideological divisions between evangelicals and mainline, conservatives and progressives. However, many conservative traditions on the cutting edge of bivocational ministry do not ordain women. Conversations are also complicated by the way in which many White, male church planters perform "white self-sufficient masculinity" (Jennings 2020, 6) in a distinctly heteronormative way. Furthermore, White liberals as well as conservatives operate within inherited structures and patterns of racism, sharing a common malformation that continues to insinuate itself into theological education and our churches. These complicated interactions are filled with potential. Will these conversations "form us in the art of cultivating belonging" (10)? Or will they merely replicate "the facilitating obsession of whiteness" in which its participants have already been formed (139)? A multivocational mindset is a necessary but insufficient view to the future that Wayman, González, Aleshire, and others invite us to imagine.

As I tie up the loose ends (Conde-Frazier 2021) of this essay, I realize that I have offered only fragments (Jennings 2020) of a larger tapestry in which ministry and theological education escape the control of churches and graduate schools. There are many other fragments to collect. There is the resonance between the boundary-breaking work of multivocational ministry and that of the diaconate, bridging church and world through a wide range of professions. There are understandings of multivocational ministry and theological education that no longer center on pastoral ministry within a congregation in a particular neighborhood: ministry beyond the pastorate, congregations beyond the walls of a building, and digital spaces as sites of ministry. Each of these fragments, and more, reminds me that the future of theological education is ours to weave.

Works Cited

Aleshire, Daniel O. 2008. *Earthen Vessels: Hopeful Reflections on the Work and Future of Theological Schools*. Grand Rapids, MI: Eerdmans.

———. 2010. "Theological Education in North America." In *Handbook of Theological Education in World Christianity: Theological Perspectives—Regional Surveys—Ecumenical Trends*, edited by Dietrich Werner, David Esterline, Namsoon Kang, and Joshva Raja, 502–13. Regnum Studies in Global Christianity. Oxford: Regnum.

———. 2011. "The Future has Arrived: Changing Theological Education in a Changed World." *Theological Education* 46, no. 2: 69–80. *ats.edu/files/galleries/2011-theological-education-v46-n2.pdf.*

———. 2021. *Beyond Profession: The Next Future of Theological Education*. Theological Education between the Times. Grand Rapids, MI: Eerdmans.

Anonymous. 2019. "A Promissory Note on Ethical Debt in Theological Education." *Religious Studies News*, January 30. *rsn.aarweb.org/promissory-note-ethical-debt-theological-education*.

Association of Theological Schools (ATS). 2020. "Standards of Accreditation for the Commission on Accrediting of the Association of Theological Schools." June. *ats.edu/accrediting/standards*.

Cascante-Gómez, Fernando A. 2017. "An Invitation to a Road Less Traveled: Theological Faculty and the Future of Theological Education." In "Theological Education between the Times," Spotlight on Theological Education, *Religious Studies News*, edited by Antonio Eduardo Alonso, 4–7. *rsn.aarweb.org/spotlight-on/theo-ed/between-the-times/theological-education-between-times-reflections-telos-theological-education*.

Conde-Frazier, Elizabeth. 2021. *Atando Cabos: Latinx Contributions to Theological Education*. Theological Education between the Times. Grand Rapids, MI: Eerdmans.

Edington, Mark D. W. 2018. *Bivocational: Returning to the Roots of Ministry*. New York: Church Publishing. *bivocational.church*.

González, Justo L. 2015. *The History of Theological Education*. Nashville: Abingdon.

———. 2020. "There's No Theological Education Pipeline Anymore." *Christian Century* 137, no. 27. *christiancentury.org/article/how-*

my-mind-has-changed/there-s-no-theological-education-pipeline-anymore.

Jennings, Willie James. 2020. *After Whiteness: An Education in Belonging.* Theological Education between the Times. Grand Rapids, MI: Eerdmans.

Jones, Robert P. 2016. *The End of White Christian America.* New York: Simon & Schuster.

Keenan, James F. 2015. *University Ethics: How Colleges Can Build and Benefit from a Culture of Ethics.* New York: Rowman & Littlefield.

———. 2018. “The Scandal of ‘Contingent’ Faculty.” *Chicago Catholic.* March 21. *chicagocatholic.com/father-james-f.-keenan/-/article/2018/03/21/the-scandal-of-contingent-faculty.*

——— and Matthew J. Gaudet. 2019. “Introduction to the Special Issue on ‘Continuity and Change in Catholic Moral Theology.’” *Journal of Moral Theology* 8, no. 1. *jmt.scholasticahq.com/article/11411-introduction.*

Lindner, Cynthia G. 2016. *Varieties of Gifts: Multiplicity and the Well-Lived Pastoral Life.* Lanham, MD: Rowman & Littlefield.

MacDonald, G. Jeffrey. 2020. *Part-Time is Plenty: Thriving without Full-Time Clergy.* Louisville: Westminster John Knox.

New Leaf Network. 2020. New Leaf Learning Centre—Negotiating New Realities. October 29. *vimeo.com/480596358/df1fc4c9ae.*

Perry, Samuel L., and Cyrus Schleifer. 2019. “Are Bivocational Clergy Becoming the New Normal? An Analysis of the Current Population Survey, 1996–2017.” *Journal for the Scientific Study of Religion* 58: 513–25. *doi.org/10.1111/jssr.12593.*

Scharen, Christian. 2019. “The Current and Future Directions of Theological Education.” *CrossCurrents* 69, no. 1. *jstor.org/stable/26756893.*

——— and Sharon Miller. 2016. “Bright Spots in Theological Education: Hopeful Stories in a Time of Crisis and Change.” *Auburn Studies 22. auburnseminary.org/report/bright-spots.*

Staudt, Kathleen Henderson. 2015. "The Itinerant Scholar-Teacher: Reflections on Twenty Years as an Adjunct Faculty Member." *Religious Education* 49, no. 2: 33–44. *ats.edu/files/galleries/2015-theological-education-v49-n2.pdf.*

Stephens, Darryl W. 2020. "Healing Congregations: A Corrective to the Metrics of Congregational Vitality." *Witness: The Journal of the Academy for Evangelism in Theological Education* 34. *journals.sfu.ca/witness/index.php/witness/article/view/59.*

Thistlethwaite, Susan Brooks. 2018. "Our Theological Schools Are Running Ethical Deficits: Here's How We Can Fix That." *Religious Studies News*, May 29. *rsn.aarweb.org/articles/our-theological-schools-are-running-ethical-deficits.*

United Church of Christ. 2018. *Manual on Ministry: A Guide to Authorizing Ministry in the United Church of Christ.* Ministerial Excellence, Support and Authorization, Local Church Ministries, A Covenanted Ministry of the United Church of Christ. *ucc.org/what-we-do/justice-local-church-ministries/local-church/mesa-ministerial-excellence-support-and-authorization/ministers/ministers_manual.*

Watson, James W., Wanda M. Malcolm, Mark D. Chapman, Elizabeth A. Fisher, Marilyn Draper, Narry F. Santos, Jared Siebert, and Amy Bratton. 2020. *Canadian Multivocational Ministry Project: Research Report. canadianmultivocationalministry.ca/master-report.*

Wayman, Benjamin D. 2021. "Imagining the Future of Theological Education." *Christian Century* 138, no. 4: 20–25. *christiancentury.org/article/features/imagining-future-theological-education.*

Wheeler, Barbara G., ed. 2019. *Disruption and Hope: Religious Traditions and the Future of Theological Education: Essays in Honor of Daniel O. Aleshire.* Waco, TX: Baylor University Press.

Wong, Maria Liu. 2017. "Engaging the *Telos* and Sharing Tales of Theological Education." In "Theological Education between the Times," Spotlight on Theological Education, *Religious Studies News*, edited by Antonio Eduardo Alonso, 19–20. *rsn.aarweb.org/spotlight-on/theo-ed/between-the-times/theological-education-between-times-reflections-telos-theological-education.*

Endnotes

1 The language of "multiple pathways" is in use in at least one US mainline denomination. The General Synod of the United Church of Christ affirmed "multiple paths for preparation and formation toward ministerial authorization" in 2005 (United Church of Christ 2018, 78).

Contributors

Ronald W. Baard, an ordained minister in the United Church of Christ, is dean of the Maine School of Ministry and teaches at New York Theological Seminary.

Phil Baisley, a recorded Friends minister, is professor of pastoral ministry at Earlham School of Religion and serves as pastor of Greenfield Friends Meeting in Indiana.

Kristen Plinke Bentley, an ordained minister with the Christian Church (Disciples of Christ), is director of the Thriving in Ministry program at Lexington Theological Seminary.

Mark D. Chapman, a lay leader at Hazelglen Alliance Church, is associate professor of research methods, director of the Doctor of Ministry program, and a lead researcher for the Tyndale Intercultural Ministry Centre at Tyndale University.

Ben Connelly, founder of the Equipping Group, is a church planter and part of the servant leader team for Salt+Light Community in Fort Worth, Texas.

Jo Ann Deasy, an ordained pastor in the Evangelical Covenant Church, is director of institutional initiatives and student research at the Association of Theological Schools in the United States and Canada.

Susan J. Ebertz, a member of the Presbyterian Church (U.S.A.), is associate professor of bibliography and academic research and director for the Reu Memorial Library at Wartburg Theological Seminary in Dubuque, Iowa.

Herbert Fain, an ordained Baptist minister, is professor of legal and social ethics at Houston Graduate School of Theology.

Norm Faramelli, a retired priest in the Episcopal Church (US), is a teacher, author, and chemical engineer, with extensive experience in transportation and environmental planning.

Kwasi Kena, an ordained elder in the United Methodist Church, is associate professor of ethnic and multicultural ministries at Wesley Seminary, Indiana Wesleyan University.

Kathleen Owens, an ordained minister in the Presbyterian Church (U.S.A.), is former moderator of the John Knox Presbytery in Wisconsin.

Anthony Pappas, a retired Baptist pastor, is a church consultant, writer, and editor and formerly served as the executive minister of the American Baptist Churches of Massachusetts.

Ed Pease, a semi-retired priest in the Episcopal Church (US), is a former bishop's deputy for congregational and clergy development, teacher, business executive, and tax consultant.

Hartness M. Samushonga, senior pastor of Millennium Harvest Church in Kingston upon Hull, England, is chief executive officer of Bivo Support International.

Darryl W. Stephens, an ordained deacon in the United Methodist Church, is director of the Pennsylvania Academy of Ministry and director of United Methodist Studies at Lancaster Theological Seminary.

Steven C. Van Ostran, an ordained Baptist pastor, serves as executive minister of the American Baptist Churches of the Rocky Mountains and previously taught at Ottawa University.

James W. Watson, lead researcher for the Canadian Multivocational Ministry Project, serves as consultant for church planting and congregational revitalization for the Salvation Army in Canada.

Ralph B. Wright Jr., an ordained minister in the Presbyterian Church (U.S.A.), spends his retirement in Patchogue, New York.

Jessica Young Brown, a lay member of the American Baptist Churches USA, is a licensed clinical psychologist and teaches in the areas of Christian education, spiritual formation, and pastoral care and counseling.

Made in the USA
Monee, IL
10 June 2022

97737506R00218